In this richly researched work, Murphy draws on the libido theory of Freud and Lacan to give a compelling psychoanalytic account of what has come to be known as asexuality. As a recently recognised phenomenon, asexuality remains profoundly under-theorised. This book, written from the perspective of psychoanalysis, opens a new chapter in thinking about what Murphy rightly calls an enigma.

Russell Grigg, psychoanalyst, member of the New Lacanian School, Melbourne, Australia

The usual view is that Freud's "pansexualism" implies that all human behaviour is sexually motivated. Lacan questioned this when he stated, "there is no sexual relation." In this important and timely book, Murphy goes even further. Starting from the undisputed evidence that there are asexual minorities in most cultures, he explores how the absence of sexual attraction can be non-pathological, demonstrating that such an exception proves that sexuality is not a rule. This brave investigation of a different desire makes us reconsider relationships, intimacy, and sexual identities.

Patricia Gherovici, psychoanalyst and author of *Transgender Psychoanalysis: A Lacanian Perspective on Sexual Difference* (Routledge, 2017)

Asexuality and Freudian-Lacanian Psychoanalysis

Asexuality and Freudian-Lacanian Psychoanalysis: Towards a Theory of an Enigma proposes that asexuality is a libidinally founded *desire for no sexual desire*, a concept not included in psychoanalytic theory up to now.

"Asexuality" is defined as the experience of having no sexual attraction for another person; as an emerging self-defined sexual orientation, it has received practically no attention from psychoanalytic research. This book is the first sustained piece of exploratory and theoretical research from a Freudian-Lacanian perspective. Using Freudian concepts to understand the intricacies of human sexual desire, this volume will also employ Lacanian conceptual tools to understand how asexuality might sustain itself despite the absence of Other-directed sexual desire. This book argues that asexuality holds a mirror to contemporary sexualized society which assumes sexual attraction and eroticism as the benchmarks for experiencing sexual desire. It also argues that asexuality may be a previously unrecognized form of human sexuality which can contribute new understandings to the range and breadth of what it means to be a sexual being.

This book will be of interest to anyone in the area of asexuality or sexuality – psychoanalysts, psychotherapists, psychologists, psychiatrists, university lecturers, researchers, students or those simply curious about the possibilities of the human sex drive.

Kevin Murphy, PhD, is a psychoanalytic psychotherapist practising in Dublin, Ireland. He is a Registered Practitioner Member of the Association for Psychoanalysis and Psychotherapy in Ireland (APPI) and a Member of the Irish Council for Psychotherapy (ICP).

Asexuality and Freudian-Lacanian Psychoanalysis

Towards a Theory of an Enigma

Kevin Murphy

Routledge
Taylor & Francis Group

LONDON AND NEW YORK

Cover image: ©iStock/Getty Images

First published 2023
by Routledge
4 Park Square, Milton Park, Abingdon, Oxon OX14 4RN

and by Routledge
605 Third Avenue, New York, NY 10158

Routledge is an imprint of the Taylor & Francis Group, an informa business

© 2023 Kevin Murphy

The right of Kevin Murphy to be identified as author of this work
has been asserted in accordance with sections 77 and 78 of the
Copyright, Designs and Patents Act 1988.

British Library Cataloguing-in-Publication Data
A catalogue record for this book is available from the British Library

Library of Congress Cataloging-in-Publication Data
LC record available at https://lccn.loc.gov/2022022302

ISBN: 978-1-032-10357-0 (hbk)
ISBN: 978-1-032-10358-7 (pbk)
ISBN: 978-1-003-21494-6 (ebk)

DOI: 10.4324/9781003214946

Typeset in Times New Roman
by Apex CoVantage, LLC

This book is dedicated to my wife, Gina, who has been a constant source of love, support and encouragement.

Contents

Preface   x
Acknowledgements   xii

Introduction   1

1   What Research Has to Say about Asexuality   19

2   Towards a Freudian Understanding   37

3   Key Freudian Concepts and Their Relation
    to Asexuality   60

4   Towards a Lacanian Understanding of Asexuality   82

5   The Challenge of Libido and the Annulment
    of Sexual Desire   107

6   Asexual *Jouissance* and the Lacanian *Sinthome*   133

7   Conclusion   155

Index   175

Preface

The idea of writing about asexuality came from working with clients in my private practice where I specialize in issues connected directly or indirectly with sexuality. A number of people came to see me who were not engaging sexually with their long-term partners. This is not unusual to encounter in a practice that deals with sexual issues, but what was different was they experienced no sexual attraction for their same-sex or opposite-sex partners. Besides that, they were remarkably unperturbed by it. They were not having sex because they did not feel sexual desire, or sexual attraction, even though they loved their partners and did not want to be with anyone else. Some said that if they never had sex again for the rest of their lives, they would be okay with that. What did bother them was the relationship pressure and societal expectation that they should feel sexual attraction because, after all, isn't that what normal people do? As a result, they were convinced there was something wrong with them, that they were somehow broken. It was through these clients that I first came to the area of asexuality. They fitted the criteria of sex-averse heteroromantic and homoromantic asexuals, but they were not self-defined asexuals in that they did not call themselves asexual nor, indeed, had they heard of this orientation.

One of the more obvious challenges of this book was whether it was possible to look at asexuality through the lens of Freudian-Lacanian psychoanalysis, which is based on a simple premise: every person has a sexual drive. It is my hope that this book will be the story of how that challenge, and the many others that were to follow, was addressed and developed into a psychoanalytical understanding of the way an asexual person might come into being. In that sense, this is not a book about asexual identity or relationships or the real difficulties of navigating the world of "compulsory sexuality", or how asexuality challenges sexual norms, which it does. It is, rather, a book about the role of the unconscious in producing an asexual subject and how Freudian-Lacanian psychoanalytic concepts might facilitate the thinking-through of this process.

A second challenge arises in how to approach asexuality as a sexual orientation without the presumption of pathology. Much like the first challenge, this is similar in that I will be using a theory born from and designed to address pathologies of one kind or another. Conscious of my position as an *allosexual* researcher (i.e., non-asexual), my intention from the outset has been to approach asexuality as objectively and respectfully as possible and to theorize it not as a dysfunction or pathology but as a potently authentic version of human sexuality, albeit one which tends to be denied this recognition. If I have begun with any assumptions, then a central one is that absence of evidence is not evidence of absence. I do not claim that this will be the only possible psychoanalytic understanding of asexuality, but I am hoping that, as the first book from this theoretical perspective, it will stimulate new ideas, discussion and further research into these areas.

Acknowledgements

I wish to acknowledge the contributions of former Associate Professor Russell Grigg and current Associate Professor Matthew Sharpe at Deakin University, Melbourne, to the shaping of the research that created this book. Professor Grigg, from the outset, brought what had begun as a relatively unformed concept to a workable idea and gave me the latitude to take that idea wherever it was necessary to go. Thanks also to Associate Professor Sharpe for his enthusiasm and belief in the theory underpinning this idea, as well as for his attention to detail, which transformed this work into a unified whole.

I would also like to thank my family for their perseverance, in particular my wife, Gina, to whom I have dedicated this book. Her support has been both unwavering and inspiring. My daughters, Alice, Georgie and Julie, were also a great support through their encouraging words, their interest in the subject matter and their regular requests for updates on the book's progress. Thanks must also go to Dr Cindy Zeiher of Canterbury University, who encouraged me to publish my research in book form. I would also like to thank Dr Dan Collins of Affiliated Psychoanalytic Workgroups (APW), who invited me to present my ideas on asexuality at successive international APW annual conferences. The fruits of that process are woven into the chapters on Lacanian theory. I would also like to thank Dr Carol Owens and Nadezhda Almqvist for inviting me to contribute on asexuality to their book, *Studying Lacan's Seminars IV and V: From Lack to Desire*. The research behind that paper is also included here. Many thanks also go to my clinical supervisor Dr Olga Cox Cameron for her work on translating French texts and for her helpful comments and views. I would also like to thank Dr Eve Watson, Course Director of the Freud Lacan Institute, whose interest and encouragement for this work were invaluable. Finally, thanks must go to my editors at Routledge, Susannah Frearson and Jana Craddock, for all their professionalism and expertise in bringing this project to fruition.

Introduction

A good place to start would be to ask, What is asexuality? "Asexuality" is defined as the experience of having no sexual attraction for another person. But under this broad definition, there are a wide variety of ways in which people experience their asexuality, and this diversity has to be borne in mind. The definition outlined is the one favoured by the Asexual Visibility and Education Network (AVEN),[1] the main internet presence for asexuality today. AVEN says that an asexual person is not drawn to people sexually and does not desire to act upon attraction to others in a sexual way. AVEN also makes a clear distinction between celibacy, which is a choice to abstain from sexual activity, and asexuality, which is an intrinsic part of who asexuals are. This latter point, AVEN says, positions asexuality as similar to other sexual orientations.

There is ongoing debate as to whether the AVEN definition adequately describes the richly varied lived experience of asexuals. The debate centres on the varying levels of heterogeneity within asexual experience and its connections with desire, attraction and sexual and/or romantic engagement. It would, to some extent, be more accurate to speak of asexualities in the plural since more and more writers and researchers point out that self-identity as asexual depends on how an individual experiences it rather than on a fixed definition.[2] As author Angela Chen points out, anyone looking for a tidy sense of what asexuality is will be disappointed.[3] The experience of being asexual can occupy a spectrum ranging from no sexual and/or romantic involvement of any kind with another person, to asexual romantic relationships between same-sex or opposite-sex individuals without sexual activity, and on to relationships which can include varying degrees of sexual activity.

In fact, research shows that asexuals masturbate at much the same statistical rate as sexual individuals. In one study, between 73% and 80% of asexual women and men, respectively, had engaged in masturbation. The average frequency was a few times a week for men and once a month for women. Equally, similar rates of asexual women (approximately 30%) and sexual women had never engaged in masturbation. Brotto et al. (2010, p. 607) suggest that sexual intercourse and masturbation that are without the element of sexual attraction might be motivated by non-sexual reasons. In terms of definitions, then, the key to whether someone is asexual or not would appear to rest on whether *sexual attraction* to another person

DOI: 10.4324/9781003214946-1

is present or absent, despite the occasional presence of sexual activity. If there is no sexual attraction, then the definition of being asexual holds.

There is also debate as to whether asexuality is a lifelong experience or whether someone identifying as asexual at a particular time of their life can also be part of the definition. The question has also been raised as to whether a person who identifies as asexual and then decides to change can still be considered asexual. Some, in turn, take issue with the AVEN definition of "asexuality" because it enshrines a focus on absence (i.e., of sexual attraction). But despite the ongoing nature of these differences, the AVEN version is the working definition that is most often used. Some researchers even extend it to include an absence of sexual attraction to "anyone or anything" (Yule et al., 2014, p. 25).

"Asexuality", as I will be using the term, is taken to be a self-defined orientation in which the asexual can engage with sexual activities even though they do not experience sexual attraction for another person. The other defining feature of asexuality is that it does not involve subjective distress as a result of not experiencing sexual desire for another person. This differentiates it completely from a sexual disorder (Brotto et al., 2010, pp. 606–607).[4] Research also suggests that asexuals do not appear to fall ill as a result of their sexual orientation (Bogaert, 2006, p. 247). In other words, they do not fall ill as a result of their libido *not* being directed externally onto another person, as Freud suggests should be the case (1916–1917, pp. 344–345). It is also important to note that asexuality is considered by many of its proponents to be innate.[5] I will be elaborating on this point and referring to asexuality as a sexual orientation because my proposal will be that rather than any form of sexuality being innate, asexuality, like heterosexuality and LGBTQIA+ orientations, is a legitimate and uniquely individual response to the persisting demand, or *Drang*, of the sexual drives (Freud, ibid.). It is a response that is impacted in the first instance by the internal experiences of the sexual drives and then secondarily through external and environmental interactions. This, again, is a point that will be elaborated on.

I mentioned previously, in working towards a Freudian-Lacanian understanding of asexuality, I will be proposing that asexuality is not a form of pathology. This is contrary to the approach that psychoanalysis has adopted towards non-normative sexualities in the past (Watson, 2011, pp. 10–15). An example of this would be the pathologizing of same-sex orientations, not by Freud, it has to be said,[6] but by those who followed after him, as outlined by Gherovici (2010, p. 185). In contrast, I will be coming to asexuality from a perspective best expressed by Dean (2000, p. 5) in his non-pathologizing approach to homosexuality (i.e., psychoanalytic enquiry may hold the potential to assist with a reconceptualization of our ideas around sexuality in general). In this context, it is worth noting that psychiatry has, relatively recently, depathologized asexuality. In the 2013 edition of the *Diagnostic and Statistical Manual of Mental Disorders* (*DSM-5*), the criteria for a diagnosis of female sexual interest/arousal disorder now come with the direction to practitioners that if a lifelong lack of sexual desire (and here, we see the political importance of definitions) is better explained by a woman's self-identification as asexual, then a diagnosis of female sexual interest/arousal disorder should *not* be made (American Psychiatric Association, 2013, p. 434). The same applies to male hypoactive sexual desire disorder where practitioners are advised that if a man's low desire is explained by self-identification as an asexual, then a diagnosis of male hypoactive sexual desire disorder is *not* made (ibid., p. 443). This move also highlights the significance of self-identification as a recognized sign of mental health and self-determination.[7]

A Brief History of Asexuality

Any focus on self-defined asexuality must take into account its relatively recent emergence into social discourse. According to Hinderliter (2009, online pagination, pp. 1–2), its first appearance was in an online blog by Zoe O'Reilly called *My Life as an Amoeba* (1997). This post allowed people to respond, and so it essentially gave rise to the first online asexual community. Another early Yahoo! Group called "Haven for the Human Amoeba" (HHA) was then formed in October 2000. In its first discussion, the group founder defined "asexual" as being "not sexual" – with reference to people. At this time, during the 2000–2001 term, a college freshman at Wesleyan University, Connecticut, David Jay, who considered himself asexual, realized there was no information at the university about asexuality. He had read *My Life as an Amoeba*, and it was this, according to Hinderliter (ibid., p. 3), which prompted him to create an internet page on his Wesleyan account, calling it AVEN – the Asexual Visibility and Education Network. AVEN is now the main asexual website on the internet today. Jay was also responsible for scripting the first definition of "asexuality". "The first instance of the present definition in HHA (Haven for the Human Amoeba) was in a discussion on defining asexualism (asexualism and asexuality were used interchangeably back then) in a post by David (Jay) in late September 2001", Hinderliter says (ibid., p. 4). While the first definition of "asexuality" was of a person who was attracted to neither gender, the definition used by the asexual community is now this: *an asexual is a person who does not experience sexual attraction.*[8] However, Hinderliter says that Jay has on one occasion referred to this definition as the one used outside the asexual community.[9] Inside the asexual community, in contrast, the preferred definition is this: *an asexual is a person who calls themselves asexual* (Hinderliter, 2009, p. 5).

The first academic enquiry into the statistical prevalence of asexuality was conducted in 2004 by Anthony Bogaert, and it found that approximately 1% of British residents defined themselves as asexual. This 1% figure is now the commonly quoted estimate for the prevalence of asexuality in any given population. However, other estimates put the prevalence from a low of 0.4% (Aicken et al., 2013, online pagination, p. 5) up to 1.05% in the UK (Bogaert, 2004, p. 282), and up to 4.8% of females and 6.1% of males in the US (Poston and Baumle, 2010, p. 527). For comparison purposes, a US Gallup poll conducted in 2016 showed that 4.1% of Americans identified as LGBTQIA+, compared to 3.5% in 2012.[10]

Asexuality and Society

Asexuality continues to strive for recognition and, indeed, acceptance. Its representative group, AVEN, acknowledges this in the use of the word "visibility" in its title. As a publicly focussed movement, therefore, it can be considered as having something in common with the burgeoning movement of queer theory.[11] Both asexual and queer proponents have a strong desire for their orientations to be recognized, and they have both had the experience of being excluded from lesbian and gay political discourse,[12] even though in the 1970s asexuality was deemed to be part of it in some instances.[13] Indeed, while asexuality occupies a politically quieter space, it shares queer theory's oppositional relationship to sexual normativity (Giffney and Watson, 2017, p. 30), engaged as it is with re-evaluating the hegemony of sexual desire's place within this norm (Miller, 2017, p. 356). The asexual stands in contradistinction to Joan Copjec's (2015, p. 41) sexually desiring subject who wants what social laws want it to want. As Miller (2017, p. 356) puts it, asexuality invites a confrontation with the idea that sexual desire is foundational to human identity.

Although asexuality has emerged at this point in history as both a quasi-politicized movement and as a self-defined sexual orientation, it would be remiss to ignore its broader place in history. Engelman (2008) believes that while asexuality's emergence now is due, in part, to its experience of increased isolation at a time of burgeoning sexuality, there have been asexual figures in history and in literature throughout the ages. She points to the Christian Virgin Mary, Joan of Arc and the Greek goddess Artemis, the huntress and, ironically, patron of both childbirth and virginity. The latter's Roman counterpart, Diana, was also considered a virgin goddess. There are other examples, such as the man on whom the movie *Lawrence of Arabia* was based, T. E. Lawrence. His friends believed he was asexual, and Lawrence himself specifically denied any personal experience of sex.[14] Florence Nightingale, whose name is included on many online lists of asexual people, led an asexual life which she dedicated to doing God's work. According to her biographer, she decided when she was relatively young to remain unattached and single (Bostridge, 2015, p. 74).

A discussion forum on the AVEN website mentions English physicist and mathematician Isaac Newton as asexual as well as Hungarian mathematician Paul Erdős.[15] In the case of Erdős, his biographer says that he did not have time for "frivolities like sex" (Hoffman, 1998, p. 22). The pop singer Morrissey has been associated with asexuality, having said that he is celibate and that he was not attracted to girls as a teenager. He has used the word "humasexual"[16] to describe his sexuality, and he is also mentioned in numerous articles on asexuality.[17] The American writer Gore Vidal was considered asexual in the later decades of his life.[18] Speaking about his 53-year relationship with Howard Austen in *The United States of Amnesia*, a 2013 documentary by Nicholas Wrathall, he said this:

> Sex destroys relationships . . . either one or the other loses interest and either one or the other wants something else. We had not taken a vow of celibacy and we were not involved with each other, that's all.[19]

The same sentiment is central to what are known as "Boston marriages", a term now used to describe long-term female-to-female relationships which do not include sex. Rothblum and Brehony (1993, p. 5) say the traditional assumption was that the women in these relationships were sexual with each other, but there is no record of whether they were. The authors, therefore, set out to reclaim the term "Boston marriage" to describe asexual lesbian relationships today.[20] In this context, the lacuna which exists in psychoanalytic research regarding asexuality is all the more conspicuous when it is recalled that the youngest daughter of the founder of psychoanalysis was in a Boston marriage for most of her adult life.

I will return to a consideration of this in Chapter 1, but to finish, asexuality also appears in works of fiction but not always in a way that is representative of asexuality as a lived experience. The character Spock from *Star Trek* and the fictional detective Sherlock Holmes are asexual figures who, according to Engelman (2008, online pagination, p. 4), represent aloof versions who apparently cannot engage in loving relationships. Also in the area of fiction, according to Miller (2017, pp. 356–357), there has been a more recent growth in the representation of asexual characters in comics and graphic novels. However, he, too, notes that the fictional depiction of asexuality as an absence or dysfunction risks stigmatizing it as a disorder or reducing it to a stereotype.

Some Questions to Be Addressed

As with any academic endeavour, it is necessary to consider questions which might need to be considered in approaching this subject. One question would be whether experiences in earliest childhood have any part to play in the formation of the asexual person as they do for the non-asexual person. If so, are these experiences part of a common set of experiences for all subjects, or are they unique to asexuals? Also, if the asexual person experiences no sexual attraction for another person, is it possible to derive a form of pleasure or, to use Lacan's term, *jouissance*[21] from this? In other words, can asexuality at some level derive a seemingly counter-intuitive pleasure from experiencing no sexual attraction? If so, how is this form of pleasure to be understood? In non-psychoanalytic asexual theory similar concepts are to be found, particularly in Przybylo's (2019) work on "asexual erotics", a term that describes pleasures which have an erotic root but which are not directly sexual. A distinction needs to be drawn between the latter's work in this area and the question being raised here. Przybylo, a prolific academic writer in this field, broadens out the meanings around "intimacy" and "relating" in order to untether erotic energies from sex (2019, pp. 1–3). In other words, the asexual person can experience the erotic in ways that do not include sex. This is an important expansion of how we might view desire, sexuality and intimacy, and would, in some respects, concur with a psychoanalytic hypothesis that a sex drive is operating unseen within asexuality. I will return to this later, but for now, the question I am raising here, in contrast, is whether asexuality can at some level derive libidinal pleasure from the experience of no sexual attraction.

In other words, can the *absence* of sexual attraction provide a form of sexual pleasure in itself?

Furthermore, if asexuality means not being sexually attracted to another person, does this indicate, speaking psychoanalytically, that no object-choice has been made? This question is relevant because psychoanalytic theory consistently maintains that the libido is plastic to the extent that it can choose *any* object (i.e., we can be attracted to any person, male, female, same sex, opposite sex or gender fluid). However, it equally maintains that *who* our libido is directed towards, and finds sexually attractive, is of slightly less importance since it is a highly individual and personal choice. Greater importance is given to the requirement that our libido must be directed towards *some* object. In short, the choice of object matters less than the act of choosing an object.

Given the very obvious absence of Other-directed sexual attraction (i.e., no object causes sexual attraction), any psychoanalytic theory of asexuality will need to establish one of two things. If object-choice *does not* occur, then why is this so and how does it come about? Alternatively, if object-choice *does* occur, then is it possible that asexuality aims at an object in a way which has not been considered so far? Does asexuality represent a new paradigm in which an asexual person can create their own meaning around the absence of sexual desire and which, in turn, establishes a different way of relating to the object understood as the other person? Furthermore, in approaching these questions, is it possible to do so, as stated, without pathologizing the asexual subject? This is intended to give a brief overview of the terrain through which this book will travel. Later in this chapter, I will map a chapter-by-chapter account of this terrain so as to offer a few signposts to mark the way.

The Research to Date

I will begin by looking into contemporary research to see what its findings tell us about the asexual person. Of interest will be anything it might have to say about the asexual subject's absence of sexual attraction and/or sexual desire. Does the research verify this absence, or is it refuted? Is it due to fear or disgust, or perhaps something else? If the asexual subject can engage in some forms of sexual behaviour, then how can this be understood in the absence of sexual attraction to and sexual desire for the Other? Does the research say anything about the possible aetiology of this orientation? Do any of the findings corroborate whether it is biological or genetic? Also, I will be looking to the research to see if there are any childhood experiences of either a sexual or an asexual nature which might throw light on this. Finally, what does the research say about the status of relationships for asexuals if there is no desire for sexual activity?

I will then review the very small psychoanalytic literature in this specific area and combine it with the field's more extensive literature on human sexuality. Much of the book will be a search through Sigmund Freud's and Jacques Lacan's theories in order to locate concepts of potential applicability to understanding the enigma of asexuality. I will be using Freud's work because it is not only foundational for Lacanian theory but also because it is predicated on the idea I mentioned earlier. This is the idea that everybody has a sexual drive which is directly or indirectly acknowledged and experienced either through its expression (physically, verbally or in fantasy), its alteration (kink, BDSM), its prohibition (sexual dysfunction, neurotic symptoms) or its weaponization (sexual abuse/violence, paedophilia). The two main contributions of this theory will be in the area of infantile sexuality, the idea that our sexuality is formed in the very earliest experiences in our lives, and in the plasticity of the sexual drive. However, Freud's theory, much like Lacan's, does not refer specifically to asexuality as a sexual orientation in which a sexual drive is theoretically present but experientially absent. The theory of Jacques Lacan, however, which builds on and advances Freud's ideas in different ways, offers concepts which allow for a closer consideration of the enigma that is asexuality.

Of further importance is the fact that the domain of sex and sexuality, for both Freud and Lacan, is not just a domain of pleasure but one which can give rise to unpleasure also, and as a result, sex can become something which creates an *impasse* (Hyldgaard, 2009, online pagination, p. 1). Sex, for psychoanalysis, is a "persisting contradiction of reality" which language is unable to deal with, and it is out of this contradiction that human experience is structured, according to Zupančič (2017, p. 3). She says, "the sexual in psychoanalysis is something very different from the sense-making combinatory game – it is precisely something that disrupts this game and makes it impossible" (ibid., p. 39). This is an aspect of Freudian/Lacanian sexual theory which I will elaborate on later. Suffice to say, it is an aspect which very often does not find its way into discourses on sexuality and is absent from most other theories about sex. Therefore, is the absence of sexual attraction for another person in asexuality due to an unconscious choice that recognizes something of the unpleasure which Freud, in particular, says is inherent in the sex drive? Being unconscious, it would then be something which drives the asexual subject, in a manner no different from sexually desiring subjects, of which they, too, would be unaware.

I will also be looking to see what the current research has to say about the unconscious phantasy[22] that may be operating within asexuality. The concept of phantasy, in the psychoanalytic sense, refers to an unconscious template which structures the subject's relation to others throughout their lives. It is, I will be proposing, a concept that offers considerable depth and value for understanding asexuality. Finally, does asexuality have something in common with hysteria, given that an aversion to sexual engagement is common to both? By extension, the further question will be whether asexuality is related to obsessional neurosis which can also represent a withdrawal of the libido from objects. I will be examining these questions to establish if it is possible to distinguish asexuality from a primarily neurotic condition, notwithstanding the place of neurosis for everyone.[23] Failure to make such a distinction, similar to a failure to distinguish asexuality from a sexual form of anorexia,[24] leaves asexuality open to negative bias and to being classified as a sexual dysfunction.

A Freudian View of Asexuality

A broad Freudian view of the sexual drive is that not only is it present for everybody but that it is a "continuously flowing source of stimulation" (1905, p. 168), even if it often goes unnoticed. This will be an important tenet which I will take as one of the book's theoretical assumptions. It would also, by extension, be a significant assumption for supporting the claim by asexuals that theirs is a sexual orientation (Gressgård, 2014, p. 125). Assuming libido is present for all subjects, it will be necessary to consider the forces that can work against the sexual drive finding its path to satisfaction through sexual activity with another person. Freud sees the alterations which instincts undergo as evidence that the human subject unconsciously defends itself against them, which will also be central to the argument in this book (i.e., the unpleasure inherent in sexuality). Furthermore, if no sexual object-choice appears to be made in asexuality, can Freudian theory shed any light on this? In this context, an area of focus will be the latency period, which is not just the final stage of psychosexual development before puberty but is also an essentially asexual phase in every person's sexual development. The question here is whether this phase has a role to play in the emergence of the asexual person. During latency, a sexual drive can be present even though the subject does not consciously experience it. Yet if the Freudian view is that the human sexual drive is constant in all subjects, then is asexual experience a form of extended latency period? Equally, and as I stated earlier, Freud is of the view that libido must inevitably be directed externally or the person risks falling ill (1916–1917, pp. 344–345), so why is it that asexuals do not fall ill as a result? In fact, one of the defining aspects of asexuality is the absence of subjective distress from having no experience of sexual attraction to others.[25]

Freud's theory of infantile sexuality is another central aspect of my approach. Sexuality and asexuality do not arrive at puberty due to hormonal changes, and in this regard, it is interesting to read testimony of some asexuals stating that they knew they were asexual before puberty (Chen, 2020, p. 81). In Freudian terms, what takes place for a sexual or an asexual person after puberty is a more sophisticated and complex repeating of what had already taken place in early infancy. This is the diphasic (i.e., two part) understanding of how human sexuality is formed and one that is specific to psychoanalytic theory. Also, to mention it again, Freud's emphasis on the disruptive possibilities of the sexual drive and their potentially traumatizing effects as it develops through infantile stages will be important in approaching an understanding of asexuality, just as it is with understanding sexually desiring subjects.

Some Specific Freudian Mechanisms

This will then lead on to a more specific consideration of Freudian psychical mechanisms and their potential role in the formation of asexuality. For example, repression is a mechanism that can be responsible for making the sex drive inoperative and so represents a resistance acting against the instinctual (drive) impulse (1915, p. 146). As well as repression, sublimation offers a potential understanding as to what is taking place in asexuality. Freud has always insisted that sexual instinctual (drive) impulses are extraordinarily plastic (1916–1917, p. 345), meaning that one component instinct can take over from another if reality frustrates their satisfaction. The question which asexuality poses is that its satisfaction is potentially derived from having no sexual drive directed externally at another person, and so it needs to be established if sublimation, which allows sexual trends to attach to non-sexual ones, can provide an insight into this. In this same context, classical Freudian concepts that are often used to explain the absence of a desire for sexual engagement with another person (i.e., female frigidity and male impotence) will also need to be considered.

Another question to be explored is whether asexuality includes a narcissistic dimension. After all, in the classic Freudian understanding, narcissism is the result of the libido which was once attached to external objects leaving those objects and setting up the person's own ego in their place (ibid., pp. 415–416). In effect, a person treats their own body in the same way in which the body of a sexual object is ordinarily treated (1914, p. 73). But if it is narcissism, then what is to be understood of relationships where some asexuals engage in sexual activities, either out of curiosity or to please their non-asexual partners, but without a feeling of sexual attraction for them? Equally, is narcissism applicable to the experience of self-directed masturbation as a non-sexual activity, that is, where their own body is the object of a sexual activity and yet is *not* treated as a sexual object?[26] Alongside the question of narcissism, the lack of sexual attraction for another person, combined with the capacity of some asexuals to engage in non-sexual but romantic relationships, leads to a consideration of idealization. This has everything to do with the object because it is the other person who becomes the romantic object of attention and, in the process, becomes elevated in the subject's mind. If an asexual engages in a romantic interpersonal relationship, it implies that to a greater or lesser extent, there is some idealization of their love object. The question for psychoanalytic theory is how this idealization occurs without including a sexual element.

The conundrum which this book is setting out to understand is how a theorized sexual drive might operate in asexuality without including sexual attraction for another person. One avenue of approach to this would be Freud's view on how the sexual drive can be experienced negatively because an increase in *internal* excitation for the child is unpleasurable (1905, p. 209).[27] In particular, Freud gives importance to the element of fright which this rise of internal excitation causes when it breaches the child's defensive shield against both internal and external stimuli; the fright in Freud's view being caused by a lack of preparedness for this rising internal excitation (1920, p. 31). In fact, he believes the most abundant source of internal excitation *is* the sexual instinct (drive) which, in turn, is repressed because of this traumatic effect (ibid., p. 34). He does not, however, extend his theory to consider a subject who might, as a result of defending against it, go on to have no conscious experience of their own sexual drive being directed at another person. In turn, while he is of the view that there is no such thing as normal sexuality (1905, p. 160, 165), his theory does not extend to a form of sexuality which might experience no sexual attraction. This is one of the limits at which Freudian theory arrives and is a point where it will be necessary to transition to Lacanian theory to extend a consideration of these issues further.

A Lacanian View of Asexuality

In the same way that Freud gives prominence to libido as the sexual energy behind human endeavour, the theories of Jacques Lacan give prominence to unconscious desire as the driving force behind action, imagination and language. In Lacan's theory, desire like libido is perpetual and constant, and is supported for every subject by a fundamental phantasy. This phantasy places the subject, divided as they are between their conscious and unconscious realities, in a relation to an intangible, invisible object which causes their desire. Lacan calls the object which causes this the *objet petit a*, or the *little o object* in English. This is an ineffable, incorporeal object which takes no specular form but which, nevertheless, has its roots in the earliest bodily objects which come to symbolize the loss of pleasure – the breast, the excrement, the phallus. The *objet petit a*, therefore, as object cause of human desire, is central to Lacanian theory as the essential support of desire in all subjects because it is the object each person constantly seeks to find again in their own way. In other words, the presence of an absent object, as cause of our desire, is essential to ensure we remain desiring subjects.

Both Lacan and Freud believe that the object of the sexual drive is unimportant once there is *some* object of the drive, and both believe the object chosen is very particular to each person. In this book, I will try to establish what kind of *objet petit a* asexuality might have within its fundamental phantasy. The latter denotes a fundamental belief within our unconscious which supports each of us in a consistent manner, in terms of how we understand ourselves and how we position ourselves with others. Lacan says the phantasy has the place of an unconscious axiom, by which he means it is our readily accepted way of seeing ourselves, one we are not aware of and one which assumes its causal power from never being contested (1966–1967, session of 21 June 1967, p. 274). Geneviève Morel explains it as "a fixed point or a centre of gravity that would support the whole of this (psychical) structure, a constant determining the life of the subject, a particular law of desire holding the key to his or her destiny" (2017, p. 3). In short, it is a self-evident truth we hold about ourselves which operates at the unconscious level and guides our choices throughout our lives. Therefore, if asexuality is a desire for no desire, then what fundamental phantasy would support a desire which is divested of phallic or sexual pleasure, or what Lacan calls phallic *jouissance*? Later, I will examine this in more detail, but for now, the point regarding asexuality is whether Lacanian theory allows for an understanding of a libidinal desire, fuelled as it is by a fundamental phantasy with the invisible *objet petit a* at its core, and including an absence of a sexual aim and sexual object, in a way that offers a form of asexual *jouissance*. Importantly, this will also necessitate examining Lacan's theory of infantile sexuality to establish if he has included somewhere within it concepts which might throw light on asexuality's disaffection with Other-directed sexuality.

Regarding infantile sexuality, Lacan believes the first infantile sexual encounter of every subject has something unpleasurable about it which can represent a structural trauma (1977, p. 55), similar to Freud's point regarding the unpleasure caused by the fright of rising internal excitation for which the infant subject is unprepared. This, it must be stressed, is distinct from the concept of sexual abuse. Here, trauma refers to any relatively ordinary experience which may overwhelm the emerging human subject as a result of flooding the infant with sensory stimulation for which it is, quite naturally, unprepared. Due to the helplessness and dependence of the human infant from its earliest stages, such an experience would, thus, fall into the category of a trauma but one that is part and parcel of the human experience. On account of this, it is also a form of trauma that is potentially capable of being experienced by all subjects, both sexual and asexual. Since the infantile period is the theorized place where human sexuality begins, I will be examining the nature of this concept of trauma and asking if and how this might contribute to the formation of an asexual orientation.

The Question of the Phallus

Any consideration of asexuality in the context of Lacanian theory will have to include the concept of the phallus, which is not an imaginary or real object, nor is it a bodily organ. It is, in Lacanian terms, the signifier of desire, in particular, the desire of the Other (2006, p. 523),[28] and is the signifier which can designate meaning effects as a whole (ibid., p. 579). Because Lacan makes the phallus an essential element for understanding and negotiating the networks of sexualized desire in relation to the Other, it will be necessary to question its place in asexuality. The perspective from which I intend to approach this question will be that the phallus is the essential signifier with which the child navigates the desire of its parents and, in the first instance, the desire of the mother. As such, a very particular relation is established between child and mother with what Lacan terms the "Imaginary phallus". I will be asking what this relation represents in asexuality and whether it evolves differently to sexual subjects. I will also examine how the place of the phallus relates to the imposition of the law of the father which prohibits the mother as object of desire. Asexuality is defined as a lack of sexual attraction for another person. In this sense, and at the risk of stating the obvious, the place of the sexualized Other would appear to be crucially different for asexual subjects. Therefore, I will be asking whether this point of difference originates in the first relation to the mother, as first Other, during infantile sexuality. Given the centrality of the breast in this context, can Lacanian theory offer a construct with which to situate a prototypical de-eroticization of this first part-object? If this is the case, the next question will be how this can transmit from the earliest oral stage through various psychosexual stages and emerge in adulthood in the form of asexuality.

A Pleasure that Is Not Obvious

The self-defined asexual experience is one in which there is no sexual attraction for another person and no subjective distress on account of it. But perhaps not all asexuals are self-defined, by which I mean, there might possibly be many people who do not experience sexual attraction for another person and who do not identify as asexual. A question which would then arise is how people in this category might sustain their sense of themselves as asexual beings in a hegemonically sex-normative world. Some of the names mentioned earlier in this context were people who were relatively prominent in their respective eras and who managed to function successfully without sexual desire, and yet they also functioned without the identificatory support of self-defined asexuality. In this regard, a concept in Lacan's later teaching which I will examine is the *sinthome* (see Lacan, 2016), a subject-specific act of artifice whereby the person creates something in their lives to allow them to function. Mostly, this is understood as an engagement with art, writing or creativity which supports the person despite any symptom they may encounter within themselves. Through his concept of the *sinthome*, Lacan posits a form of *jouissance* which is no longer prescribed by the other person. Consistently for him, man's desire is the desire of the Other (1977, p. 235), and yet his later theorizing proposes an innovative way in which a subject can, essentially, find a way to be independent of the Other. I will be asking whether this concept offers an understanding of how a non-identified asexual subject can derive a different and, as yet, unconsidered form of *jouissance*, one that establishes and supports a new relation between the subject and the Other. In terms of the word *symptom*, it is important to bear in mind that, in psychoanalytic terms, everybody has the potential to have a symptom (Lacan, 1974–1975, session of 18 February 1975, pp. 97–99). Indeed, Collette Soler's (2003, p. 86) interpretation of this idea, no doubt taking her lead from Freud's question in this regard, goes so far as to encompass "normative heterosexuality" itself as a symptom.[29] Through the personal invention of a *sinthome*, therefore, the subject can create a solution which ties the three Lacanian registers of human existence together – the Real which are experiences that are beyond words; the Symbolic which is the register of language, law and culture; and the Imaginary which comprises the subject's experience of their body, interior life and relationship with the Other. The question to be addressed in this regard is what the theory of the *sinthome* can offer in understanding that form of asexuality which does not identify as asexual.

Just like sexual subjects, asexual subjects desire careers, recognition, self-expression and, apart from those asexuals who define themselves as a-romantic (Carrigan, 2011, p. 468), relationships with others. In short, they are desiring beings, and the energy of this desire is libido. Therefore, in order to theorize a libido which is not sexually directed at another person, it will be necessary to ask if this Other-directed component of libido is sublimated, repressed or annulled, and if so, how this comes about. Furthermore, when we listen to asexuals speaking about their asexuality, it becomes apparent that there is something absolute about the way sexual attraction is elided.[30] The latter is not part of their experience nor is the sexual activity of others very often understandable for them.[31] The absolute nature of this absence of sexual desire for another person, and the absence of any understanding of the attractiveness of sexual engagement, would suggest that something of a foreclosure has taken place. If this is so, it will be necessary to ask if "foreclosure" rather than "annulment" is the appropriate term. A further challenge in this regard is that, within Lacanian psychoanalysis, the term "foreclosure" is usually associated with psychosis. Therefore, in order to assist in an understanding of the asexual orientation without the assumption of pathology, it will be necessary to interrogate the foundations of this term "foreclosure" and ask whether its invariable association with psychosis is justified and sustainable.

A Summary of the Book

The book has seven further chapters, and in Chapter 1, I will look at the current research being carried out which, despite it being a relatively new field and comparatively small, is, nevertheless, of a high quality and offers insightful material. The psychoanalytic theory on asexuality is practically non-existent by comparison but is useful nonetheless. In Chapter 2, I will examine Freud's theories of the instincts and of libido in an exploratory survey of the conceptual resources available for an understanding of asexuality. Of importance are ideas such as how the drives are capable of a variety of ways of finding satisfaction. I will also examine sublimation, auto-eroticism and, as stated, the much-overlooked presence of an asexual period in every sexual person's development, namely, the latency period.

Libido has an unpleasurable aspect to it, despite the popularly held view to the contrary, and so in Chapter 3, I will focus on Freud's idea that trauma can be experienced from internally generated libidinal demands. I will also examine the role of narcissism in withdrawing libido from external objects as well as Freud's concept of the ego ideal as an agency that can include a desire for no desire. I will also look at repression and its potential role in asexuality along with the concept of inhibition and its classically understood role in male impotence and female frigidity.

In Chapter 4, I will begin a three-chapter theoretical exploration of Lacanian theory and its broad array of conceptual tools. In particular, I will consider how Lacan's theory offers a perspective on the universal concept of psychical lack as an absence which creates desire. I will examine the central place of this absence within Lacan's concept of the unconscious fundamental phantasy which, as stated, is the postulated imaginary construct acting as support for human desire. I will also highlight his theorizing of infantile sexuality and how a symbolic reversal of dependency on another person for the satisfaction of need can come about. Here, I will be proposing that the lack of Other-directed sexual desire, which is definitional for asexuality, might not be an absence, per se, but instead an actively orientated desire for no sexual desire. This would allow for the stigmatization of asexuality as a lacking orientation and a negative space to be considered in a new light.[32]

In Chapter 5, I will explore Lacan's theory of the infant's experience of the first Other and the concept of the Imaginary phallus. Becoming the Imaginary phallus for the mother is, he believes, a pivotal moment whereby the pre-Oedipal child seeks to become what it imagines its primary caregiver, usually the mother, desires and so models its own desire accordingly. I will offer a reading of this pivotal moment in order to see if it can provide a foundation for an asexual relation to the Other. This chapter will also examine how Lacanian theory can accommodate the paradoxical asexual experience of an active libidinal desire aimed at nothing.

In Chapter 6, I will, as stated, refine the concept of annulment when referring to the absence of sexual attraction for another person and propose that it is necessary to consider the term "foreclosure" as more appropriate, provided it can be separated from its Lacanian association with psychosis. I will also show how the *sinthome*, a later conceptual development in Lacan's work, might offer a fruitful and robust way of understanding the enigma of asexuality within a predominantly sexual discourse, particularly in the case of asexual people who have not self-identified as asexual.

Chapter 7 is the concluding chapter in which I will draw together the various theoretical strands of the previous chapters in order to propose that asexuality is a valid sexual orientation, that it is libidinally driven and that its libido is directed towards a very specific albeit previously unconsidered object which causes asexual desire. I will be concluding that asexuality is the result of the earliest pre-Oedipal encounters with libidinal excitation (i.e., the drive) which are experienced as unpleasurable. I will further conclude that this unpleasure egresses forward through infantile psychosexual stages until it emerges in adulthood as the foreclosure of sexual desire for another person.

Notes

1 See AVEN's website for this definition and other information about asexuality, at asexuality.org.
2 The collection of essays edited by Cerankowski and Milks (2014) captures the plurality of the asexual lived experience. See also Przybylo (2019, p. 11).
3 "The ace way of thinking has many new terms and nuances. Like anything that is honest, it can be messy" (Chen, 2020, p. 6).
4 See also Prause and Graham (2007, p. 350).
5 Engelman, 2008, online pagination, p. 1; Scherrer, 2008, p. 631; Bogaert 2012, pp. 150–155.
6 See Freud's (1951 [1935]) comments on homosexuality in 'Letter to an American Mother'.
7 Chen (2020, p. 90) makes the point that asexuality is granted this exception status while still remaining within the DSM while at the same time hypoactive sexual desire

disorder, or low sex drive, is further pathologized when the only thing that separates the two is a conceptual shift in self-identification.

8 AVEN website, accessed at www.asexuality.org/.

9 There are different views of what the definition of asexuality should include. See Carrigan et al., 2014, pp. 3–4, 25.

10 Available at: https://news.gallup.com/poll/201731/lgbt-identification-rises.aspx. Accessed 1 November 2021.

11 See Kurowicka (2015).

12 For queer theory, see Giffney and Watson (2017, pp. 30–31). For asexuality, see Mosbergen, D. (2013).

13 A newspaper article titled "Gay Front Seeks Campus Recognition" in *The Florida Alligator* published in 1971 said membership of the Gay Liberation Front was open to asexuals, bisexuals, homosexuals and "confused heterosexuals". Available at: bit.ly/3tVOZCs pic.twitter.com/3AQxy3CUXh [Accessed 1 November 2021].

14 Available at: https://en.wikipedia.org/wiki/T._E._Lawrence [Accessed 1 November 2021].

15 Available at: www.asexuality.org/en/topic/19214-famous-asexual-people/ [Accessed 1 November 2021].

16 Available at: www.rollingstone.com/music/music-news/morrissey-unfortunately-i-am-not-homosexual-97985/ [Accessed 1 November 2021].

17 For Morrissey and more, see www.thetalko.com/15-famous-people-who-are-asexual/, and see also www.ozy.com/flashback/asexual-lives-of-achievement/31647, which also lists Immanuel Kant, Jane Austen and Hans Christian Andersen. [Both sources accessed 1 November 2021].

18 Available at: www.timteeman.com/2015/11/08/inside-gore-vidals-cliffside-palace-of-sex-scandal-and-celebrity/ [Accessed 1 November 2021].

19 Available at: www.youtube.com/watch?v=wnQh3wrnXtE [Accessed 1 November 2021].

20 Faderman (1985, p. 190 ff) says the term "Boston marriage" arose in the 19th century in America and that novelist Henry James intended "The Bostonians" (1885) to be a study of such a relationship between two women which he found to be common practice in New England.

21 *Jouissance* is understood as a libidinized pleasure that goes beyond the law of the Pleasure Principle. The latter is a "law" whereby we enjoy only enough to satisfy our needs. *Jouissance*, instead, goes on to seek more pleasure to the point where pleasure turns to unpleasure. Lacan describes *jouissance* as a pleasure which brings suffering and is, therefore, a painful pleasure. Braunstein (2003, p. 102) says the concept of *jouissance*, from Lacan's introduction of it in 1958, "became a term rich in nuances, a term that would get progressively more complicated, multiplying and defining itself until it was transformed into the foundation of a new psychoanalysis: a 'notion' without which all else becomes inconsistent". For a comprehensive examination of this "notion", see Leader (2021).

22 "Phantasy" is used in this book to denote a fundamental axiom which unconsciously supports the structure of each subject in a consistent manner. Lacan says, "the phantasy has no other role, you have to take it as literally as possible and what you have to do, is to find in each structure, a way to define the laws of transformation which guarantee for this phantasy, in the deduction of the statements of unconscious discourse, the place of an axiom" (*Seminar XIV*, session of 21 June 1967, p. 274).

23 Freud says, "you may quite well say that we are *all* ill – that is, neurotic – since the preconditions for the formation of symptoms can also be observed in normal people" (SE XVI, 1916–1917, p. 358).

24 Carnes (1997, p. 1, 39, 49 and 52) describes sexual anorexia as a distressing, lifelong and pathological avoidance of sex, but this is not asexuality.

25 A distinction needs to be made between distress at experiencing no sexual desire, of which there appears to be none in asexuality, and distress at being asexual in a sexual world. Chen (2020, p. 92) says, "plenty of aces (asexuals) are distressed about being ace – without the cause of that distress being a problem in itself".

26 Scherrer (2008, p. 627) quotes a respondent who says they do not connect masturbation with anything sexual. For similar comments, see also Brotto et al., 2010, p. 607; O'Donnell (2008).

27 Freud takes up this subject again at greater length in *The Economic Problem of Masochism* (1924, pp. 159–161).

28 The word "Other" with a capital *O* is used to signify a person or persons in the subject's experience from whom desire and recognition is sought. "Now, everything that is signifying to us always occurs in the locus of the Other" (Lacan, 2017, p. 238, and see p. 268).

29 In a footnote added to *Three Essays on Sexuality* in 1915, Freud says, "Thus from the point of view of psycho-analysis the exclusive interest felt by men for women is also a problem that needs elucidating and is not a self-evident fact" (1905, p. 146).

30 A research participant says, "I would say I've never in my life had a dream or a fantasy, a sexual fantasy, for example, about being with another woman. So I can pretty much say that I have no lesbian sort of tendencies whatsoever. You would think that by my age I would have had some fantasy or dream of something, wouldn't you? . . . But I've never had a dream or a sexual fantasy about having sex with a man, either. That I can ever, ever remember" (Prause and Graham, 2007, p. 344).

31 Another participant says, "I guess I'm wondering what other people are thinking and other people are feeling and am I the only one who's not doing this?" (ibid., p. 345).

32 See Chen (2020, p. 180).

References

Aicken, C. R. H., Mercer, C. H. and Cassell, J. A. (2013) 'Who reports absence of sexual attraction in Britain? Evidence from national probability surveys', *Psychology and Sexuality*, 4(2), pp. 121–135. Available at: www.tandfonline.com/doi/full/10.1080/19419899. 2013.774161 [Accessed 1 November 2021].

American Psychiatric Association. (2013) *Diagnostic and statistical manual of mental disorders*, 5th Edition. Arlington, VA: Author.

Bogaert, A. F. (2004) 'Asexuality: Its prevalence and associated factors in a national probability sample', *Journal of Sex Research*, 41(3), pp. 279–287.

Bogaert, A. F. (2006) 'Toward a conceptual understanding of asexuality', *Review of General Psychology*, 10(3), pp. 241–250.

Bogaert, A. F. (2012) *Understanding asexuality*. New York: Rowman & Littlefield.

Bostridge, M. (2015) *Florence Nightingale, the woman and her legend*. London: Penguin.

Braunstein, N. A. (2003) 'Desire and jouissance in the teachings of Lacan', in Rabaté, J.-M. (ed.), *The Cambridge Companion to Lacan*. Cambridge: Cambridge University Press, pp. 102–115.

Brotto, L. A., Knudson, G., Inskip, J., Rhodes, K. and Erskine, Y. (2010) 'Asexuality: A mixed-methods approach', *Archives of Sexual Behaviour*, 39(3), pp. 599–618.

Carnes, P. (1997) *Sexual anorexia – Overcoming sexual self-hatred*. Minnesota: Hazelden.

Carrigan, M. (2011) 'There's more to life than sex? Difference and commonality within the asexual community', *Sexualities*, 14(4), pp. 462–478.

Carrigan, M., Gupta, K. and Morrison, T. G. (2014) *Asexuality and sexual normativity: An anthology*. New York: Routledge.

Cerankowski, K. J. and Milks, M. (eds.). (2014) *Asexualities – Feminist and queer perspectives*. New York: Routledge.

Chen, A. (2020) *ACE – What asexuality reveals about desire, society and the meaning of sex*. Boston: Beacon Press.

Copjec, J. (2015) *Read my desire: Lacan against the historicists*. New York: Verso.

Dean, T. (2000) *Beyond sexuality*. Chicago: University of Chicago Press.

Engelman, J. (2008) *Asexuality as a human sexual orientation*. Available at: https://seren dipstudio.org/exchange/serendipupdate/asexuality-human-sexual-orientation [Accessed 1 November 2021].

Faderman, L. (1985) *Surpassing the love of men – Romantic friendship and love between women from the renaissance to the present*. London: The Women's Press.

Freud, S. (1905) 'Three essays on sexuality', in *A case of hysteria, three essays on sexuality and other works*, Standard Edition VII. London: Vintage/Hogarth.

Freud, S. (1914) 'On narcissism: An introduction', in *On the history of the psycho-analytic movement, papers on metapsychology and other works*, Standard Edition XIV. London: Vintage/Hogarth.

Freud, S. (1915) 'Repression', in *On the history of the psycho-analytic movement, papers on metapsychology and other works*, Standard Edition XIV. London: Vintage/Hogarth.

Freud, S. (1916–1917) *Introductory lectures on psycho-analyses*, Standard Editions XV–XVI. London: Vintage/Hogarth.

Freud, S. (1920) 'Beyond the pleasure principle', in *Beyond the pleasure principle, group psychology and other works*, Standard Edition XVIII. London: Vintage/Hogarth.

Freud, S. (1924) 'The economic problem of masochism', in *The ego and the id and other works*, Standard Edition XIX. London: Vintage/Hogarth.

Freud, S. (1935) 'Letter to an American mother', *American Journal of Psychiatry* (1951), p. 107. Available at: https://sourcebooks.fordham.edu/pwh/freud1.asp [Accessed 1 November 2021].

Gherovici, P. (2010) *Please select your gender: From the invention of hysteria to the democratizing of transgenderism*. New York: Routledge.

Giffney, N. and Watson, E. (eds.). (2017) *Clinical encounters in sexuality – Psychoanalytic practice and queer theory*. New York: Punctum Books.

Gressgård, R. (2014) 'Are there issues particular to asexuality research which differentiates it from other forms of sexualities research?' in Carrigan, M., Gupta, K. and Morrison, T. G. (eds.), *Asexuality and sexual normativity: An anthology*. New York: Routledge.

Hinderliter, A. C. (2009) *Asexuality: The history of a definition*. Available at: www.asexu alexplorations.net/home/history_of_definition.html [Accessed 1 November 2021].

Hoffman, P. (1998) *The man who loved only numbers*. London: Fourth Estate.

Hyldgaard, K. (2009) 'Sex as fantasy and sex as symptom', *The Symptom Online Journal for Lacan.com* (10), Spring. Available at: www.lacan.com/symptom10a/sex-as.html [Accessed 3 November 2021].

Kurowicka, A. (2015) 'The queer identity for the twenty-first century? An exploration of asexuality', in Oleksy, E. H., Różalska, A. M. and Wojtaszek, M. M. (eds.), *The personal of the political: Transgenerational dialogues in contemporary European feminisms*. Cambridge: Cambridge Scholars Publishing, pp. 203–216.

Lacan, J. (1966–1967) *The logic of phantasy*, Seminar XIV, unpublished (Gallagher, C., trans). Available at: www.lacaninireland.com [Accessed 21 November 2021].

Lacan, J. (1974–1975) *RSI*, Seminar XXII, unpublished (Gallagher, C., trans). Available at: www.lacaninireland.com [Accessed 6 December 2021].

Lacan, J. (1977 [1964]) *The four fundamental concepts of psycho-analysis*, Seminar XI (Miller, J-A., ed.) (Sheridan, A., trans). London: Penguin.

Lacan, J. (2006 [1966]) *Écrits – The first complete English edition* (Fink, B., trans). New York: W. W. Norton.

Lacan, J. (2016 [1975–1976]) *The sinthome*, Seminar XXIII (Miller, J.-A., ed.) (Price, A. R., trans). Cambridge: Polity.

Lacan, J. (2017 (2015) [1957–1958]) *Transference*, Seminar VIII (Miller, J.-A., ed.) (Fink, B., trans). Cambridge: Polity Press.

Leader, D. (2021) *Jouissance – Sexuality, suffering and satisfaction*. Cambridge: Polity.

Miller, N. E. (2017) 'Asexuality and its discontents: Making the "invisible orientation" visible in comics', *Inks: The Journal of the Comics Studies Society*, 1(3), Fall, pp. 354–376. Ohio: The Ohio State University Press.

Morel, G. (2017) 'Fundamental phantasy and the symptom as a pathology of the law', *The Centre for Freudian Analysis and Research Web Journal*, pp. 1–19. Available at: https://cfar.org.uk/wp-content/uploads/2017/05/Morel.pdf [Accessed 6 December 2021].

Mosbergen, D. (2013) 'LGBT+, asexual communities clash over ace inclusion', *Huffington Post,* 21 June (updated 6 December 2017). Available at: https://www.huffpost.com/entry/lgbt-asexual_n_3385530 [Accessed 3 December 2021].

O'Donnell, B. (2008) 'We're married, we just don't have sex', *The Guardian*, 8 September. Available at: www.guardian.co.uk/lifeandstyle/2008/sep/08/relationships.healthandwellbeing [Accessed 4 November 2021].

O'Reilly, Z. (1997) 'My life as an amoeba', *Zoe O'Reilly Blog*, 30 May. Available at: http://web.archive.org/web/20030210212218/http://dispatches.azstarnet.com/zoe/amoeba.htm [Accessed 1 November 2021].

Poston, D. L., Jr. and Baumle, A. K. (2010) 'Patterns of asexuality in the United States', *Demographic Research*, 23, pp. 509–530. Available at: www.demographic-research.org/volumes/vol23/18/23-18.pdf [Accessed 1 November 2021].

Prause, N. and Graham, C. A. (2007) 'Asexuality: Classification and characterization', *Archives of Sexual Behaviour*, 36(3), pp. 341–355.

Przybylo, E. (2019) *Asexual erotics: Intimate readings of compulsory sexuality*. Columbus, OH: Ohio State University Press.

Rothblum, E. D. and Brehony, K. A. (eds.). (1993) *Boston marriages – Romantic but asexual relationships among contemporary lesbians*. Amherst, MA: University of Massachusetts Press.

Scherrer, K. S. (2008) 'Coming to an asexual identity: Negotiating identity, negotiating desire', *Sexualities*, 11(5), 1 October, pp. 621–641.

Soler, C. (2003) 'The paradoxes of the symptom in psychoanalysis', in Rabaté, J-M. (ed.), *The Cambridge Companion to Lacan*. Cambridge: Cambridge University Press, pp. 86–101.

Watson, E. (2011) *Touching the void: A psychoanalytic critique of the encounters between lesbian sexuality and psychoanalysis*, unpublished PhD thesis. Dublin: School of Medicine and Medical Science, College of Life Sciences, St. Vincent's University Hospital, University College Dublin, Ireland.

Yule, M. A., Brotto, L. A. and Gorzalka, B. B. (2014) 'Mental health and interpersonal functioning in self-identified asexual men and women', in Carrigan, M., Gupta, K. and Morrison, T. G. (eds.), *Asexuality and sexual normativity: An anthology*. New York: Routledge, pp. 25–40.

Zupančič, A. (2017) *What is sex?* Cambridge, MA: MIT Press.

Chapter 1

What Research Has to Say about Asexuality

Asexuality has been brought to public attention through asexual individuals recounting their experiences in books and blogs, forming communities on the internet[1] or, in some cases, raising awareness through activism and forging alliances with LGBTQIA+ communities.[2] This, in turn, has brought asexuality to the attention of academic researchers seeking to understand asexuality on its own terms from a variety of theoretical perspectives. What I intend to do in this chapter is to focus on what this research has to say about asexuality, its attributes, its characteristics and its challenges both at an individual and collective level. Research on asexuality comes almost exclusively from disciplines other than psychoanalysis, and before any consideration can be given to psychoanalytic theory, it is essential, in my view, to listen to what asexual people have said and what researchers have found in terms of the lived experience of being asexual. In this sense, the value of the selected research which follows lies not only at the level of individual asexual experience but also in the way it elaborates on more general and commonly occurring characteristics.

The Early Study

In 1980, a study titled "Theories of Sexual Orientation" was published by researcher Michael Storms which is generally accepted to be the first to include the term *asexuality* as it is used now. In it, a model of sexuality was developed which classified heterosexuals as individuals who are highly attracted to the other sex (i.e., high in heteroeroticism), homosexuals as individuals who are highly attracted to the same sex (i.e., high in homoeroticism), bisexuals as individuals who are highly attracted to both sexes (i.e., high in both heteroeroticism and homoeroticism) and asexuals as individuals who are not attracted to either sex (i.e., low in both heteroeroticism and homoeroticism). Using a two-dimensional model of sexual orientation, Storms distinguished between individuals who are bisexual (those who score high on both heteroeroticism and homoeroticism) and individuals who are asexual (those who score low on both dimensions). In a radical call for asexuality to be included in sexual research, he said that failing to differentiate bisexuals from asexuals would obscure the results of research on sexual

DOI: 10.4324/9781003214946-2

orientation (ibid., p. 790). He added that his two-dimensional model of erotic orientation concurred with a Freudian view of bisexuality whereby bisexuals would have high levels of both homosexual and heterosexual eroticism. More generally, his results demonstrated a strong connection between a person's erotic fantasy content and his or her sexual orientation (ibid., p. 791). Storms concluded that if erotic fantasy was an important determinant of sexual orientation, researchers like him still had no idea what produces erotic fantasy (ibid.).[3] Storms's important inclusion and recognition of asexuality, however, did not progress to any greater understanding of this orientation.

The research which is generally regarded as the first to discover the prevalence of asexuality is by Anthony Bogaert. Using data from a national probability sample in the UK, he found that approximately 1% of British residents defined themselves as asexual (2004, p. 282), a figure most often cited for the percentage of asexuals in a given population. The survey was prompted by the need for sexual information about the general population in the wake of the AIDS epidemic, and it was among the most representative of sexuality surveys. Up to this time, Bogaert says that sexual aversion disorder and hypoactive sexual desire disorder (HSDD) had been studied more frequently. He distinguishes asexuality from these conditions because in both sexual aversion disorder and HSDD, there usually is or was a sexual attraction towards partners of either or both gender(s). However, this is inhibited or blocked by either an aversion for genital contact with, or a low sexual desire for, these partners. He says that asexuality, in contrast, can be defined as the *absence* of a traditional sexual orientation, in which an individual exhibits little or no attraction to males or females (ibid., p. 279). He notes two further things in his study: that asexuality is a lifelong orientation, an aspect that some disagree with, and that the lack of sexual attraction does not necessarily include a lack of sexual behaviour with either sex, which most other researchers agree with (ibid.).

While 1.05% of the 195 participants reported being asexual, this was very similar to the rate of same-sex attraction (both exclusive same-sex and bisexuality combined; 207 or 1.11%). However, there were more gay and bisexual men than asexual men and more asexual women than lesbian and bisexual women. Relative to sexually active people, asexuals had fewer sexual partners, had a later onset of sexual activity (if it occurred) and had less frequent sexual activity with a partner currently. Overall, asexual people had less sexual experience with sexual partners, and Bogaert interpreted this fact as providing some validation of the concept of asexuality. He speculates about whether the rate of asexuality is actually higher than reported given that some of the participants who declined to participate in this survey (about 30%) could also be asexual. His findings also show that a variety of factors, from demographic (gender, social class, education and race-ethnicity), to physical development (height and menarche[4] onset), to health and religiosity, statistically predicted asexuality. Even physical development and health variables – late menarche, health problems in women and shorter stature and health problems in men – independently predicted asexuality. His study also found that a sizable minority (33%) of asexuals were in long-term relationships, and another 11%

had had at least one long-term relationship in the past. He believed that such partnerships in asexual people may occur for a variety of practical reasons (e.g., economic and child-rearing), along with the fact that some, perhaps many, may still have a romantic/affectionate attraction to others and, thus, desire to form a romantic bond with them. Another important finding was that, although asexual people reported a relatively low level of sexual activity with a partner (e.g., 0.2 per week vs. 1.2 per week for sexual people), some still engaged in sexual activity with a partner, perhaps if only to please that partner. Thus, distinctions between sexual attraction and other aspects of relationships (e.g., romantic attraction and sexual behaviour) may be important within the context of definitional/conceptual issues surrounding asexuality, just as they are for categories of sexual orientation (i.e., heterosexuality, homosexuality and bisexuality).

In a 2006 paper, Bogaert (p. 241) described asexuality as an "overlooked phenomenon", and perhaps conscious of any unintended implications of his 2004 findings regarding physical health and atypical prenatal development as predictors of asexuality,[5] he clarified that these should not be used to pathologize asexuality. The earlier view, in pointing towards a weak biology alongside a possibly atypical physiology, could have lent itself to a pathologizing *credo* when, in fact, physical health and prenatal development only accounted for a small percentage of variation in the prediction of asexuality. Also, he said that until recently, a lack of sexuality was not perceived negatively (ibid.). Rather, sexual activity, particularly if excessive or occurring within a nonreproductive context (e.g., masturbation), was perceived as a health and societal problem. In addition, even today, lack of interest in sex is promoted within certain religious groups and cultures (ibid.). He said this:

> If . . . we avoid a general tendency to pathologize and recognize that some people may be quite content to live as asexual beings, it may in fact serve to remove the stigma and possible distress associated with such inclinations.
>
> (ibid.)

While HSDD does require a clinical focus, he believes asexuality should not necessarily be deemed a pathological state (ibid., p. 249).

Asexuality and Subjective Distress

According to Prause and Graham (2007, p. 341), asexuality raises questions concerning the role of "personal distress" in defining sexual desire problems. Their study attempts to better characterize the way the label *asexual* is used and to investigate what distinguishes those who identify as asexual from those who do not. Implicit in the debate about what constitutes a normal level of sexual desire is an assumption that *some* level of sexual desire is normative. As such, they ask whether low or absent sexual desire is necessarily to be associated with pathology. In other words, should a diagnosis of a disorder be assigned on the basis of cognitions or behaviours (the way a person thinks or acts) in the absence of evidence that these are maladaptive (citing Rubin, 2000). They point out that the current evidence does not suggest that thoughts or actions associated with asexuality necessarily signal a problem yet note that the term *asexual* can be used as a pejorative label (ibid., 2007, p. 342). Their research was designed to better characterize individuals who self-identify as asexual and to measure the level of subjective distress among asexuals on the basis, as other authors have noted, that subjective distress is a symptom required for many psychiatric diagnoses. The study found that self-identified asexuals were not particularly sexually fearful but that they had a lower excitatory drive. Interestingly, the study did not find, as Bogaert (2004) did, a gender or relationship status difference between sexuals and asexuals. The data also indicated that a higher percentage of asexuals had completed at least a college degree as compared to non-asexuals, and this was not accounted for by the group age difference. The Bogaert study found the opposite. Also, there was no significant difference in the lifetime number of sexual partners reported by asexuals and non-asexuals, whereas in Bogaert (2004), asexuals reported fewer sexual partners. Both groups of participants reported that asexuals would differ most from non-asexuals by their no/low sexual desire and their no/low sexual experience, but the quantitative data suggested that asexuals actually differed most in their sexual desire and sexual arousability levels, and not the amount of their sexual experience. The authors say it remains to be determined to what extent asexuality is problematic in the absence of individual, personal distress. This point applies to self-defined asexuals – that is, those people who have recognized and accepted their asexual orientation.

Researching Asexual Identity

Picking up on a statement by sex therapist Ellen Cole (1993, p. 187) that one of the most pervasive social assumptions is that all humans possess sexual desire, sociologist and diversity scholar Kristin Scherrer (2008, p. 621) comments that there is little academic literature exploring those people who do *not* possess it. She says that asexuality challenges notions of the pervasiveness of sexuality and presents a unique opportunity to explore the negotiation of identity and desire (ibid., p. 622). Of the 89 participants who responded to her question, "what does this identity mean to you?", 39 or 44% said that their asexual identity means that they do not experience sexual attraction or sexual desire (ibid., p. 626). The remaining 56% put forward alternative understandings. Of these, 27 said that a lack of interest in sexual behaviour was a defining component of their asexual identity and that this was not necessarily associated with sexual attraction. Scherrer points out that for some, an asexual identity is *not* about a lack of sexual attraction but rather is based on an intent *not* to participate in sexual behaviours. A smaller group of participants offered definitions of their asexuality that contained relatively limited information about the meaning of their asexual identity, such as, "It is just who I am". She found 13 participants who described themselves as not experiencing sexual desire or attraction, but at the same time, when describing an "ideal relationship", they declared interest in some sort of physical intimacy with another or others. Regarding masturbation, while her study did not explicitly ask about it, ten participants mentioned it, with some making the distinction between sex in relation to others and the sexual encounter with the self (ibid., p. 628). Despite this distinction, they still considered masturbation to be an expression of sexual desire that they were *not* interested in (ibid.).[6] For Scherrer, this disconnect between masturbation and sexuality is an interesting divorce given masturbation's historical connection to sex. It reinforces findings by Prause and Graham (2007) who found that two of the four self-identified asexual people in their sample did engage in masturbation while defining it as non-sexual.

Scherrer argues that sexual essentialism is a widespread assumption of modern society, and so the idea that the desire for sex is a natural and essential characteristic is present in many of her participants' descriptions of their asexuality, with many describing themselves as *naturally* asexual (2008, p. 628). While the internet facilitates the discovery of a language for asexuality, she finds it interesting that this identity mostly revolves around the *lack* of sexuality. For Scherrer, some respondents compare an asexual identity with a lack rather than the presence of a characteristic, as many identities are. Because it is defined as a *lack* of behaviour or desire, she says asexuality has escaped attention, a clear departure from the experiences of other marginalized sexualities. Asexual identities are also defined in opposition to celibacy and celibate identities which are described as a choice,[7] and so for many of her participants, the "naturalness" of their asexuality is an important aspect of how they see their identity. Many participants also reported that it was only after encountering on the internet the language of asexuality and an asexual community that they took on the identity. The discovery involved not only a language to describe themselves and a community offering support and acceptance, but it also involved a way of thinking about their asexuality as an essential characteristic of themselves (ibid., p. 631).

Asexuality and Sexual Activity

In a dual study of asexuality, Brotto et al. (2010) examined relationship characteristics, frequency of sexual behaviours, sexual difficulties and distress, psychopathology, interpersonal functioning, and alexithymia[8] in 187 asexuals recruited from the AVEN website. This survey of 54 men and 133 women found that sexual response was lower than normative data but was not experienced as distressing. Between 73% of women and 80% of men had engaged in masturbation. The average frequency was a few times a week for men and once a month for women. Similar rates of asexual women in this study (approximately 30%) and women in a study of sexual individuals had never engaged in masturbation. Some 27% of the sample engaged in sexual intercourse and provided a variety of reasons for this, some of which were unrelated to sexual attraction (ibid., p. 607). The authors say that sexual intercourse and masturbation that are stripped of sexual attraction might be motivated by issues such as stress reduction, relationship maintenance, partner pressure or broader societal expectations (ibid.). Social withdrawal was found to be the most elevated personality subscale, but interpersonal functioning was in the normal range. Alexithymia was elevated in 12% of the survey, but again, social desirability was in the normal range. A second part of the study was designed to expand upon the quantitative findings with 15 asexuals from the first study going through in-depth telephone interviews. The findings of this second study suggest that asexuality is best conceptualized as a lack of sexual attraction, even though respondents varied greatly in their experience of sexual response and behaviour. Asexuals partnered with sexuals acknowledged having to "negotiate" sexual activity (ibid., p. 599). There were not higher rates of psychopathology among asexuals, but the authors say a subset might fit the criteria for schizoid personality disorder. There was also strong opposition to viewing asexuality as an extreme case of sexual desire disorder (HSDD).

About 80% of the men and women selected *asexual* when presented with a forced-choice question about their sexual orientation. "This is despite the fact that we recruited from AVEN, a web-community devoted to asexuals, and that participants had to personally endorse the asexual label before being routed to questionnaires", they say (ibid., p. 606). The nature of their relationships, for those asexual individuals who were currently in a relationship, helped to interpret why not all participants selected asexual as their orientation. The majority described their relationships with a focus on the romantic as opposed to the sexual. They say that the 11% who did not endorse asexual as their label may have been deterred by the focus on *sexual* in asexual and preferred to conceptualize themselves and their relationships as a romantic orientation.

In terms of the age of first sexual interest and of intercourse debut, many individuals indicated that they could not recall the onset of sexual interests. The authors believe this lack of recollection of first sexual interests and experiences is important as puberty generally marks a significant point for the development of sexual feelings and behaviours. They further add that this suggests, perhaps, a developmental trajectory whereby the lack of sexual interests in early adulthood may set the stage for later lack of sexual desire or excitement. The study found that 73% of the sample had never engaged in sexual intercourse, and this replicates the findings of Bogaert (2004). The fact that one-third of a sample of individuals with a mean age of 30 had never been in an interpersonal relationship is also noteworthy. The authors speculate that problems in child-parent attachment may lead to problems in how the person later develops intimate relationships as an adult. They propose that asexuals may have been avoidant as children, leading to insecure attachment and to viewing relationships as awkward and uncomfortable as adults.

The majority (90%) of the sample reported that they did not experience sexual distress (ibid.), and whereas it has been speculated that asexuality might overlap with sexual desire disorder (Prause and Graham, 2007), this supports the speculation by Bogaert (2006) that asexuality and desire disorder can be differentiated on the basis that the person with low desire can experience distress whereas the asexual does not (Brotto et al., 2010, p. 606). Of significance, however, is the finding that for both women and men, sexual distress and any experience of sexual desire were positively correlated. In other words, the study found that distress was reported to increase with increasing desire. These paradoxical correlations, the authors say, suggest that the presence of a desire response is distressing for the asexual individual because sexual desire might be experienced as "the mind defying one's true intentions" (ibid.). As masturbation frequency did not differ markedly from comparable normative data, it suggested that the "motivations for masturbation may not stem from an intrinsic desire or sexual excitement" (ibid., p. 609). There was also a consistent theme to how asexuals defined asexuality. A "lack of sexual attraction" was evident in nearly all individual responses as participants distinguished this lack of attraction from other aspects of sexual response which may still have been present, such as, again, sexual desire. If sexual desire or arousal were present, asexuals argued that they were not directed at anyone. The study also differentiated a persistent or lifelong lack of sexual attraction from the normative decline in sexual attraction that takes place with relationship duration (ibid.).

It also found that asexuality did not appear to be a fear-mediated construct – that is, that the absence of sexual attraction was not as a result of a fear of being sexually involved with another person. It found, too, that the lack of sexual activity was not related to avoidance or disgust. There was also a great deal of variety in sexual behaviours among asexuals, with some participants having frequent sexual intercourse and some having never engaged in it. The motivations for engaging in sexual activity were, in some cases, an effort to "seem normal" (ibid., p. 614). However, the study also supported other research which found that asexuals had low levels of sexual arousability or excitement. While suggesting that a more thorough examination of the construct of distress might be necessary for future research, the authors say that it might also be at the heart of differentiating the problematic lack of sexual desire to be found in hypoactive sexual desire disorder compared to the non-distressing lack of attraction to be found in asexuality. The fact that all asexuals interviewed believed that asexuality was biological and that there may be a genetic component to it also deserves further study, they say.

Citing current theorists, they posit that asexuals may lack "cognitive causal attribution" and so their physiological arousal does not become directed towards any target. They point to theorists who prefer a biological explanation for the development of sexual attraction, suggesting a link with disruptions in the process of adrenal maturation (adrenarche)[9] between the ages of six and ten. Alternatively, they say, asexuality may develop from a central mechanism that "prevents the activation of neural receptors by these androgens thus preventing proliferation" (ibid.). This is pointing towards a hormonal aetiology similar in scope to that suggested by Bogaert (2004, p. 280, 284) regarding the possible role of the hypothalamus. Describing asexuality as a "poorly understood construct", the authors say that the majority of their participants could not recall onset of any sexual attractions during childhood and, instead, reported feeling different from their peers who verbalized sexual attractions. This supports their theory regarding possible aberrations in the period of adrenarche (ibid., p. 616). The point they highlight regarding the lack of recall of the onset of any sexual attractions supports a view of asexuality as a predominantly lifelong orientation. It also suggests that whatever the reason for having no sexual attraction, its beginnings can be placed at an indeterminate point before the onset of puberty.

Diversity within Asexuality

A study which focusses on the identities and lived experience of self-identified asexuals was conducted by researcher Mark Carrigan who chose this area because of the diverse range of experiences which fall under the popular AVEN definition of an asexual (2011, p. 464). While conceding that the AVEN definition has been highly influential, he contends that it also conceals a significant degree of heterogeneity as to the personal reasons that individuals self-define as asexual (ibid., p. 467). Carrigan believes that before any understanding of these reasons is possible, it is important to gain some acquaintance with the terms that asexuals use to describe themselves. He lists the identifications he found within the emerging asexual discourse with many accepted as conversational terms among asexuals while others, such as "sex-averse and "a-fluid", are more rarely encountered. In his compilation, a central distinction is made between romance and sex which, he says, may be counter-intuitive from the perspective of a mainstream sexual culture that regards the latter as the culmination of the former. Many asexuals, however, feel attraction but without any sexual component to it, instead regarding it as romantic and/or emotional. Others feel attraction that is distinctly aesthetic (ibid., p. 468).[10]

Within those grouped as romantic asexuals, Carrigan says that the variations include heteroromantics who only feel romantic attraction to the opposite sex, homoromantics to the same sex, biromantics to both sexes and panromantics without reference to sex or gender. He says that some romantic asexuals actively seek relationships because closeness, companionship, intellectual and emotional connection are desirable to them (ibid., p. 469). Others are simply open to the possibility, given their experience of romantic attraction, without actively seeking it or assigning it any priority in their lives. Aromantic asexuals, in contrast, experience no romantic attraction and have no desire to pursue romantic relationships. He says that Scherrer found something similar in that "self-identified aromantic asexual individuals tend to describe their ideal relationships as primarily friendship-like" (ibid.). In other cases, though, he notes that romance may be actively and viscerally rejected, as with the respondent in his study who wrote of their disgust at ideas associated with romance and their annoyance at the priority commonly ascribed to them within people's lives (ibid., p. 469).

Carrigan also found that attitudes with regard to sex varied among asexuals, in that those who are sex-positive endorse sex as positive and healthy, sometimes with a concomitant intellectual and/or cultural interest, albeit without experiencing sexual desire or seeking to engage in it themselves (ibid.). He found that those who are sex-neutral are simply uninterested in sex. However, some in this category may be willing to have sex in certain contexts. As well as pleasing a partner, it may be a source of intimacy and confirmation without being enjoyed in a way that is, per se, sexual. He says this latter qualification is supported by the findings of Brotto et al. (2010) that asexuals who have sex do not find it brings them closer to their partners. For others, it may be a "chore", a term that came up in numerous interviews and in replies to Carrigan's questionnaires (ibid.). The third group of attitudes he found are those who are sex-averse or anti-sex, where the *idea* of sex, let alone the actual practice of it, is deeply problematic. Yet here, too, there is variety, with some mildly uncomfortable about sex, some slightly revolted by it and some who find it both disgusting and deeply distressing (ibid.).[11]

Asexuality and Science

Asexuality theorist Ela Przybylo (2012, p. 224) examines the role of scientific research in shaping the "possibilities and impossibilities of what counts as asexuality". She says asexuality, like all sexualities, is culturally and historically contingent and has not existed at any other time in Western history, at least not as "asexuality" per se (ibid., p. 225). She also believes that asexuality, like most sexualities, is "in significant and intricate ways carved into existence by science" (ibid.). Earlier studies of asexuality, for all their faults, accepted asexuality as another "hue of human sexuality" (ibid., p. 227), unlike more contemporary studies which demonstrate a "tangible claiming of asexual territory" as a modern "discovery" by science (ibid., p. 226). She says the first depictions of asexuality saw Michael Storms engage in a remodelling of Alfred Kinsey's sexuality scale, producing as a by-product the sexual orientation of asexuality. Kinsey's work had hinged upon one sole axis of sexuality – the heterosexual-homosexual continuum. He did not investigate what he termed group X – those having "no socio-sexual contacts or reactions" (citing Kinsey et al., 1948, p. 656) and who did "not respond erotically to either heterosexual or homosexual stimuli and (did) not have overt physical contacts with individuals of either sex in which there is evidence of any response" (citing Kinsey et al., 1953, p. 473). Nor, she points out, did Kinsey use the term *asexuality*.

Przybylo also contends that while Storms named *asexuality*, he "hardly acknowledged this act of naming", being more interested in the area of bisexuality (ibid., p. 227). In Masters and Johnson's *On Sex and Human Loving* (Masters et al., 1986), she says sexologists William Masters, Virginia Johnson and Robert Kolodny linked asexuality with negative and pathological traits. The disinterest in the asexual category in the late '70s and early '80s suggests that it was not "a site of meaning making, intellectual enquiry or identity formation" (ibid., p. 229). She further postulates that this flags the very contingency and "constructed-ness" of sexuality in terms of sexual ideals and practices. She says this:

> these studies' negligence towards asexuality reminds us that asexuality, like all sexualities, is not immutable and ever present in the same form. Today's flourishing of asexual interest and meaning-formation . . . puts into sharp relief the absence of such conversations in the past.
>
> (ibid.)

Przybylo says Bogaert's work, because it was the first outright study of asexuality, is of great importance, and a lot of what was to follow built on it to a greater or lesser extent. But it presents itself as "value-free" and "neutral" while at the same time being limited in its "reliance on biological explanations of asexuality" and what she calls "a psychosocial rehearsal of confining sexual *gender* roles". She adds, "In other words, it seems that the price paid for the legitimisation and depathologisation of asexuality is high – the rehearsal of limiting and normative standards of gender, as well as a veritable binding of asexuality to the body" (ibid., p. 231). Like Bogaert, she doubts whether the 1% figure, as indicative of asexuals in a given population, is accurate or reliable, believing the true figure may be considerably higher (ibid.).[12]

Przybylo also questions the general trend of contemporary sexology in establishing the *differences* between men's and women's biological sexual response. In contrast, she observes that Masters and Johnson had as "one of their major ideological tenets: the similarity between women and men" (citing Irvine, 2005, p. 60). Przybylo asks why it is that this difference is based on classifying women as less aware of their bodies, less capable of coordinating their bodies with their minds and more sexually receptive and pliable? She says these current patterns within scientific sexological discourse reflect something of contemporary sexual politics (ibid.). While the scientific research on asexuality is instrumental in legitimizing asexuality, she says, "it does so through the reproduction of normative, essentialist, and harmful notions about (a)sexuality and sexual difference" (ibid., p. 239). The outcome is that women are rendered as more receptive, pliable and less sexually coordinated than men, and asexuality becomes mapped on and in the biological body. These naturalized views of sexual difference take precedence and are framed in what may appear to be a progressive and generous analysis of asexuality, she says.

Taking the various findings and viewpoints from this selection of research, the composite picture of an asexual subject which emerges is a person who does not feel sexual attraction for another person; does not experience subjective distress due to this absence and has experienced this for most, if not all, their lives. Also, the asexual person in this research is not, generally speaking, characterized by fear or disgust at sex and can, in some cases, engage in romantic, non-sexual relationships or, at times, in consensual sexual acts. The contemporary self-identified asexual can also consider their asexuality to be a biological or genetically determined orientation, has no recollection of childhood sexual attractions and can engage in self-directed masturbation which they consider to be a non-sexual activity.

Psychoanalytic Writing on Asexuality

Moving to psychoanalytic writing in this area, research on asexuality as a self-defined, distress-free, lifelong orientation is almost completely lacking, and there are only a handful of papers which touch on the area either directly or indirectly. One paper which is occasionally cited negatively by writers on asexuality is by psychoanalysts Hansen de Almeida and Brajterman Lerner.[13] In it, the authors are credited with stating that there is no such thing as asexuality (1999, p. 491). While this sentiment is undoubtedly contained within their paper, this is not a paper on asexuality but on gender identity. The term "asexuality" is used in the concluding paragraphs, but it is conflated with the term "gender neutrality", and the authors are making the point that to identify as non-sex (i.e., neither male nor female) is a "fantasy" in their opinion (ibid.). Their point is not that asexuality does not exist but rather that to identify as a neutral gender is an omnipotent fantasy of denial that leads to the "annihilation" of gender identification (ibid.). It is occasionally cited as an example of psychoanalysts proposing a repudiation of self-defined asexuality, but in this paper, this is not the case.

One paper which does appear to offer such a repudiation, assuming its title is to be understood as signalling such an intent, is Jean-Louis Chassaing's "The Position of the Resigner" (2008). In it he notes, presumably ironically, that asexuals appear to be "happy" in their orientation (ibid., p. 101) and asks why this would not be the case, having rid sex from their lives (ibid., p. 102). Speculating that asexuality is positioned somewhere between a denial and a disavowal, he offers the view that asexuality has by-passed the tensions inherent in sexual relations (ibid., p. 103). As such, asexuality represents, in his opinion, an example of the perfect mastery of the sexual Real, by which he means that the enigmatic challenges which sexuality poses are avoided. He asks the reasonable question, but does not appear to answer it, as to what happens to the object relation (i.e., the other person) in asexuality (ibid., p. 106). This is a topic which I believe to be of significance, and I will return to it more fully in the following chapters. Chassaing says it remains to be seen if asexuality is a fashionable fad and, therefore, transient (ibid.). He concludes by commenting that the phallus as signifier of desire, and a central component of Lacanian theory, needs to be defended because of its importance in the symbolization of lack which drives desire (ibid., p. 107). For him, the pacifying effects of the phallus through speech and language offer a path through the challenges of sexuality, and he implies that this is preferable to the "perverse complexity" of escaping castration which asexuality represents (ibid.). This point is an occasionally encountered psychoanalytic viewpoint when theorists are confronted with non-normative sexualities and view them as an escape from, or a shelter from, castration.[14] Yet according to Leader, the fundamental phantasy which is a component of *every* subject's psychical structure could "be defined as an apparatus that allows the subject to shelter from castration" (2021, p. 111). In other words, given that all subjects have a fundamental phantasy, heterosexual subjects seek a shelter from castration, too.

Meanwhile, Éléonore Pardo also refers to the place of the phallus and to the possibility of asexuality as a "temporary fad" (2010, online pagination, p. 1). She agrees that asexuals can be considered as free from sex but only in terms of sexual activity and sexual desire. What she believes unites them is the fact of having put in practice "a denial, thus bringing about a degradation of phallic signification", a point similar to Chassaing's earlier. She does, however, ask an interesting question as to whether they constitute a new form of contemporary subjectivity. Asexuals are sexed beings (i.e., male or female) – there is no third possibility – but as spoken beings (*parlêtre*), they have the possibility to play with their sexed being to elude what she calls the real "fatality" of sex (ibid., p. 6). She says this is possible as an "imaginary assemblage" because on the imaginary level, anything is possible in matters of sex, sometimes to the extent of asserting one thing and at the same time its opposite. She asks if asexuals are not without sex but rather alone in sex, a state that appears to reference being transfixed in an imaginary and narcissistic dimension which, in turn, works against the sexual drive being directed at another person (ibid.). I will examine the place of narcissism later in the book, but I will be drawing different conclusions.

In a contemporary culture of spectacle and consumption, Pardo says the subject falls under the illusion of being able to compensate for any lack by consuming the objects at hand. As this filling of the lack with real objects operates at the level of the imaginary, it eludes castration. This resonates again with a theme within psychoanalysis, mentioned earlier, of non-normative sexuality being viewed as a shelter from castration. This, she argues, leads to a confrontation with forms of *jouissance* outside of the body that are impossible to interpret. But in what represents a departure from the lived experience of asexuals, she says that this process "leaves the psyche wide open to the manifestations of anxiety" (ibid., p. 7). She goes on to say that the common justification of asexuality that "I have been born like this" is a very modern trap, a catch-all phrase, for being biologically programmed and having no choice, even though this involves a form of depersonalization (ibid.). Be that as it may, there is one point here on which I will concur and elaborate later, namely that sexuality and asexuality are not biologically programmed. Apart from the essentialist connotations which it introduces, it ignores the social roots of the human subject and is counter to a psychoanalytic perspective which prefers to understand gender and the choices around sexuality as unrelated to biology, or indeed to binary notions of heteronormativity.

For Pardo, asexuality can be seen as an effect of the human subject being unable to "temper his jouissance" to the point where "sexual difference appears more or less secondary" (ibid., p. 8). She says that in order to become a subject, the human being must encounter sexual difference, experienced as fundamentally traumatic and unassimilable. Yet asexuality implies an encounter of a different kind, she believes. It is still traumatic but comes from the outside, through social discourse and imagery dominated by sex, stripped of its symbolic dimension and in a Real that may lead to "terror" (ibid.). As a phenomenon, she says asexuality shows that in silencing its eroticism, a body is left to claim, in the public arena, the identity which it cannot grasp symbolically. As such, for her, asexuality is a contemporary form of a new subjectivity, where the symbolic is missing and the imaginary takes over. This, she says, disrupts the position of the Other, as sexual partner, whereby a pleasure of the drives can be attained by the asexual which is different from any satisfaction of need (ibid.). I will be concurring with some elements of this, but I will be proposing that asexuality does not arise due to an inability to "grasp symbolically" the sexual real. I will also be proposing that while self-defined asexuality is, in part, responding to the adverse effects of a social discourse which is dominated by sex, social discourse is not the primary cause of asexuality.

Kristian Kahn (2014, p. 47, 72, fn. 23) positions the asexual as an artist figure with potential to exist productively at the margins of heteronormative culture and whose asexual orientation, just like art, is the result of sublimation. The asexual, he says, is on the "cusp" of the imaginary and the symbolic registers, and is an individual who does not strive for *jouissance* with another person. Rather, he says, the asexual can be viewed as autoerotic or "self-containing" (ibid., p. 64). He includes Lacan's concept of the *sinthome* (see Lacan, 2016) and applies it to the asexual experience generally, a point on which I will differ. As a result, for Kahn, asexuality as "sinthomatic" views the Other, whose desire is what we desire, as "meaningless" since the *sinthome* provides all the consistency necessary for carrying out a "productive psychological, social, and cultural role". He says that not only is the asexual able to straddle the imaginary and symbolic realms, just as the artist can, he or she is also able to bring "meaning into being through recourse to living at the level of the sinthome" (ibid., p. 67). From this perspective, he says the asexual-as-artist, due to an embodiment of the *sinthome*, exists in an a priori position beyond the pleasure principle as well as "beyond the restrictive mandates of the symbolic realm of language, heteronormative logic, and subjects barred from the objects they desire" (ibid., p. 71). He believes this allows the asexual to see *jouissance* "as nothing more than an illusory fantasy", a link to Lacan's concept of misrecognition which takes place in the founding act of identity during the Mirror Stage in infancy. For Kahn, the asexual prefers instead the "transgressive space afforded by the *sinthome* – the place of artistry, the place where desires and fantasies can mean whatever the subject wants them to mean" (ibid.). Again, while I will be working with similar theoretical constructs, I will be proposing a different understanding of asexuality.

As can be seen, just a few psychoanalytic papers take asexuality for their subject matter, and only Kahn's takes an inclusive and testing stance with regard to how psychoanalytic theory might accommodate and account for this sexual orientation. Within the other papers, there is evidence of a reliance on either anecdotal data or unquestioning adherence to psychoanalytic theoretical principles. As a result, they struggle to explain the concept of a sexual drive which is absent without recourse to characterizing it, to a greater or lesser extent, as dysfunctional. This book will seek to offer an alternative view to this.

As I mentioned in the previous chapter, the little available literature on asexuality within psychoanalysis is all the more curious given that Freud's youngest child, Anna, appeared to represent a non-sexual orientation without subjective distress. One might ask how a theory rich in ideas about human sexuality could have had a blind spot on a topic which, on the face of it, was an implicit element in the life of its founder's daughter. Anna was in a non-sexual relationship for 50 plus years with Dorothy Tiffany Burlingham, a separated mother of four and the granddaughter of the founder of Tiffany & Co., the American luxury retailer (Young-Bruehl, 1988, p. 443).

It has never been stated in her biographies or other psychoanalytic writing that Anna Freud was asexual, and it is difficult to be definitive on the subject. Some believe she "closely resembled" a lesbian (Roudinesco, 2016, p. 249), but if so, the indicators suggest she was an asexual lesbian. Her biographer is of the view that, in spite of their lifelong relationship, Anna Freud did not have a sexual relationship with Dorothy Burlingham or anyone else. Furthermore, those in her professional circle were of the opinion that the relationship between the two women was "chaste" (Young-Bruehl, 1988, pp. 137–138). Among her wider network, however, there were rumours about her being a (sexual) lesbian, and Anna was reputedly annoyed at this gossip because she did not want to be "labelled homosexual", presumably in the sexually desiring sense (ibid., p. 196). This rumour arose in spite of the fact that none of the acquaintances of the two women had ever seen them caress or embrace (ibid., p. 443).

In another biography of Anna, there is a veiled reference to asexuality contained in a case history of a patient which her biographer says could be "generally applicable" to her (Peters, 1985, p. 19). Describing a young woman patient who did not experience sexual desire, Anna states that it was not due to repression nor did it stop the young woman from taking an affectionate interest in the love life of her women friends and colleagues. Anna wrote the case history to illustrate a concept she created called "altruistic surrender" in a chapter of her book *The Ego and the Mechanisms of Defence*. In it she writes that the patient, "gratified her instincts" not directly but "by sharing in the gratification of others" (1937, pp. 136–137). In doing so, she says the patient's efforts could only be called altruistic. Of interest here is her description of how libidinal gratification is derived through non-sexual means, the origin of which appears to be distanced from either sublimation or repression (i.e., no sexual drive is being sublimated or repressed). In an interview which was published a year after her death, she describes her concept of altruistic surrender in the following terms:

> in the type of altruism I described the person seeks out the wishes in the outside world to represent his own wishes. . . . This is to me the important thing – the individual is not critical of the fulfilment so long as it is not his own person involved, and the super-ego which is so critical of, let us say,

exhibitionism says, "Well for the other person it's quite all right, it's nice." There comes the vicarious pleasure.

(Sandler and Freud, 1983, pp. 339–340)

Her lack of Other-directed libido did not escape her father's attention. When she was 19 years of age, Sigmund Freud successfully intervened to discourage her would-be suitor, the psychoanalyst Ernest Jones, telling him that she was not ready for marriage or courtship of any kind. In the course of a short letter, Freud opined that Anna was still "far away from sexual longings" at this point in her life (Freud and Freud, 2014, p. 87). In his equally short and acquiescent reply, Jones displays his sex-normative bias when he points out that she is a "beautiful character" who will be a "remarkable woman later on, provided that her sexual repression does not injure her" (ibid.). In October 1918, when she was 23 years old, Freud began treating his daughter in the first of two periods of psychoanalysis with the objective to "awaken her libido" (Roudinesco, 2016, p. 249) which is ironic given his lifelong belief in and practice of sexual abstinence (ibid., p. 128).[15] However, the point is that while Anna may not have experienced sexual attraction, in that era, it could only be seen as an inhibition with symptomatic connotations. The possibility that this might have been a viable form of sexuality was not given any consideration.

In a 1924 letter to a trusted female colleague, Freud again referred to his concern and his hope that he could find a way to "drive her libido from the hiding place into which it has crawled" (Appignanesi and Forrester, 1992, p. 278).[16] The following year, in another letter to the same colleague, he again referred to his concerns for Anna's "suppressed genitality" (ibid.). By 1927, despite being proud of his youngest daughter's growing intellectual achievements as a theorist and clinician specializing in child psychoanalysis, he was still worrying about her lack of sexuality. In a further letter to the same colleague, he was more to the point stating that she had "no sexual life" (Gay, 1988, p. 541). Despite his concerns, however, her "flight from sexuality" never resolved in the way that he, or indeed Ernest Jones, would have hoped and preferred (Appignanesi and Forrester, 1992, p. 279). To the end of her life, it is believed that Anna Freud did not engage sexually with anyone. The approach of those around her was to quietly consider her as either an exemplary form of female sexual frigidity[17] or else discreetly view it as a case of repressed lesbianism.

In the next two chapters, I will explore her father's work and examine whether, despite being an explicit theory of sexuality, it offers any conceptual foundations on which to build an understanding of asexuality.

Notes

1 As well as AVEN (www.asexuality.org/), there are a growing number of asexual community blogs, such as https://asexual.blog/, www.asexuals.net/asexuality-blog/, https://asexualagenda.wordpress.com/, and https://asexualadvice.tumblr.com/.

2 See Chen (2020, p. 184) and Przybylo (2019, p. 8).

3 This is interesting, as Freud sees phantasy as central to sexuality. In the Little Hans and Rat Man case studies, sexuality, phantasy and childhood are inextricably linked and go on to influence adulthood. See 1909, p. 206, fn. 1; and see 1919, p. 204. Also, the *Standard Edition* translations spell it with a *ph* to emphasize that it is produced by the unconscious, and so we remain unaware of it and its effects. "Fantasy" is usually reserved for the conscious experience of images and constructs which can also reveal unconscious desires. Lacan's English translations use both, depending of the translator.

4 The beginning of menstruation, or menarche, in girls and the beginning of sperm production, or spermarche, in boys.

5 In his 2004 paper, he says, "Both stature and the timing of puberty are interesting in this regard because they are partially regulated by the hypothalamus (e.g., Grumbach and Styne, 1992). Indeed, the fact that homosexual men may differ from heterosexual men in height and pubertal timing has provided support for the notion that the development of sexual attraction processes is affected by biological factors (e.g., prenatal hormones) originating prior to birth" (p. 280).

6 See also Yule et al., 2014, pp. 93–94.

7 The AVEN website states, "Unlike celibacy, which is a choice to abstain from sexual activity, asexuality is an intrinsic part of who we are, just like other sexual orientations".

8 The inability to recognize emotions or their subtleties and textures.

9 Adrenarche is a process related to puberty in which the adrenal glands secrete very low levels of androgens and which can occur as early as 5 years of age.

10 An asexual respondent in Scherrer's study says, "I just don't feel sexual attraction to people. I love the human form and can regard individuals as works of art and find people aesthetically pleasing, but I don't ever want to come into sexual contact with even the most beautiful of people" (2008, p. 625). See also Brinkley, 2017.

11 One of Carrigan's respondents says, "I find the idea of sex utterly disgusting. I honestly think I would vomit if I ever had sex" (2011, p. 468). Another says, "I believe I differ from many other repulsed (as opposed to indifferent) asexuals in that it is purely the idea of myself having sex that I find disgusting. The idea of others doing it does not bother me in the slightest, apart from finding depictions of female sexuality a little uncomfortable as it reminds me of myself" (ibid., p. 470). The altruism in this latter point also resonates with Anna Freud's concept of altruistic surrender mentioned later.

12 She says the 1.05% is "not particularly accurate or reliable", as many authors (Chasin, C. J. D., 2011; Hinderliter, 2009; Prause and Graham, 2007) have suggested.

13 For example, see Engelman, 2008, online pagination, p. 3.

14 For an example, see *Queer as a new shelter from castration,* Geldhof and Verhaeghe, 2017, p. 214.

15 See also Gay (1988, pp. 162–164).

16 The letter was to Lou Andreas-Salomé when Anna would have been 29 years of age. See also Freud's excerpted letter to Anna on this topic (Appignanesi and Forrester, p. 276).

17 In contrast, Freud's close colleague and fellow psychoanalyst, Princess Marie Bonaparte, great-grandniece of Emperor Napoleon I of France and, after marriage, Princess George of Greece and Denmark, was distressed by her lifelong sexual frigidity. A contemporary of Anna's, she was part of Sigmund Freud's inner circle and one of his most loyal and trusted friends. Despite a strong sexual desire, psychoanalysis and surgical interventions failed to reverse her inability to experience vaginal pleasure. See Appignanesi and Forrester, 1992, p. 338.

References

Appignanesi, L. and Forrester, J. (1992) *Freud's women*. London: Weidenfeld and Nicolson.

Bogaert, A. F. (2004) 'Asexuality: Its prevalence and associated factors in a national probability sample', *Journal of Sex Research*, 41(3), pp. 279–287.

Bogaert, A. F. (2006) 'Toward a conceptual understanding of asexuality', *Review of General Psychology*, 10(3), pp. 241–250.

Brinkley, N. (2017) 'Aesthetic attraction and being on the asexual spectrum', *Archer Magazine*, 19 November. Available at: https://archermagazine.com.au/2017/04/aesthetic-attraction/?fbclid=IwAR2KjQE2laj36Uq3WcSTPgXWOAL1vRQdObJQBOjjdw7g jMZiwiw1mS447eQ [Accessed 31 December 2021].

Brotto, L. A., Knudson, G., Inskip, J., Rhodes, K. and Erskine, Y. (2010) 'Asexuality: A mixed-methods approach', *Archives of Sexual Behaviour*, 39(3), pp. 599–618.

Carrigan, M. (2011) 'There's more to life than sex? Difference and commonality within the asexual community', *Sexualities*, 14(4), pp. 462–478.

Chassaing, J.- L. (2008) 'La position du demissionnaire', *Eres/La revue lacanienne*, 2(2), pp. 101–107.

Chen, A. (2020) *ACE – What asexuality reveals about desire, society and the meaning of sex*. Boston: Beacon Press.

Cole, E. (1993) 'Is *sex a natural function*: Implications for *sex* therapy', in Rothblum, E. and Brehony, K. (eds.), *Boston marriages: Romantic but asexual relationships among contemporary lesbians*. Amherst, MA: University of Massachusetts Press, pp. 187–193.

Chasin, C. J. D. (2011) 'Theoretical issues in the study of asexuality', *Archives of Sexual Behavior*, 40(4), August, pp. 713–723.

Engelman, J. (2008) *Asexuality as a human sexual orientation*. Available at: https://seren dipstudio.org/exchange/serendipupdate/asexuality-human-sexual-orientation [Accessed 1 November 2021].

Freud, A. (1937) *The ego and the mechanisms of defence*. London: The Hogarth Press.

Freud, S. (1909) 'Notes upon a case of obsessional neurosis', in *Two case histories: Little Hans and the Rat Man*, Standard Edition X. London: Vintage/Hogarth.

Freud, S. (1919) 'A child is being beaten', in *An infantile neurosis and other works*, Standard Edition XVII. London: Vintage/Hogarth.

Freud, S. and Freud, A. (2014) *Correspondence 1904–1938*. Cambridge: Polity.

Gay, P. (1988) *Freud: A life for our time*. London: Macmillan.

Geldhof, A. and Verhaeghe, P. (2017) 'Queer as a new shelter from castration', in Giffney, N. and Watson, E. (eds.), *Clinical encounters in sexuality – Psychoanalytic practice and queer theory*. New York: Punctum Books, pp. 211–221.

Grumbach, M. M. and Styne, D. M. (1992) 'Puberty: Ontogeny, neuroendocrinology, physiology, and disorders', in Wilson, J. D. and Foster, D. W. (eds.), *Williams textbook of endocrinology*, 8th Edition. Philadelphia: W. W. Saunders, pp. 1139–1221.

Hansen de Almeida, R. and Brajterman Lerner, R. C. (1999) 'Gender identity: Its importance in the analytic practice. A theoretical view'/'Identidade de genero: Sua importancia na pratica analitica. Uma visao teorica', *Revista Brasileira de Psicanalise*, 33(3), pp. 485–494.

Hinderliter, A. C. (2009) *Asexuality: The history of a definition*. Available at: www.asexu alexplorations.net/home/history_of_definition.html [Accessed 1 November 2021].

Irvine, J. M. (2005 [1990]) *Disorders of desire – Sexuality and gender in modern American sexology*. Philadelphia: Temple University Press.

Kahn, K. (2014) 'There's no such thing as a sexual relationship – Asexual sinthomatics', in Cerankowski, K. J. and Milks, M. (eds.), *Asexualities – Feminist and queer perspectives*. New York: Routledge.

Kinsey, A. C., Pomeroy, W. B. and Martin, C. E. (1948) *Sexual behaviour in the human male*. Philadelphia: W B Saunders Company.

Kinsey, A. C., Pomeroy, W. B., Martin, C. E. and Gebbard, P. H. (1953) *Sexual behaviour in the human female*. Philadelphia: W B Saunders Company.

Lacan, J. (2016 [1975-76]) *The sinthome,* Seminar XXIII, (Miller, J.-A., ed.), (Price, A. R., trans). Cambridge: Polity.

Leader, D. (2021) *Jouissance – Sexuality, suffering and satisfaction*. Cambridge: Polity.

Masters, W. H., Johnson, V. E. and Kolodny, R. C. (1986) *Masters and Johnson on sex and human loving*. New York: Little, Brown.

Pardo, E. (2010) 'Asexuality, contemporary phenomenon?' *Recherches en psychoanalyse* (10), pp. 251a–256a. Available at: www.cairn.info/revue-recherches-en-psychanalyse-2010-2-page-251a.htm [Accessed 6 November 2021].

Peters, U. H. (1985) *Anna Freud – a life dedicated to children*. New York: Schocken Books.

Prause, N. and Graham, C. A. (2007) 'Asexuality: Classification and characterization', *Archives of Sexual Behaviour*, 36(3), pp. 341–355.

Przybylo, E. (2012) 'Producing facts: Empirical asexuality and the scientific study of sex', *Feminism & Psychology*, 23, May 2013, pp. 224–242, first published on 20 April 2012.

Przybylo, E. (2019) *Asexual erotics: Intimate readings of compulsory sexuality*. Columbus, OH: Ohio State University Press.

Roudinesco, É. (2016) *Freud – In his time and ours* (Porter, C., trans). Cambridge, MA: Harvard University Press.

Rubin, J. (2000) 'William James and the pathologizing of human experience', *Journal of Humanistic Psychology*, 40(2), pp. 176–226.

Sandler, J. and Freud, A. (1983) 'Discussions in the Hampstead index on the ego and the mechanisms of defence', *Bulletin of the Anna Freud Centre*, 6(4), pp. 329–349.

Scherrer, K. S. (2008) 'Coming to an asexual identity: Negotiating identity, negotiating desire', *Sexualities*, 11(5), 1 October, pp. 621–641.

Storms, M. D. (1980) 'Theories of sexual orientation', *Journal of Personality and Social Psychology*, 38(5), pp. 783–792.

Young-Bruehl, E. (1988) *Anna Freud*. London: Macmillan.

Yule, M. A., Brotto, L. A. and Gorzalka, B. B. (2014) 'Sexual fantasy and masturbation among asexual individuals', *The Canadian Journal of Human Sexuality*, 23(2), pp. 89–95.

Chapter 2

Towards a Freudian Understanding

It might reasonably be asked why a consideration of asexuality would begin with a Freudian theory of sexuality. Yet if asexuality is to be considered a sexual orientation, then it would seem reasonable to, first, refer to a theory of sexuality as much as possible. A second obvious reason is that in psychoanalytic theory there exists a substantial body of knowledge regarding sexuality than is to be found anywhere else. Third, as stated earlier, Freudian theory contains within it a paradoxical, often overlooked but decidedly clear, thematic regarding the negative aspects of sexuality. Or to put it another way, Freud's writings challenge, and have always challenged, the popular assumption of sexuality as an unambiguously pleasurable or, indeed, knowable phenomenon.[1] Instead, the man who is reputed to have said that sex is everywhere points in equal measure to the potential of sexual libido as disruptive and potentially unpleasurable. He conceptualizes libido as a theorized sexual energy which is both a constant within the human subject and a "plastic" or flexible form of energy (Freud, 1916–1917, SE XVI, p. 345) which is capable of finding satisfaction in a variety of ways.[2] This means that *every* subject has a sexual drive, and it is a point which might, at first sight, appear problematic in approaching asexuality. However, I will be proposing that for the asexual person, both the object of the sexual drive and the aim of the sexual drive are so remote that it has been difficult, if not impossible, to recognize that there is a sexual drive operating. In blogs, books, research questionnaires, conversations and interviews, most asexuals convey the message that to a greater or lesser extent they are desiring subjects, and even if it is not a conventionally understood sexual desire, I will be proposing that it is nevertheless a desire which has libidinal roots.

In terms of the roots of human sexuality, then, Freud (1921, p. 137) points to earliest infancy or what he calls the period of infantile sexuality. He defines "infantile sexuality" as comprising "all the feelings" that a child has for its parents and caregivers which drive the child's sexual impulses. These sexual impulses are expressed in the child's wish for signs of affection from the adults around it, such as the desire to kiss, touch and look at them. But he says, infantile sexual impulses are also to be found in such things as the child's curiosity about the adults' bodies and how they work. It finds expression, too, in the more familiar Freudian tropes of the child's wish to marry its mother (for the boy) or have a child (for the girl)

DOI: 10.4324/9781003214946-3

with its father. For Freud, these are sexual impulses which display a combination of tender and jealous feelings along with sexual intentions. In a fundamental way, he says the child makes the person it loves into the "object" of all its "still not properly centred sexual needs", hence the phrase "sexual object" for the person who causes us to desire sexually (1905, pp. 135–136). The general characteristics of infantile sexual instincts (drives) are that they are numerous, they derive from a great variety of organic sources within the body, they act independently of one another and they only achieve a more or less complete synthesis, for Freud, relatively late at puberty (ibid., p. 125). This is a condensed restating of Freud's theory that the sexual instincts (drives) develop, for all subjects, through oral, anal and phallic stages up to the age of 6 years or so and then enter a period of latency, or quietness, until puberty when the fragmented instincts fuse together into a genital sexuality.[3]

Against a theoretical backdrop such as this, one of the challenges which it inadvertently presents for asexuality is that to be without a sex drive is to be almost a non-person. This is probably best exemplified in a religious article which poses the following question: "What do you call a person who is asexual? Answer: Not a person. Asexual people do not exist" (Nantais and Opperman, 2002, online pagination, p. 1). In contrast to this, Freud has long argued that the sexual instincts (drives), rather than being the measure of normality, the ingredient for a happy life or the source of unequivocal pleasure, are more nuanced in that they can also be problematic (1896, SE I, p. 222) and can have an unsettling quality (1912, SE XI, p. 190).[4] The sexual drives can just as easily be "breakers of the peace" which constantly produce "tensions whose release is felt as pleasure" (1920, SE XVIII, p. 63). He says that this aspect of the sex drive has caused civilization to suppress it (1908, SE IX, p. 186). In later chapters, I will be returning to this idea of disruption when considering the theories of Jacques Lacan, but for the moment, Freud's theory sees the sexual drive as so troublesome that it needs to be suppressed. Not only that, he sees its troublesome quality as being due to the unacceptable nature of sexual feelings because they might derive from within our families of origin. He believes this latter aspect, "derived from eroticism", is responsible for renunciations of the sexual drive (ibid., p. 187) which can take the form of enforced sexual abstinence or neurotic illness (ibid., p. 196).[5]

Freud also sees the sexual drive as including a quota of aggression and even repugnance (ibid.) which also makes its very presence challenging. This is why he has long believed there is something ineffable, unsayable, about sexuality (1930, p. 105, also fn. 3), and this, in turn, has fundamental implications for subject formation. So even before asexuality is considered, this also has important implications for how sexuality can be perceived and understood, and this is a point taken up by current theorists which I will come to later. If there is something unsayable about human sexuality, then we are always dealing with something which defies convenient definitions and normative categorizations. The word "sexual" becomes not just a multi-layered concept but also an enigmatic one. As Freud says, the thing we call "sexual" is something which allows us to contrast male and female, to search for pleasure, to reproduce the species, but all the while having within it something that is unsettling, at times improper and, at other times, something which must be kept secret (1916–1917, SE XVI, p. 304).

The other aspect of sexuality which is central to Freud's thinking is its plasticity – that is, its ability to take different forms and finds a variety of ways of achieving satisfaction. He sees this as the reason why some people prefer same-sex partners, some eschew partners altogether (ibid.) and some use fantasy to gain pleasure.[6] This latter point is of importance to asexuality because I will be proposing in later chapters that, contrary to what appears to be the case, there may be an unconscious libidinal fantasy operating at a fundamental level within this sexual orientation. On the subject of fantasy, Freud believes that sex used for purposes other than sexual reproduction has been a feature of human sexuality from time immemorial, in all periods of history and among all peoples (ibid., p. 307).

When asexuality is criticized for being an exception in terms of human sexuality, it is worth remembering Freud's view of homosexuality. He says that homosexual urges, far from being exceptions in terms of human sexuality, are in fact part of the sexuality in every single neurotic (ibid., p. 304). He also says that those who self-identify as homosexual are only a fraction of those who are latent homosexuals (ibid., pp. 307–308). Current USA statistics, cited earlier, suggest that the population of self-defined asexuals is on a par with the LGBTQIA+ population. It remains an open question as to whether the numbers of asexuals, as Freud suggests regarding homosexuality, is a fraction of those who self-define themselves as such. Homosexuality is an important example for Freud of both the plasticity of sexuality and its polymorphously perverse origins[7] in the infantile stages (1905, p. 234). I am proposing that asexuality is equally important for the same reasons; it supports the theory of plasticity of the sexual drives, and it could, quite possibly, also be part of every person's sexuality.

Freud doesn't use the word "asexual" often, and never in the sense of self-defined asexuality, but in one of the few instances where he does use the word, he says that because society's educative processes ensure that "almost all infantile sexual activities" are forbidden, people really believe the lives of children are asexual (ibid., p. 312).[8] However, in what amounts to a challenge for both an understanding of self-defined asexuality and a challenge in theorizing its apparent absence of sexual desire, Freud believes there is no such thing as an asexual childhood. It only appears to be this way because the period up to the age of 5 or 6 years, the period of infantile sexuality, is "covered in most people by the veil of amnesia" (ibid.). Freud believes the majority of experiences before the start of the latency period[9] are forgotten due to this infantile amnesia (1916–1917, SE XV, p. 176). The reason for forgetting these experiences is that they relate not only to early sexual life but also to the Oedipal relation to parents which needs to be repressed. This could offer a different perspective on the recurrent experience of asexuals in studies as something they are born with (Bogaert, 2004, p. 284; Brotto et al., 2010, p. 615). Infantile amnesia erases any memory of early sexuality, and so asexuality would, similar to sexually desiring orientations, appear as if the person is born with it. Also, the fact that these earliest sexual experiences are covered over by amnesia due to the effect of repression corroborates the argument that they involve a degree of unpleasure. I hope to show, as the theory builds through the following chapters, that while the Freudian concept of infantile sexuality remains a core element of this book (i.e., as a universal phenomenon), the subjective experience of it, and passage through it, is not the same for everyone and that one of its outcomes can be the formation of an asexual subject. Leader (2021, p. 145) suggests that the infant's "interpretation of bodily sensation – especially when it is difficult to localize – forms part of early experiences of arousal, and may have profound effects on the shaping of sexualities".

Asexuality and the Sexual Drive

The universality of the human sexual drive does not mean that it is unequivocally experienced or expressed in conventional ways. Freud's most comprehensive contribution to this field is his *Three Essays on Sexuality* (1905) in which he says that there is no natural link between the sex drive and its satisfying object – that is, the sexual drive is independent of its object or person on whom it focusses for sexual satisfaction. Nor is the sex drive's origin likely to be due to that object's "attractions" (ibid., p. 148). The object, in other words, is not important, other than the fact that *some* object is necessary. While this might seem, again at first sight, an obvious point to make, it is, in fact, a radical rethinking of human sexuality, and I will be arguing later in the book that it has a pivotal role in understanding asexuality. It is another frequently overlooked element of Freud's non-binary thinking with regard to sexuality in what is his seminal work on the subject. The two ideas, that there is no natural link between the drive and its object, and the equally radical notion that it can be *any* object once there is *some* object, are not out of place in contemporary queer theory.[10] In fact, Dean (2003, p. 245) is of the opinion that ideas such as the instinct's independence of its object means that Freud can be credited as the "intellectual founder of queer theory". For our purposes, these concepts, and the latter concept in particular, are central to any consideration of asexuality. It is generally assumed that asexuality, per its definition, does not have an object, and I will be offering an alternative perspective on this later in the book. If psychoanalytic theory believes there must be *some* object in asexuality, even though alternative asexual theories do not include an object, it will be necessary to consider what kind of object this can be. Equally, and it is another challenge of theorizing asexuality using a sexual theory, within Freudian theory, there are no conceptual clues as to what the object of asexual desire might conceivably be.

What we do know from Freud's theory, however, is that the object is a contingent choice that varies depending on the individual, while the "essential and constant" aspect is the drive itself (1905, p. 168).[11] This underlines the notion that what is of most importance for Freud is the constancy of a sexualized desire. In other words, we could argue that for Freud, the human subject is driven by a desire for desire itself and that this is fundamental because, as he says, the object can be *any* object and it is not the "attractiveness" of the object that causes the sexual drive to mobilize. Again, these are the often overlooked and yet clearly delineated concepts within Freud's theory whether we consider sexuality or asexuality. If asexuality is the lack of sexual attraction for any person, then quite obviously, there is no verifiable object. Because Freudian theory excludes the possibility of a viable (i.e., non-pathological) sexual orientation in which a person does not experience sexual desire and makes no sexual object-choice, it is only with the later conceptual tools of Jacques Lacan that this particular conundrum can be explicated more fully in the chapters that follow. For now, Freud's view is that the word "libido" is "properly reserved for the instinctual (drive) forces of sexual life" and that it is not, and cannot be, an "asexual libido" but only a sexual libido (1916–1917, SE XVI, p. 312, 413).

Yet even for sexual subjects, the sexual drive has many idiosyncrasies. Full sexual release through orgasm with another person is not always necessary, and sexual excitation does not have to move towards this goal – that is, it can be sublimated into other activities and towards other goals. Having detached the fixed nature of the sexual object from the sexual drive, he is now detaching the so-called normal sexual aim from the drive also (1905, p. 170).[12] So if the object, as other person, is not a constant, then neither is the aim of sexual satisfaction. Going further, he even says that a constant sexual drive is not always a positively experienced phenomenon. It can just as easily bring with it a feeling of disgust, one of the factors in restricting the sexual aim (ibid., p. 152). As well as disgust, he also points to the element of cruelty that can be present in the sexual instinct (drive) (ibid., p. 159). He notes the capacity for some people to find pleasure in pain, either inflicted on themselves (masochism) or in inflicting it on others (sadism). The presence of a sadistic component in the sexual instinct (drive), he believes, can dominate an individual's entire sexual activity, as we find in perversion (ibid., pp. 157–160). It emerges as predominant in the pregenital oral stage where gaining erotic mastery over the breast as object coincides with its destruction (1920, SE XVIII, p. 54). The Freudian view is that the sadistic instinct (drive) takes on the "function of overpowering the sexual object" in carrying out the sexual act (ibid.). Notwithstanding the predominantly male perspective, Freud is not only including an aggressive/sadistic component as an experiential contingency within relatively conventional reproductive sex, but he is also including the idea that sadism/aggression can begin at the earliest oral stage of psychosexual development. The point of interest here is that the sexual drive can include not just less-positive aspects but unpleasurable ones also. This terrain of the earliest stages of psychosexual development is formative of sexuality and, as I am proposing, of asexuality, but it can, quite obviously, produce uniquely different outcomes. Freud's point is that the infant's sexual drive is directed at *some* object, and the particular relation it establishes to that object at this earliest stage of infantile sexuality remains influential in determining all later relations to subsequent objects (others). Meanwhile, the inclusion of a destructive presence within the sexual drives (ibid.) illustrates that the sexual instinct (drive) is not solely seeking out and deriving a conventional satisfaction, but it is also combining opposing instinctual trends of both pleasure and pain (1905, p. 160). In short, this flexibility shifts any understanding of human sexual desire into a decidedly non-normative framework which holds out the potential for yet unconsidered possibilities.

Outward Trajectory of Libido

In Freud's theory, the object of sexual satisfaction is contingent, which means it becomes the object only because it is best fitted to make satisfaction possible (1915, p. 122). While his theory allows for the possibility of the object to be an object in fantasy, it does not allow for the option which is found in asexuality, namely, the possibility that sexual desire is directed at no object. Looked at another way, Freudian theory does not allow for the possibility that the object towards which asexual libido might be directed is this very absence itself. I will be taking up this point in more detail in later chapters, but for now, what Freudian theory does offer is a particularly important understanding with regard to the *choice* of object. While there must be *some* object, irrespective of what it is, a further refinement is necessary because this does not mean it can be just *any* object. It is, rather, an object that is highly specific in terms of what the individual desires, and it is determined by the history of each individual, particularly childhood history. In later chapters, this perspective on the very specific choice of object will be built upon and extended more fully.

If sexual excitation not only arises from the sexual areas of the body but "from all bodily organs" (ibid., p. 217), this clearly conveys that the human subject is hardwired to experience sexual excitation. However, directing this libido onto another person is not similarly arranged. The libido, in Freud's view, is originally connected or attached to the subject's own ego in a narcissistic libidinal cathexis which he describes as "the original state of things" (ibid., p. 218). The subject only later directs this libido outwards onto others, and even then, essential parts of it remain behind in the ego. His point is that an inwardly directed libido is the original way it is organized, and finding an object externally happens later. As I have been considering, in the case of asexuality the libido, for all intents and purposes, does not appear to extend outwards to external objects. Some asexuals do report that they experience excitation arising from the "sexual areas", but interestingly, they do not connect it with sexual desire for another person (Prause and Graham, 2007, p. 346). For Freud, libido must inevitably be directed externally, or the person risks falling ill (1916–1917, SE XVI, p. 342). Yet as stated, one common finding of the research in Chapter 1 is that asexuals do not experience subjective distress on account of having no sexual desire for another person. An extension of this is that they are not any more prone to medical or psychological conditions than sexually desiring people. If so, then, the question which arises is how and why this is the case, and one possible inference might be that, as hypothesized earlier, asexuals actually do have a libido which is directed at *something*.

At a time when the first beginnings of sexual satisfaction are still linked with the taking of nourishment, the sexual instinct (drive) finds a sexual object outside the infant's own body in the mother's breast (1905, p. 222). Freud is of the view that a child's interaction with the person responsible for their care amounts to an "unending source of sexual excitation and satisfaction from his [*sic*] erotogenic zones". Since in most cases it is the mother, Freud says that she, in turn, regards what she does as an "asexual" pure love in "teaching the child to love" and to grow up with "vigorous sexual needs" (ibid., p. 223). This is one of the clearest statements from Freud that illustrates how, for classical psychoanalysis, a subject beginning life without a sexual drive aimed at an external object (i.e., another person) is an unthinkable construct.

Asexuality and Libidinal Sublimation

Yet since asexuality experiences no sexual desire aimed at an external object, it is necessary to theorize that the libido must be capable of a transformation such as this. Is such a possibility included within the existing psychoanalytic canon? As stated, Freud does insist that sexual instinctual (drive) impulses are what he calls "extraordinarily plastic" (Freud, 1916–1917, SE XVI, p. 345). One can take the place of another, or one can take over another's intensity. If the satisfaction of one is frustrated by reality, the satisfaction of another can bring "complete compensation" (1923, pp. 44–45).[13] This is because the sexual instincts (drives) have the capacity to change their object and take another which is more easily attainable. This ability to displace or find a substitute has practical benefits in avoiding or reducing frustration. Therefore, Freud argues, if this displaceable energy is desexualized libido, it can also be described as *sublimated* energy or what he calls a "desexualized Eros" (ibid., p. 44). Lacan will have a different position on this which I will come to later, but for now, this sublimated energy would still retain the main purpose of *Eros* in establishing unity, or in a tendency towards unity, which is particularly characteristic of the ego and can be found in platonic or social relationships (ibid., p. 45). This is close to what asexuality represents in terms of a desexualization of its aim and object. Freud extends the concept of displaceable energy, or sublimation, to the activity of thought processes. If they, in the wider sense, are included among these displacements, then thinking is also "supplied" from the sublimation of erotic motive forces (ibid.). While he appears to be offering a suitable theorization of asexuality with this concept of desexualized libido, he is in reality offering an account of sublimation which transforms existing sexual trends into non-sexual trends. He is also positing a mode of transformation of the sexual instinct which is controlled by the ego and, as such, would be under conscious control. This would mean that an asexual person would be choosing to consciously function through an array of sublimated activities and actions as a way of *not* engaging with sexual activity. The repeated experience of asexuals included in the research shows that asexuality is not a conscious choice, such as we find in celibacy. This, in turn, means that if asexuality is a choice of any kind, then it is happening at the level of the unconscious because the asexual is unaware of it. Nor does the asexual person experience a sexual trend, to use Freud's phrase, in the first instance. For this reason, it would appear that asexuality, rather than being a form of sublimation, is taking up a wholly different relation to the sexual drive, one which moves beyond the concept of sublimation and towards a satisfaction of a radically different kind.

For Freud, sexual instincts (drives), from the beginning to the end of their development, work towards obtaining pleasure, and they retain this original function unaltered. What is of interest in any consideration of the aetiology of asexuality is how the "other instincts" – that is, the ego-instincts (drives) – come into play.[14] They may have the same aim to start with as the sexual instincts (drives), but Freud says that "under the influence of the instructress Necessity" (1916–1917, SE XVI, p. 357) (i.e., reality), they learn to replace the pleasure principle by a modification of it. The task of avoiding unpleasure now becomes almost as important as obtaining pleasure. The ego learns to renounce immediate satisfaction, postpone pleasure by putting up with a little unpleasure and abandon certain sources of pleasure altogether. An ego like this becomes, Freud says, "reasonable" and is no longer governed by the pleasure principle. Instead, it obeys the reality principle which also seeks pleasure, but this time, it is a pleasure "assured" because it takes account of reality, even if pleasure has to be postponed or diminished in order to achieve it (ibid.). This understanding moves us closer to the domain of asexuality because now, the seemingly all-powerful sexual instincts (drives) can be influenced or held in check by the ego instincts (drives). Also, the ego instincts (drives) are tasked with avoiding "unpleasure", which in the case of asexuality can sometimes, but not always, even equate to the "idea" of sex. As one asexual respondent says, "I find the whole idea of sexual contact slightly repulsive" (Carrigan, 2011, p. 470).

The Reversal of Libido

If Freud's theorizing places the ego in the role of mediating agency for the activity of sublimation, this is because he believes that the ego deals with the first object-cathexes of the id (and later ones) by taking the libido into itself and binding it to itself by means of identification (1923, p. 46). The subject identifies, in the sense of incorporating something into itself, with the person to whom it has libidinally attached. This transformation of erotic libido into ego-libido by definition involves a desexualization, as far as Freud is concerned. As a process, he has famously said that sublimation places social aims higher than sexual ones, the latter in his view being "self-interested" (1916–1917, SE XVI, p. 345). Sublimation, therefore, is a special case of the way in which sexual trends are attached to non-sexual ones and, from an asexual perspective, means that sexual satisfactions can be transformed into non-sexual satisfactions. Again, from an asexual reading, it is important not to conflate the two issues at stake here. Sexual satisfactions can transform into non-sexual ones, but that does not have to mean that the latter are without a libidinal element, a point which Lacan will categorically address as I will come to later. Freud, however, explains his process as the ego "getting hold" of the libido that has been invested in the object, setting itself up as the love-object, and desexualizing or sublimating the libido of the id. This theory, that ego-libido can draw object-libido back to itself, represents an important amplification of the theory of narcissism, which I will be examining in more detail. It suggests the possibility, particularly in terms of asexuality, that the eventual outward move-ment of the libido to external objects (1905, p. 218)[15] can undergo a transforma-tion or even a reversal at an early stage of infantile sexual development. The process which brings this about will also be examined in the following chapters, and in particular, the concept of reversal will be further traced and highlighted in Lacan's work.

To reiterate briefly, for the purposes of understanding asexuality, Freudian sublimation has its limitations. Freud himself theorizes that the active libidinal drive operating within the human subject seeks objects from which to derive satisfaction. This, for him, means that "there is a limit to the amount of unsatis-fied libido that human beings on the average can put up with" (1916–1917, SE XVI, p. 346). He is of the view that sublimation is only able to deal with satis-fying more than a certain fraction of libido. As sexual energy, libido "makes a person's satisfaction depend on the attainment of only a very small number of aims and objects" (ibid.). In other words, if a person desires sexual release, then sublimated forms of release may not suffice. On the point that not everybody has the same capacity to sublimate, Freud says only a small number of people are "gifted with the capacity" to do so (ibid.). In particular, he is referring to a per-son's ability to create, through sublimation, artistic or other works that contrib-ute to civilization, something which is also not within every person's capability. Equally, for those who *are* able, it ignores the anecdotal evidence that great art-ists and leaders can display high levels of sexual activity irrespective of the level of creativity or sublimated activity they participate in. In *Beyond the Pleasure Principle* (1920), Freud is direct on this point: "No substitute or reactive forma-tions and no sublimations will suffice to remove the repressed instinct's persist-ing tension" (p. 42). More specifically, in the context of asexuality, the place of sublimation in its aetiology may well prove to be based on a false premise. The capacity to exchange an originally sexual aim, directed at an external, independ-ent object (Laplanche and Pontalis, 1973, p. 433), for another non-sexual one assumes the existence of an original sexual aim that is diverted. The testimony of asexuals, puzzling as it may seem, is the opposite: for them, it is a predomi-nantly lifelong experience in which there never has been a sexual aim directed towards an external object (Brotto et al., 2010, p. 609). If asexuals appear to be essentially satisfied with their non-sexual orientation, this suggests that while some role for sublimation has to be assumed, it will be necessary to understand why no existing sexual trend is evident. This will require looking for something other than, or beyond, sublimation to theorize the cause and the satisfaction of their hypothesized libido.

Asexuality and the Constant Demand of the Drive

In terms of libido as sexual energy, Freud says there are two important aspects of human instincts (drives). One is his often-quoted definition that an instinct (drive) is a concept that appears on the frontier between the mental and somatic (i.e., mind and body). This is to emphasize that the instinct (drive) emanates as a representative of stimuli originating from *within* the organism that are seeking to satisfy bodily needs. In other words, from deeply rooted, biologically generated somatic agitations comes a pressure that demands to be satisfied in some way. When this demand "reaches the mind", as he puts it, it is as "a demand upon the mind for work in consequence of its connection with the body" (1915, pp. 121–122). But this demand, as I will further outline, is not always experienced as pleasurable. The second important point he makes is that every instinct (drive) is a piece of activity because something is being urged to happen, to take place, in order to quell the somatic agitation that is percolating to consciousness. Even when he considers passive instincts (drives), and asexuality could easily be characterized as a relatively passive position in relation to libido, he says, "we can only mean instincts (drives) whose *aim* is passive" (1905, p. 122). In other words, the libido remains active, but its aim is passive. Freud gives some examples of a sexual instinct whose *aim* is passive such as the aim to be hurt in masochism or to be looked at in scopophilia (exhibitionism). Extending this line of thinking away from a focus on paraphilias, this allows for the possibility, and one which will be considered more fully in later chapters, that asexuality has an active libido but with the aim of *not* experiencing sexual attraction for or *not* seeking sexual satisfaction with another person. Freudian theory, therefore, allows for the important possibility that asexuality could be considered a sexual orientation with an active libido that is aimed at *not* experiencing sexual desire.

One reason why an active libido might be aimed at *not* experiencing sexual desire is to be found in Freud's first observation regarding the instincts (drives). While the aim of the adult sexual instinct (drive) is pleasure (ibid., p. 149), an important point to be extrapolated from his theory is that there are "motive forces" (1915, p. 126) which work against an instinct (drive) being carried through to satisfaction in an unmodified form. This, and the vicissitudes which the drives can undergo, are what he considers to be methods of *defence* [emphasis in original] against those same instincts (drives) (ibid., pp. 126–127). In other words, he is saying that the repeated demand on the mind to act, which is a fundamental characteristic of the sexual drive in its broadest sense, might need to be defended against even for sexual subjects. This is a radical idea not only for its time but also when placed within contemporary discourses on sex and sexuality because the concept that the human sex drive might need to be defended against is not usually found outside of psychoanalytic theory. I propose to return to this more fully in Chapter 3 and in later chapters. For now, if the theoretical position of the asexual could, on the face of it, be arrived at via an unconscious defence against the sexual drive, then the possibility remains that the sexual instinct (drive) undergoes a vicissitude whereby rather than being repressed, its aim, and its choice of object, is for *no* sexual pleasure or sexual satisfaction.

Active Libido and Desexualization

With regard to a non-sexual object, Freud says that the sexual drives can be satisfied without recourse to an object outside of the person. At the beginning of mental life, the ego is libidinally invested (cathected) with the instincts (drives) and is capable, to some extent, of satisfying them on its own, or what Freud terms "auto-erotic". At this early stage of infantile sexuality, the outside world is not of interest to the child in terms of satisfaction. The ego is associated with what is pleasurable and the outside world with what is either indifferent or unpleasurable (ibid., p. 135). Due to the instincts (drives) for self-preservation, however, the ego must eventually acquire objects from the external world and, paradoxically, cannot avoid feeling internal instinctual (drive) stimuli for a time as unpleasurable. In order to quell the latter unpleasurable experiences, pleasurable objects from the outside are introjected and internal unpleasurable sensations are projected outward.

The key outcome of this, according to Freud, is that the ego, whose first function was to distinguish between internal and external, through what he calls the "reality-ego",[16] now becomes a "pleasure-ego" which prioritizes pleasure above all other considerations (ibid., p. 136). What Freud's observation implies is that, for the pleasure-ego, the external world is divided into a part that is pleasurable, and this part it incorporates into itself. The other part of the external world remains the part into which it has projected its own hostile or unpleasant aspects. This means the ego coincides with pleasure, and reality coincides with unpleasure. Put another way, reality becomes desexualized. Brodsky (2011, p. 74) says, "Freud distinguishes . . . between ego and reality according to sexualization and desexualization. It is thus that he gives a complicated idea of the desexualization of reality and the desexualization of libido".[17]

For Freud, when the stage of objects in the external world begins for the infant, the relation to the object is placed along the dimension of pleasure and unpleasure. If the object becomes a source of pleasure, he says, an action is made to bring the object closer and to incorporate it into the ego, and he calls this the "attraction" exercised by the pleasure-giving object (1915, p. 137). However, it will be necessary to establish if the process also occurs in this way in asexuality or if, perhaps, the opposite is the case. Do the earliest infantile experiences include the possibility that the first partial object, understood as the breast, is desexualized because it is not experienced as the pleasure object? If this is a potentially foundational experience which can produce an asexual subject, then Freudian theory does not advance any concepts which would allow this line of thinking to be taken further. As such, I will be returning to this question using Lacanian theory in the following chapters.

Asexuality and Pre-Oedipal Influences

What Freudian theory does advance, in contrast, is a focus on the importance of infantile sexuality in shaping what will become adult sexuality. When Freud speaks of infantile sexuality, he is referring to the infant's first impulses that make their appearance "attached to other vital functions", such as sucking at the mother's breast (1916–1917, SE XVI, p. 313). As far as he is concerned, this early sexual experience has significance for everyone, without exception. The importance of the first object's influence on the choice of every later object cannot be overstated and is one which has a profound effect and influence in even "the remotest regions of our sexual life" (ibid., p. 314). The path of infantile sexuality moves from the breast and oral eroticism, to the faeces and anal eroticism, and then to the genitals and phallic eroticism, including infantile masturbation which, in psychoanalytic terms, is an infantile pleasure derived from touching the genitals. After this, there is the latency period in which there are, ordinarily but not exclusively, no expressions or experiences of sexuality. The final stage is the genital stage, or puberty, when the latency period ends and where sexuality re-emerges but in a form that will be closer to adult sexuality.

In psychoanalytic thinking, therefore, this is the diphasic, or two-part, nature of human sexuality. Sexuality, in this view, does not begin at puberty but has already had an infantile phase, its first iteration. After the latency period has ended and puberty has begun, the second phase of human sexuality starts to emerge. For this reason, adult sexuality is based on and shaped by early infantile experiences, as well as by the repressions of incestuous impulses which bring about the dissolution of the Oedipus complex,[18] thus ushering in the latency period (1905, p. 177, fn. 1, p. 200, 222).[19] Freud is, therefore, consistently pointing to the earliest time in infantile development as the place where human sexuality is laid down. He believes that from the third year of life, a child's sexual life is similar to an adult's except for the primacy of the genitals. He is referring to the inevitable traits of perversion and, despite the lesser intensity, the whole trend towards satisfaction of the sexual drive. Yet in an obvious reference once again to the importance of the pre-Oedipal phase, he says that "the most interesting phases of sexual or libidinal development" take place *earlier* than the third year of life (1916–1917, SE XVI, p. 326). What this means for sexuality, and asexuality, is that a time of life about which we will have no memory has been instrumental in creating the form which adult sexuality will take.

As I mentioned, the first object of the oral component of the sexual instinct (drive) is the mother's breast which satisfies the need for nourishment.[20] The erotic component which is satisfied simultaneously through sucking, Freud says, "makes itself independent with the act of sensual sucking [*lutschen*]; it gives up the outside object and replaces it by an area of the subject's own body" (1916–1917, SE XVI, p. 326). This is an example of the sexual drive starting as a bodily need but becoming independent of need and so taking on a sexualized component, by which Freud means the pleasure derived from the act of sucking alongside, and now independent of, the satisfaction of the biological need for food. Of particular interest here, from the perspective of asexuality, is the movement Freud is describing in which the object as external is given up, and the emphasis instead is placed on the libidinal pleasure associated with a part of the subject's own body, in this case the mouth. An auto-erotic choice, if it can be called that, is made that favours the sexual pleasure of the object experienced as self as opposed to one predicated on the object as external to the self. The sexual component of the oral instinct (drive) becomes auto-erotic "from the first", as do the anal and other erotogenic instincts (drives) (ibid.).

After this, Freud says, the course of sexual development for sexually desiring subjects has two aims: firstly, libidinal satisfaction moves to an external object from the infant's own body through the "abandonment of auto-eroticism". Secondly, what he terms the "unification of the various objects of the separate instincts (drives) and their replacement by a single object", that is, a whole, external Other's body (ibid.). What Freud is pointing to here is how the subject, primarily, and from its earliest instinctual (drive) experience, turns towards its own body for sensual pleasure despite the presence of an external object (i.e., the breast). Then secondarily, the infant must turn to an outside object for erotic satisfaction and leave auto-eroticism behind. Freudian theory does not extend to considering the possibility that at this point of turning to an external object for infantile sexual satisfaction, an alternative asexual experience might evolve in which there is no seeking of sexual satisfaction in the Other. I will, therefore, examine this possibility in later chapters from the perspective of Lacanian theory.

The Obstacle to Genital Primacy

In Freud's theory, the diffuse streams of the component instincts (drives) of infantile sexuality finally come together under the "primacy of the genitals" at puberty. But now the libido comes up against the resistance of the preconscious system.[21] In other words, he theorizes that there are conditions under which genital primacy does not take place. He says this occurs because reality's effect is to constrain libidinal urges, and by reality, he means the child's interaction with external objects – that is, the ordinary frustrations and prohibitions imposed by its primary caregivers. This resistance due to the effects of reality can lead to a regression to the stages before genital primacy, of which there are two types (ibid., p. 343). One type returns from a higher to a lower stage of development as a result of repression (ibid., p. 342) and never fully occupies the genital stage. The second type involves repression of the genital organization, often found in hysteria. This version remains at the final genital stage but a symptom, as a substitute satisfaction, is formed.[22] In either case, Freud says, "people fall ill of a neurosis" because they are unable to satisfy their libido, and their symptoms are a substitute for this frustrated satisfaction (ibid.). I will be proposing in later chapters that regression does not fully explain asexuality because with the first type, there should be signs of regressed infantile sexuality at earlier fixation points, and there does not appear to be, unless the presence of masturbation is considered as such. The second type would assume a return of the repressed in the form of neurotic symptoms which, again, there does not appear to be.

Freud himself argues that not every frustration of a libidinal satisfaction makes the person neurotic (ibid., p. 344). Further, he says that the nature of frustration is seldom universal and absolute. In order to create pathogenic effects, he says, frustration must affect the mode of satisfaction which "alone the subject desires, of which alone he is capable" (ibid., p. 345). In other words, frustration only emerges when it blocks a path to satisfaction which is desired by the person in the first place. The experience of asexuality appears to be that, since there is no sexual satisfaction being desired in the first place, there is no path to sexual satisfaction being blocked. Freud believes that for sexually desiring subjects, there are many ways of tolerating deprivation of satisfaction without falling ill as a result (ibid.). A reasonable proposition with regard to asexual subjects would equally be that they are not "falling ill" by being deprived of sexual satisfaction because, to begin with, they are not seeking it.

Asexuality and Infantile Object-Choice

The concept of not seeking sexual satisfaction is implicit within the definition of an asexual, and this prompts the question as to whether pleasure, and indeed satisfaction, can be derived without a conventional object-choice being made. Does Freudian theory allow for such a possibility? One manifestation of infantile sexual activity, mentioned earlier, is thumb sucking, which Freud defines as a rhythmic repetition of a sucking contact by the mouth or lips (ibid., pp. 180–181). In thumb sucking, the instinct (drive) is not directed at another person but obtains its satisfaction from the subject's own body or, as stated, auto-erotically. Freud identifies three characteristics of auto-erotic satisfaction: it attaches to one of the vital somatic functions, it has (as yet) no sexual object (auto-erotic) and its sexual aim is dominated by an erotogenic zone (ibid., p. 182). The literature on asexuality suggests that there is diversity in terms of sexual activity whereby some engage auto-erotically, some engage sexually with a partner, albeit reservedly so, and some do neither. On balance, however, many appear to find masturbation acceptable (Brotto et al., 2010, p. 607; Scherrer, 2008, pp. 627–629) but without any apparent subjectively experienced eroticism directed either at another person or through fantasy (O'Donnell, 2008, p. 1). An asexual describes it thus:

> I might have gotten a book on women's sexuality. I was like "let's try to do some masturbation here and see if this goes anywhere." And it's like, "umm, no this is just boring." So it was like that's the extent of it. It was just boring.
>
> (Prause and Graham, 2007, p. 345)

The presence of masturbation suggests an unconscious sexual instinct (drive) operating auto-erotically but without an attraction to a sexual object as other person. Freud says many people who are abstinent only remain so with the help of masturbation, a satisfaction he believes is linked with the auto-eroticism of early childhood (1905, pp. 191–192). This underpins his view that the aim of infantile sexuality is to gain satisfaction by stimulation of a particular erotogenic zone which has been "selected in one way or another" (ibid., p. 184). To be satisfying, Freud says the stimulation of an erotogenic zone must have been previously experienced as such (ibid.). In other words, there must have been an original satisfaction which left behind a need for its repetition. He says the repetition of the satisfaction has two aspects: the first is a feeling of tension which is unpleasurable, and the second is a need to stimulate an erotogenic zone to remove this tension (ibid.). In sexually desiring subjects, he says the aim is to remove the unpleasurable tension in the erotogenic zone by finding an external stimulus which produces satisfaction. Asexuality stands in contrast to this since there is no external stimulus holding out the promise of satisfaction of a sexual need. There is also no apparent sexual need requiring satisfaction. This gives rise to the question as to whether the asexual subject has found a unique way of responding to the infantile experience of unpleasurable rising tension.

Asexuality's apparent lack of sexualized object-choice – *object* understood here as "other people" (ibid., pp. 191–192) – is a conundrum because, for Freud, object-choices are made during infantile sexuality at the end of the Oedipus complex. In other words, the type of person we are attracted to and the gender of that person have their roots in the earliest experiences we have. The Oedipus complex takes place in the final stage of infantile sexuality, or the phallic stage, in which every person between the ages of about 3 and 6 years experiences an unconscious desire for the death of the parent of the same sex and a sexual desire for the parent of the opposite sex. Freud theorizes that this universal experience plays "a fundamental part in the structuring of the personality, and in the orientation of human desire" (Laplanche and Pontalis, 1973, p. 283). For psychoanalysis, because it is a conflictual event which can have perplexing outcomes, the Oedipus complex is a major determinant of and contributor to pathological categories.

Since the calmer latency period follows this period of libidinized discord, the next stage at which object-choice resumes its significance is puberty when the infantile object-choice of either one or other caregiver, usually a parent, is dispensed with and a new object-choice is made. This new object-choice, however, is based on the original choice, but this time, the choice is for a person outside of the Oedipal configuration and also with a sensual current attached to the pre-existing affectionate current. "Should these two currents fail to converge, the result is often that one of the ideals of sexual life, the focussing of all desires upon a single object (person), will be unattainable", Freud says (1905, p. 200). In terms of asexuality, this is an interesting concept because, while some asexuals eschew all sexual contact and even emotional relationships (Carrigan, 2011, p. 470), many asexual relationships remain based on the affectionate current which, according to

Freud, is also libidinally underpinned (1905, p. 200).[23] This supports the proposition that infantile sexuality is part of the asexual experience. It also suggests that an element of infantile sexuality (i.e., the affectionate current) persists through latency and into puberty where it contributes to the formation of the adult asexual. As stated, Freud is saying that the human subject is biologically constructed to experience sexuality. Therefore, if substantial psychophysical forces of infantile sexuality combine to produce hetero- and LGBTQIA+ forms of sexuality,[24] it is conceivable that equally substantive, but as yet unconsidered, combinations of infantile sexual experiences produce an asexual subject.

Freud postulates that all intense emotional responses "including even terrifying ones, trench upon sexuality" (ibid., p. 203).[25] If this is the case and even strong emotions are connected to sexuality, then this will be of importance when I come to explore in more detail the Freudian idea that the sexual instinct (drive) needs to be defended against. I will do this through a more detailed examination of the concept of internally generated infantile trauma.[26] For the moment, and supporting the point earlier about powerful formative forces within the subject, Freud says that the human body even at the infantile stage makes the "fullest provisions" for "setting in motion the process of sexual excitation" (ibid., p. 204). The sensory surfaces are first and foremost the place where it begins through both the skin and the sense organs, in particular the erotogenic zones. In fact, his overall point in this regard is that there may well be "nothing of considerable importance that can occur in the organism without contributing some component to the excitation of the sexual instinct (drive)" (ibid., p. 205). From a psychoanalytic perspective, there appears to be no consideration given to the absence of the experience of infantile sexuality and of the libido as the ubiquitous energy of the sexual instinct (drive). As stated earlier, this is why it will be necessary to use Lacanian theory to hypothesize how the *not* experiencing of sexual attraction might occur and how satisfaction of this apparent absence might be achieved in asexuality.[27]

Asexuality and the Latency Period

While the very idea of an active, Other-directed libido being absent might be mystifying for those unfamiliar with asexuality, it is nevertheless part of every sexual person's passage towards adult sexuality. The experience of an apparently absent libido is to be found in the latency period of all subjects to a greater or lesser extent. This gives rise to the question as to whether asexuality could be a form of extended, or even permanent, latency period. Freudian theory states that the first "configuration" of the child's love takes place in the Oedipus complex (1921, p. 138), but the repression which brings the complex to an end means that the sexual aspect of the object-choice is "unutilizable" during the latency period which follows. Instead, the sexual current becomes an "affectionate current" in sexual life (1905, p. 200). However, as stated, concealed behind this affection are the "sexual longings of the infantile component instincts (drives)" (ibid.). Within the parameters of Freudian theory, then, this allows for the possibility of a sexual drive operating in the background, as it does in the latency period, while overt sexual interest or activity with others is absent. On this basis, asexuality shares a number of common features with latency – the lack of interest in sexuality, the apparent absence of sexual object-choice and the possibility of a sexual drive operating behind affection.

During latency, Freud says that whatever of the first period of love during the Oedipus complex is left over shows itself as a "purely affectionate emotional tie", relating to the same people in the subject's life (i.e., the parents or primary caregivers). The difference now is that during latency, this tie can no longer be described as "sexual" (ibid.). Indeed, the adult relationships of some asexuals are characterized, similar to the latency period, as comprising strong affectionate bonds that do not include a sexual tie to other people (Thompson, 2012, pp. 54–55). It is during latency that forces which impede the sexual instinct (drive) are built up (Freud, 1905, p. 177) through the diversion of the sexual instinct (drive) from sexual aims, to new, non-sexual aims. This comes about by a process of sublimation as the child's ego turns away from the object-cathexes with the parents and replaces them with non-sexual identifications with other objects in his or her world. Now the libidinal trends of the Oedipus complex are in part "desexualized and sublimated . . . and in part inhibited in their aim and changed into impulses of affection" (1924, p. 177). This is the repression, referred to earlier, which brings the Oedipus complex to an end and ushers in the relative calm of the latency period. But in Freud's view, the sexual impulses do not stop just because the latency period begins. Instead, the sexualized energy produced by these impulses is used for other purposes such as contributing to social feelings and, through being prohibited from satisfaction by repression and reaction-formation, for the purpose of building up barriers against sexuality (1905, p. 232). In short, the latency period is a time when the sex drive is active.

Freud emphasizes that the experience of latency will differ depending on the individual. A fragment of sexuality may break through, or some sexual activity may persist until puberty when the sexual instinct (drive) emerges again with greater intensity (ibid., p. 179). In later chapters, I will expand on this idea to propose that not only does the passage through infantile sexuality differ for asexuals but also that the re-emergence of "sexuality" post-latency can take on its characteristic absence of sexual desire. For now, the point of interest is that Freud includes a phase of sexual development in every subject which, to a greater or lesser extent, is the conscious experience of no sexual desire. At the same time, a sexual instinct (drive) is operating which is sublimated into other areas of the subject's life. The latency period offers an example of how a libidinal force can be operating and yet unnoticed while the subject is involved in a variety of non-sexual activities and experiences.

However, in order to ensure that asexuality does not become associated with the concept of an extended, or permanent, stage of latency and, therefore, become categorized as a developmental anomaly, it is necessary to offer a distinction between the two. The main point of difference between asexuality and an extended, or permanent, latency period is that, for sexually desiring subjects, latency is inaugurated by a repression which brings the Oedipus complex to an end. I will be proposing in later chapters that this is not the case for asexuality, on the basis that repression is not the mechanism which ensures the desexualization of the libidinal trends within asexuality. I will be proposing, in contrast, that the libidinal trends within asexuality are desexualized, not at the Oedipal stage but during the earlier pre-Oedipal phase, and that even then, repression as originating cause is not a factor. This, in turn, would mean that the passage of the asexual subject through the latency period would be qualitatively different to that of the subject who goes on to desire sexual contact with others. In other words, I will be proposing that the asexual enters the latency period with an already different orientation to the sexual drive.

Asexuality and the Incest Taboo

Given that the pause in sexually orientated experiences which latency represents allows for the erection of barriers and restraints on sexuality, the most important of these barriers for Freud is the one against incest. It is the barrier against any possibility of continuing to choose the mother or father figure as the sexual object post-puberty (ibid., p. 225, and fn. 3).[28] He goes on to say, however, that it is "in the world of ideas" (ibid.) that the choice of object is first made and that, equally, the sexual instinct (drive) of post-pubertal subjects is "almost entirely restricted to indulging in phantasies" (ibid., p. 226). He defines "phantasies" as ideas which are *not* destined to be carried out (ibid.), which have their roots in infantile sexuality, which can persist through latency in the unconscious and which have a crucial role to play in symptom and dream formation. He sums up his line of thinking by saying that the Oedipus complex, as the infantile psychical engagement with one's caregivers (usually mother and father), represents the peak of infantile sexuality and, through its after-effects, exercises a decisive influence on the sexuality of adults (ibid., fn. 1).

The point of interest is how, for Freud, sexuality is determined not in a fixed biological sense but through a fluid inter-dynamic relation between the child and its adult caregivers that combines physical and erotically charged experiences together with perceptual encounters in terms of what is seen and heard. These are combined with fantasized or imaginary components as the child seeks to put sense and meaning onto their experiences. The theory posits that every subject undergoes the Oedipus complex and must do so in their own unique way (ibid.). It also posits that repression has taken place which has effectively removed all possibility of sexual excitation being experienced or converted into desire for the child's parents. Nevertheless, Freud says that sexual love and what "appears to be" non-sexual love for parents come from the same sources (ibid., p. 227). This emphasizes the sexual underpinning of non-sexual love. The presence of an affectionate trend which does not include a sexual trend places the root of what Freud terms a "sexually anaesthetic" (ibid.) orientation firmly within infantile sexuality.

In his view, there is no doubt that every object-choice in adulthood is based, albeit less closely, on the prototypes of mother and father (ibid., p. 228). The importance of this in determining a later choice of sexual object means that any "disturbance" in the child's relations to his parents will, in his view, "produce the gravest effects" on adult sexual life (ibid.). If, therefore, every object-choice in adulthood is based on the prototypes of mother and father, what does this imply about the nature of the relationship with these prototypes at the infantile stage? While I will be returning to this question in later chapters, for now, Freud says the child's affection for its parents is the "most important infantile trace" which directs object-choice; but it is not the only one. He allows for the "innumerable peculiarities" of erotic life to have an input into this choice in adulthood, along with the "compulsive character" of falling in love with someone. But he adds, these factors are "unintelligible" unless seen as the "residual effects of childhood" (ibid., p. 229, fn. 1). The Freudian view carries the implicit understanding that libido is seeking to avoid unpleasure and achieve pleasure through discharge via sexual activity with another person. However, the theory also states that any factor that impairs sexual development brings about a regression, which Freud describes as a return of the libido to an earlier phase of development which *was* pleasurable. On this point, I will be proposing a different trajectory in that not only is asexuality *not* a case of impaired sexual development but also, rather than regression to an asexual phase, the opposite takes place. My proposition is building towards the concept that, based on what Freud so far includes of the unpleasure inherent in the sexual drive, early infantile sexuality unconsciously *begins* as unpleasurable for the asexual and that this progresses forward through various psychosexual stages into adulthood. Needless to say, it will be necessary to establish if Lacanian theory supports this proposition or not, but for the moment, and in Chapter 3, I will examine specific Freudian concepts in order to further evaluate, include or discount their significance for asexuality.

Notes

1 Sexuality theorist Jeffrey Weeks points out that Freud's concept of consciousness being constantly undermined by unconscious forces outside our rational control is "the most radical theoretical challenge this century to the fixity of gender and sexual identities" (1991, p. 94).

2 Regarding my use of the term "satisfaction", it might be helpful to include Juliet Mitchell's point that the object that is longed-for and which promises satisfaction begins as an object which is lost (1982, p. 6). Any satisfaction that might subsequently be attained will always contain this loss within it. Therefore, there is something fundamentally impossible about satisfaction itself. She links it to Freud's statement that potentially, the sexual drive is "unfavourable to the realization of complete satisfaction" (1912, pp. 188–189).

3 Lacan will differ on this point. For him, they do not achieve complete synthesis under the rubric of genital sexuality.

4 See also Zupančič, 2017, pp. 7–8.

5 In "'Wild' Psycho-Analysis" (1910, p. 223), Freud says sexual satisfaction is not a solution to neurotic symptoms since a "good number" of people are unable to find satisfaction in it and "unsatisfied sexual trends . . . can often find only inadequate outlet in coitus or other sexual acts".

6 This can include a range of behaviours from masturbation to what, today, is termed "kink", slang for unconventional sexual preferences or behaviours.

7 The phrase "polymorphously perverse" emphasises that human sexuality begins in all subjects from a diffuse and diverse set of psycho-physical component sexual drives and is capable of manifesting in a variety of ways. In this Freudian view, even bodily organs, as well as the functions they perform, have a sexual significance (See 1916–1916, SE XVI, p. 308).

8 Appignanesi and Forrester argue that, from the mid-1940s to the 1970s, the British school of psychoanalysis desexualized not just the "psychoanalytic child" but also the "sexual mother" (1992, p. 454).

9 The latency period begins when the Oedipus complex ends at around the age of 5 or 6 years of age and continues until puberty.

10 Queer theorist Nikki Sullivan says Freud sees sexuality "less as an essence than as a drive" with a "whole range of possible sexual aims, object choices and states of psychosexual being" (2003, p. 14).

11 Here, he describes the instinct (drive) as a "continuously flowing source of stimulation" (ibid., p. 149, and footnote 1).

12 He comes to this idea through his focus on the perversions (i.e., anything that is not reproductive sex) and believes that even in "the most normal sexual process", it is possible to detect rudiments of perversion (1905, p. 171).

13 Here, he also says that erotic instincts appear to be more plastic than destructive instincts.

14 Instincts have four components for Freud: the pressure (*Drang*) or demand for work, which is constant; the aim (*Ziel*) which is always satisfaction; the object (*Objekt*) is the thing through which the instinct achieves its aim; and the source (*Quelle*) which is the somatic process that begins in the body and whose stimulus is represented in mental life by an instinct. See 1915, pp. 122–123.

15 See also Freud, 1916–1917, SE XVI, p. 416. His changing view on whether the id or the ego is the reservoir of libido (1923, pp. 63–66) does not alter his point that ego-libido, not object-libido, is the original state of things.

16 For the distinction of an "inside" and an "outside", see *Formulations on the Two Principles of Mental Functioning* (1911), *Negation* (1925) and Chapter 1 of *Civilization and its Discontents* (1930).

17 Lacan (1977 [1964]) takes issue with Freud's notion of a desexualized libido but agrees with his idea that the "approach of reality involves a desexualisation" (see *The Four Fundamental Concepts of Psychoanalysis, Seminar XI*, session of 29 April 1964, p. 155). My proposition concurs with Lacan in that there is no desexualized libido, particularly in asexuality, but there is a desexualized aim and object of the sexual drive.

18 The Oedipus complex occurs during the phallic stage between the ages of circa 3–6 years.

19 Freud places final object-choice at the dissolution of the Oedipus complex. He also says many variations are possible of the standard Oedipus complex which will have a very important bearing on the development of the individual (1924, p. 179).

20 Lacan emphasizes that it can be just as easily a feeding bottle as a breast (2020, p. 176).

21 The preconscious belongs to Freud's earlier topological explanation of the psychical system and will become part of the ego in his later topology.

22 Symptom is used here in the clinical sense to indicate a disorder. Freud (1926, SE XX, p. 91) defines it thus: "A symptom is a sign of, and a substitute for, an instinctual

satisfaction which has remained in abeyance; it is a consequence of the process of repression. Repression proceeds from the ego when the latter – it may be at the behest of the super-ego – refuses to associate itself with an instinctual cathexis which has been aroused in the id". Symptom formation is the moment of the genesis of neurosis and is the sign of a return of the repressed (See also Laplanche and Pontalis, 1973, p. 446).

23 He says, "Only psycho-analytic investigation can show that behind this affection, admiration and respect there lie concealed the old sexual longings of the infantile component instincts which have now become unserviceable".

24 We can also include the place of social forces here as formative of adult sexual orientations because the centrality of object-choice in Freud's theory by definition involves the input of other people as representatives of social/cultural influences (i.e., laws, conventions, customs, practices and beliefs).

25 There may also be a prima facie relatedness between this concept and asexual writer Ela Przybylo's (2019) concept of "asexual erotics".

26 Infantile sexual trauma, as I will be using it, will refer not to abuse from an external agent but to the internal "menacing" demands of the libido in the context of the prematurity of the human infant and its relatively long state of dependence (See Freud, 1919, SE XVII, p. 210 and 1916–1917, SE XVI, p. 364).

27 This is analogous to Lacan's (2014 [1962–1963]) distinction between his view of anxiety and Freud's. For Freud, anxiety is fear without an object, but for Lacan, anxiety is not without an object. Lacan says of this object that the subject "is not without having it, but elsewhere, right where he is, it's not to be seen" (see *Anxiety, Seminar X*, session of 9 January 1963, pp. 88–89). I will be proposing that asexuality has a similar object that is not seen.

28 The Oedipus complex ends and the latency period begins only when the child has understood that incestuous thoughts or feelings have had to be abandoned.

References

Appignanesi, L. and Forrester, J. (1992) *Freud's women*. London: Weidenfeld and Nicolson.

Bogaert, A. F. (2004) 'Asexuality: Its prevalence and associated factors in a national probability sample', *Journal of Sex Research*, 41(3), pp. 279–287.

Brodsky, G. (2011) 'Sexual reality', *Hurly-Burly, The International Lacanian Journal of Psychoanalysis* (5), March, pp. 61–77.

Brotto, L. A., Knudson, G., Inskip, J., Rhodes, K. and Erskine, Y. (2010) 'Asexuality: A mixed-methods approach', *Archives of Sexual Behavior*, 39(3), pp. 599–618.

Carrigan, M. (2011) 'There's more to life than sex? Difference and commonality within the asexual community', *Sexualities*, 14(4), pp. 462–478.

Dean, T. (2003) 'Lacan and queer theory', in Rabaté, J.-M. (ed.), *The Cambridge Companion to Lacan*. Cambridge: Cambridge University Press, pp. 102–115.

Freud, S. (1896) 'Extracts from the Fliess papers, draft k', in *Pre-psycho-analytic publications and unpublished drafts (1886–1899)*, Standard Edition I. London: Vintage/Hogarth.

Freud, S. (1905) 'Three essays on sexuality', in *A case of hysteria, three essays on sexuality and other works*, Standard Edition VII. London: Vintage/Hogarth.

Freud, S. (1908) 'Civilized sexual morality and modern nervous illness', in *Jensen's 'Gradiva' and other works*, Standard Edition IX. London: Vintage/Hogarth.

Freud, S. (1910) "'Wild' Psycho-Analysis", in *Five lectures on psycho-analysis, Leonardo da Vinci and other works*, Standard Edition XI. London: Vintage/Hogarth.

Freud, S. (1911) 'Formulations on the two principles of mental functioning', in *Case history of Schreber, papers on technique and other works*, Standard Edition XII. London: Vintage/Hogarth.

Freud, S. (1912) 'On the universal tendency to debasement in the sphere of love', in *Five lectures on psycho-analysis, Leonardo da Vinci and other works*, Standard Edition XI. London: Vintage/Hogarth.

Freud, S. (1915) 'Instincts and their vicissitudes', in *On the history of the psycho-analytic movement, papers on metapsychology and other works*, Standard Edition XIV. London: Vintage/Hogarth.

Freud, S. (1916–1917) *Introductory lectures on psycho-analyses*, Standard Editions XV–XVI. London: Vintage/Hogarth.

Freud, S. (1919) 'Psycho-analysis and the war neuroses', in *An infantile neurosis and other works*, Standard Edition XVII. London: Vintage/Hogarth.

Freud, S. (1920) 'Beyond the pleasure principle', in *Beyond the pleasure principle, group psychology and other works*, Standard Edition XVIII. London: Vintage/Hogarth.

Freud, S. (1921) 'Group psychology and the analysis of the ego', in *Beyond the pleasure principle, group psychology and other works*, Standard Edition XVIII. London: Vintage/Hogarth.

Freud, S. (1923) 'The ego and the id', in *The ego and the id and other works*, Standard Edition XIX. London: Vintage/Hogarth.

Freud, S. (1924) 'The dissolution of the Oedipus complex', in *The ego and the id and other works*, Standard Edition XIX. London: Vintage/Hogarth.

Freud, S. (1925) 'Negation', in *The ego and the id and other works*, Standard Edition XIX. London: Vintage/Hogarth.

Freud, S. (1926) 'Inhibitions, symptoms and anxiety', in *An autobiographical study, inhibitions, symptoms and anxiety, lay analysis and other works*. Standard Edition XX. London: Vintage/Hogarth.

Freud, S. (1930) 'Civilization and its and discontents', in *The future of an illusion, civilization and its discontents and other works*, Standard Edition XXI. London: Vintage/Hogarth.

Lacan, J. (1977 [1964]) *The four fundamental concepts of psycho-analysis*, Seminar XI (Miller, J-A., ed.) (Sheridan, A., trans). London: Penguin.

Lacan, J. (2014 [1962–1963]) *Anxiety*, Seminar X (Miller, J.-A., ed.) (Price, A. R., trans). Cambridge: Polity Press.

Lacan, J. (2020 [1956–1957]) *The object relation*, Seminar IV (Miller, J.-A., ed.) (Price, A. R., trans). Cambridge: Polity Press.

Laplanche, J. and Pontalis, J. B. (1973) *The language of psycho-analysis* (Nicholson-Smith, D., trans). London: Hogarth Press/Institute of Psycho-Analysis.

Leader, D. (2021) *Jouissance – Sexuality, suffering and satisfaction*. Cambridge: Polity.

Mitchell, J. (1982) 'Introduction – 1', in Mitchell, J. and Rose, J. (eds.), *Feminine sexuality – Jacques Lacan and the école freudienne*. New York: Norton, pp. 1–26.

Nantais, D. S. J. and Opperman, S. S. J. (2002) *Eight myths about religious life*. Available at: http://ozvocations.catholic.org.au/thinking/visionmag/myths.html [Accessed 6 November 2021].

O'Donnell, B. (2008) 'We're married, we just don't have sex', *The Guardian*, 8 September. Available at: www.guardian.co.uk/lifeandstyle/2008/sep/08/ relationships.healthandwellbeing [Accessed 4 November 2021].

Prause, N. and Graham, C. A. (2007) 'Asexuality: Classification and characterization', *Archives of Sexual Behaviour*, 36(3), pp. 341–355.

Przybylo, E. (2019) *Asexual erotics: Intimate readings of compulsory sexuality*. Columbus, OH: Ohio State University Press.

Scherrer, K. S. (2008) 'Coming to an asexual identity: Negotiating identity, negotiating desire', *Sexualities*, 11(5), 1 October, pp. 621–641.

Sullivan, N. (2003) *A critical introduction queer theory*. New York: New York University Press.

Thompson, J. (2012) 'No sex please, we're homoromantic', *Diva Magazine*, May, pp. 54–55. London: 505 Albert House, 256–260 Old Street, EC1V 9DD.

Weeks, J. (1991) *Against nature – Essays on history, sexuality and identity*. London: Rivers Oram Press.

Zupančič, A. (2017) *What is sex?* Cambridge, MA: MIT Press.

Chapter 3

Key Freudian Concepts and Their Relation to Asexuality

Freud points to a non-sexual or asexual emotional tie between people in which the ego is capable of setting up an object inside itself that it has lost or perceives itself to have lost through having had to give up that object (1923, p. 28). For him, this "introjection" is a form of regression to the oral phase, whereby the external object is introjected so that it becomes easier for the ego to give it up. The example of the Dora case study illustrates how she withdraws her libido from the forbidden object of her father in a regression to an identification with him, or at least to an identification with a trait of his personality (i.e., his cough) (1921, pp. 106–107). Identification is, therefore, the earliest and original form of emotional tie with the object, even earlier than object cathexis (ibid., p. 107). Freud speculates that an identification of this kind might be the only way the id, from which erotic impulses derive, can give up its objects. He believes this process is a "very frequent one" especially at early stages of development (1923, p. 29). The capacity to transform itself into the loved object (ibid., p. 30) through taking the libido back into itself makes the ego a "precipitate of abandoned object-cathexes" and one which contains the "history of those object-choices" (ibid.).

Freud is describing the id's loss of the sexual object and the manner in which this loss is mitigated by the ego assuming the features of that lost object. He says that, from one point of view, this is a method by which the ego can obtain control over the id by forcing itself on the id as the love-object. In terms of asexuality, it allows for the possibility that even at early stages of development, object-libido can be withdrawn from the subject's libidinal object-choices, and this is a concept which will take on greater relevance in the following chapters. For now, this transformation of libido, in Freud's view, implies an "abandonment of sexual aims, a desexualization – a kind of sublimation, therefore" (ibid.). This is a desexualization of the child's relation to part of its external reality (i.e., the sexual object), which can be easily recognized as a feature of asexuality. But this is not to say that desexualization implies that there is no sexual drive in operation because quite obviously, in order for desexualization to occur, there has to be a sexualized entity, with a sexual drive, to begin with.

Freud's idea is that all sexual tendencies, whether towards love partners, parents, siblings or, even, the self, are an expression of a sexual drive with sexual

DOI: 10.4324/9781003214946-4

satisfaction as its aim (1921, p. 90). In the case of siblings, parents and others who are deemed by the ego to be inappropriate objects of the drive, the sexual drives are diverted from this aim (ibid.). Nevertheless, they preserve enough of their "original nature" to allow their true identity to be recognized; by which he means that the sexual drives can be detected in, say, the longing for closeness with, or altruistic tendencies towards, others (ibid., p. 91).[1] In short, there is always something sexual taking place, even when it appears not to be. As mentioned in Chapter 2, affectionate feelings are the successor of a "completely sensual object-tie" with the person in question or with that person's prototype or *imago* (ibid.). The concept of affection being the repressed derivative of earlier sexual trends also means that asexuality might, therefore, be considered a sexual orientation. To restate, for Freud, affectionate emotional ties have sexual aims even though they have been diverted from those sexual aims (ibid., p. 138). Another support for this concept of the sexual behind the non-sexual can be found in Freud's view of the ego instincts (drives) which take the person's own ego as their object and so are to be counted among the sexual instincts (drives) (1920, p. 61, fn. 1).

Freud also finds an active libido in a non-sexual context in his study of groups (1921, pp. 93–99).[2] This time, however, he reasons that if narcissistic self-love is tempered (i.e., lessened or reduced) within groups, then this is proof that group formation represents a "new" kind of libidinal tie among group members, where narcissism or ego-libido is reduced (ibid., pp. 102–103). In groups, there is "no question" of sexual aims because the love instincts have been diverted from this aim. It is identification which ties people together, but, he says, this is, nonetheless, a *libidinal* tie. However, it is worth pointing out that in psychoanalytic theory, any subjective identity which this might bring for both the asexual and the non-asexual cannot be a guarantee of subjectivity since it is based on two structural foundations which, particularly in Lacanian terms, lack solidity. These are language, which is fluid in terms of meaning, and the ego, which is based on misrecognition from the outset.[3]

Sexual Independence from the Other

In the Freudian sense, therefore, identification is a way of creating a libidinal bond with another person or persons but without a sexual aim. In the Oedipus complex, Freud's example is of the boy identifying with the father as his ideal and then forming a sexual object-cathexis towards the mother. In the Freudian understanding, identification not only comes *before* object-cathexis, but it is also ambivalent from the start, capable of turning from being tender to just as easily being hostile (1921, p. 105). It can take place with any new perception of "a common quality shared with some other person who is not an object of the sexual instinct (drive)" (ibid., p. 108). He says that "all the ties" which a group depends on have the characteristic of instincts (drives) that are inhibited in their aims (ibid., p. 140). In his view, therefore, the tie that binds the members of a group is in the nature of this kind of identification, based on an "important emotional common quality", as he calls it. This common quality, he suspects, lies in the emotional tie to the leader of the group. This, again, takes place through the process of introjection, but in this context, the leader comes to stand in or substitute for the original lost object, usually understood as the mother figure (ibid., pp. 108–109).[4]

However, despite the seeming asexual nature of these ties, something of the sexual persists for the individual within groups (ibid., p. 141), and since it is libido which ties people together, it does not matter whether the libido is of a homosexual, heterosexual or, we might add, asexual nature. This, Freud argues, is because "it is not differentiated according to the sexes, and particularly shows a complete disregard for the aims of the genital organization of the libido" (ibid.). Asexuality, like group formation, can involve some of these elements, in particular the existence of a love-tie that does not involve a sexual element. However, the obvious distinction which needs to be made is that groups, at least for Freud, are comprised of sexual individuals who come together in asexual formations. In contrast, the group that comprises asexual individuals is asexual before the group is formed but who are nevertheless and paradoxically, at least according to Freudian theory, forming ties which are libidinal ties.

Asexuality and the Ego Ideal

Taking up Freud's point of an apparently desexualized libido, the question arises as to whether this concept has anything to offer. For him, desexualization can be brought about by sublimation which takes place through the mediation of the ego (i.e., the conscious mind). In sublimation, sexual object-libido (Other-directed) is changed into narcissistic libido (self-directed) and given a new aim, other than sexual satisfaction (1923, p. 30). In this theorization, he is emphasizing that the desexualization of the libido is the abandonment of sexual aims (ibid., p. 30). He is also describing the ego's ability to withdraw the dependence for satisfaction of the sexual drive, either partially or totally, from the "influence of other people" (1921, p. 69). While this aspect of Freudian theory offers a plausible understanding of how a libidinal investment in objects can be absent in asexuality, it still does not throw any light on why, for asexuality, there is no conscious experience of the sexual drive. To put it simply, if sublimation has a conscious dimension to it, since it is mediated by the ego, then the questions remain as to how and why sexual desire is not registered in the consciousness of the asexual. After all, for sublimation to be consciously seeking out substitute non-sexual satisfactions, an inherent sexual drive has to have been acknowledged by the subject. I will be returning to a theoretical consideration of these questions using Lacanian theory in the following chapters.

In terms of sexually desiring subjects whose libido is directed towards sexual aims, the transition to such a libidinal investment directed towards an object involves a reduction of narcissistic libido. In Freudian theory, in order to facilitate the giving up of infantile narcissism, the subject forms an ideal which is a "substitute" for the lost narcissism of early childhood when the child was their own ideal

(1914, p. 94). This ego ideal ensures self-directed narcissism can redirect to object cathexes (investments), and it is the result of the earliest identifications with caregivers in the child's "pre-history" (1923, p. 31), emphasizing the importance of pre-Oedipal factors. Since it is the hoped-for perfection onto which the subject's lost narcissism of childhood is displaced (1914, p. 94), the ego ideal contains within it something intrinsically of the subject. It also heightens the demands of the ego to achieve the standard this ideal sets. Therefore, directing the libido towards an object-cathexis (i.e., the binding of the libido to the object) is a question of whether this process is concurrent with one's ego ideal or, conversely, counter to one's ego ideal (ibid., p. 99). This means that the unconscious libidinal binding to the object is a question of whether it is ego-syntonic[5] – that is, in harmony with what the ego wants (ibid.).

In this way, then, the ego ideal can impose "severe conditions upon the satisfaction of the libido" (ibid.) through its choice of objects and can reject some objects because, judged against the ego ideal, they are incompatible. In asexuality, this allows for the possibility that the ego ideal may impose conditions on the satisfaction of libido if not just the object but also the aim via the object of sexual satisfaction is counter to the ego ideal. In this regard, Freud's comment that people strive to attain happiness through becoming the ideal of perfection they once were in childhood (ibid.) takes on a different meaning, particularly if that ideal is a non-sexually desiring one. In effect, the possibility now arises that the asexual can choose objects that are compatible with their ego ideal which may include the ideal of no sexual desire. The asexual experience, in general, suggests that a sexual drive has rarely, if ever, been experienced in their lives. This further suggests that the ego ideal of asexuality has not included the concept of sexual attraction for another person from an early age, if at all. Quite obviously, to propose that a non-sexually desiring ideal can potentially operate within asexuality, it will be necessary to theorize how this can take place, and I will be doing this in the following chapters.

For now, in Freud's theory, behind the ego ideal which, through repression, brings the Oedipus complex to an end (1923, p. 31), lie hidden the first and most important identifications of the child with the parents (ibid.).[6] In both sexes, Freud believes, the outcome of the Oedipus complex can be an identification with the father, with the mother or both (ibid., p. 33).[7] Identification with one (i.e., modelling itself on one parent) will strengthen the object-cathexis (i.e., libidinal attachment) with the Other. In Freud's schema of a simple, positive (his term) Oedipus complex, for example, the identification with, or the becoming like, the parent of the same sex preserves the object-relation (libidinal attachment) to the parent of the opposite sex (ibid., p. 34). As mentioned earlier, the broad outcome of the Oedipus complex is to form a "precipitate" in the ego, consisting of abandoned object-cathexes which, for Freud, unite to form an ego ideal or super-ego (ibid.). This ego ideal or super-ego then confronts the ego when it is not reaching the standards set by the incorporated ideal (ibid.). The point of interest here is that an ego ideal can be formed, not simply as a residue of earlier object-choices of the id but as an energetic reaction-formation *against* those choices (ibid.). In asexuality, a non-sexually desiring subject appears to come into being despite identifications and object-choices that can relate to sexually desiring objects. However, Freud's theory includes the proposition that the ego is not just influenced to "be like" the parental role model (i.e., sexually desiring). It can equally be influenced *not* to "be like" the parental role model (i.e., not sexually desiring). This is through the action of the super-ego seeking to maintain the sought-after standard which the ego ideal represents. If this is the case, it opens the possibility that the ego ideal in asexuality can take up the position of withholding permission to be like the parental model, thus representing a divergence from a traditional sex-normative identificatory position.[8] It can also allow for the possibility that, through the influence of the ego ideal, there is a preference to take up a non-sexually desiring position with regard to the Other. In Freud's view, the ego ideal is the heir to the Oedipus complex (1923, p. 36), by which he means that it is formed from the identifications with the parents into a model to which the child attempts to conform, a model which combines both prohibitions and ideals. The ego ideal facilitates the child in moving beyond its state of narcissism and is responsible for the repression which brings the Oedipus complex to a close. For Freud, therefore, the ego ideal is the expression of the "most powerful impulses" and the "most important libidinal vicissitudes of the *id*" (ibid.). I will be proposing that the asexual ego ideal is also the expression of powerful impulses and important libidinal vicissitudes of the id but in a way that does not include sexual desire, and again, I will be returning to this in the following chapters.

Libido as Internal Enemy

What, then, are these powerful impulses of the id that Freud is referring to? If we take a step back for a moment, he believes the setting up of the ego in the place of the object in narcissism cannot be considered as either exceptional or trivial since it was probably "the universal and original state of things" (1916–1917, SE XVI, p. 416).[9] Indeed, many sexual instincts (drives) begin by finding satisfaction autoerotically in the subject's own body (ibid., p. 314). Object-love only later develops out of narcissism and even then, without narcissism disappearing completely, a point I will consider further in this chapter. Narcissistic libido is understood to be "an amount of sexual energy attached to the ego itself and finding satisfaction in the ego just as satisfaction is usually found only in objects" (1919, p. 209). Its discovery is, for Freud, a legitimate development of the concept of sexuality (ibid., p. 210). But it is through the existence of narcissistic libido that an important discovery of the trauma inherent in the sexual drive was made; hence, the powerful forces of the id, which I mention earlier. Freud found that the same sexual aetiology applying to the transference neuroses could be applied more broadly to the narcissistic neuroses. In other words, traumatic neuroses could be included in the orbit of psychoanalytic investigation because of Freud's intuition of the connection between fright, anxiety and narcissistic libido (ibid.). His reasoning is as follows: while traumatic neuroses and war neuroses brought a strong focus on the real trauma which soldiers and people in danger experienced from external threats, they appeared to have nothing in common with the internal psychical threats experienced in the transference neuroses (ibid.). Then he found a link between war neuroses, traumatic peace-time neuroses and narcissistic neuroses on the one hand, and transference neuroses on the other. Freud proposes that the link is the existence of narcissistic libido which makes the ego a "loved" object. In both categories of neuroses, the ego as the loved object is being threatened and/or overwhelmed. In traumatic and war neuroses, the ego is defending itself from an external danger. In the transference neuroses, the enemy is internal, and it is the libido whose demands are experienced as "menacing" (ibid.).

In terms of asexuality, then, Freud's work on narcissism brings with it the concept of libido as having the potential not only to be disruptive but also to be the internal enemy. As such, it can threaten to overwhelm the ego, and anything that threatens to overwhelm the ego must be defended against. Again, the conventional understanding that libido can only be experienced as pleasurable is being radically opposed. Freud says the main defence system available for dealing with this internal threat is repression which "lies at the basis of every neurosis, as a reaction to a trauma – as an elementary traumatic neurosis" (ibid.). But since Freudian theory does not extend to a consideration of this concept's potentially formative role in producing an asexual orientation, this point about trauma as internally generated and intrinsically linked to the sexual drive will be taken up again in the following chapters. I will also be considering if repression is the only possibility for dealing with early infantile trauma associated with a potentially threatening libido.

To emphasize Freud's position on the traumatic potential of infantile sexuality, he says that such experiences are "momentous" because they take place "in times of incomplete development", and that is why they are liable to have "traumatic effects" (1916–1917, SE XVI, p. 361). This now opens the possibility that the structurally traumatic effect of the sexual drive can produce very different outcomes in terms of choice of sexual orientation.[10] Regarding asexuality, Freud is describing a template for what can be experienced as internally generated trauma due to an increase in libidinal excitation for which the infant is unprepared. Since being prepared constitutes the last line of the child's defences against internally generated stimuli, he believes the difference between being unprepared and being prepared is possibly a decisive factor in determining the outcome in terms of trauma (1920, pp. 31–32). As stated, however, his theorizing does not extend to a consideration that this experience could lead to a radically different relation to the sexual drive, whereby having a desire for no sexual desire could become the ideal. Again, this is something which will be taken up in the following chapters.

The Reduction of Libidinal Excitement

Freud's concept of the pleasure principle is a theorized mechanism for reducing libidinal excitation in order to keep the quantity of excitation as low as possible or at least constant (ibid., p. 9). Accordingly, pleasure is *in some way* [emphasis in original] connected with the diminution, reduction or extinction of the amounts of stimulus while unpleasure is connected with their increase (1916–1917, p. 356). He further argues that if this principle holds, then anything that might increase excitation is bound to be felt as unpleasurable (1920, p. 9). The asexual experience seems to be consistent with this principle because "unpleasure" corresponds to rising sexual excitation (Brotto et al., 2010, p. 607). While registering no sexual attraction for other people, asexual subjects appear to have developed a way of unconsciously maintaining sexual excitation at its lowest possible level. Sexual subjects, in contrast, deal with the unpleasure of rising sexual excitation by seeking discharge of this rising tension through sexual activity, either through masturbation or in relation to another person.

In *Beyond the Pleasure Principle*, Freud (1920) nuances his idea that the pleasure principle dominates mental processes. If it did, he reasons, then many of our mental processes would be accompanied by pleasure, which in fact they are not. There is instead a "beyond" of the pleasure principle which, pursuing satisfaction, produces unpleasure. He now says that the most that can be said is that there exists in the mind a *tendency* towards the pleasure principle. This tendency, in turn, meets with opposition from the reality principle, which seeks to postpone satisfaction of instinctual (drive) and sexual impulses, abandon some impulses altogether or tolerate unpleasure until satisfaction can be achieved (ibid., pp. 9–10). As the ego develops, the other mechanism which inhibits the pleasure principle is repression. It holds back sexual drives that are not compatible with the aims of the ego, or with the reality principle, and cuts them off from the possibility of satisfaction (ibid., p. 11). If these drives succeed in getting around repression to find a direct or substitutive satisfaction, then this is also felt by the ego as "unpleasure". His hypothesis is that these sexual impulses were repressed by the ego in the first place on account of being unpleasurable. Their return to find another form of satisfaction is no less so (ibid.). His theorizing again suggests how internal libidinal excitations can be experienced as unpleasurable and need to be defended against. In his view, the human mental apparatus is shielded against the amounts of excitation impinging on it from the outside, but there is no such shield against excitations coming from within. This, he believes, is because excitations coming from within are not considered atypical or alien compared to stimuli from the external world (ibid., p. 29). For Freud, this produces two things: first, internal feelings of pleasure and unpleasure predominate over external stimuli. Second, a particular way is adopted to deal with "any internal excitations" which produce too great an increase of unpleasure. This "way" of dealing with them, he says, is to treat them as if they *are* coming from the outside so that a defensive shield can be erected against them.

The Trauma of the Sex Drive

What is of interest here is that, as stated, an increase in internal excitation is equated with unpleasure (1905, p. 209).[11] Freud's objective is to understand the effects produced by any "breach in the shield against stimuli" and the problems that follow in its train, with particular importance given to the element of fright caused by the lack of preparedness for any such breach in the shield (1920, p. 31). Viewed in terms of asexuality, then, he is describing a template for the experience of internally generated trauma due to an unexpected increase in, or uncomfortably high levels of, libidinal excitation (ibid., p. 30).[12] The most abundant sources of internal excitation are the instincts (drives) and, in particular, the sexual instinct (drive) which is met with repression for the very reason that it has a traumatic effect (ibid., p. 34). In addition, Freud theorizes that a repressed instinct (drive) never stops looking for complete satisfaction, and no substitute or reactive formation or, indeed, sublimation can remove the persisting tension caused by the demand for satisfaction (ibid., p. 42). The asexual subject, however, appears to register no persisting tension as a result of any repressed sexual drive, especially if asexuality's absence of subjective distress is taken into account. The question that arises then, and it will be addressed more fully in the context of Lacanian theory, is how this can occur.

The conundrum of the sexual drive which Freud highlights is how the tension of sexual excitement is an unpleasurable feeling and yet is also felt as pleasurable. He asks how this unpleasurable tension and the feeling of pleasure are to be reconciled (1905, p. 209). In one piece of research on asexuality mentioned in Chapter 1, anxiety was shown to increase among asexual subjects as sexual excitation increased. Freud, in seeking an answer to his conundrum, says the kind of pleasure derived from the excitation of "erotogenous zones" is "fore-pleasure", and he links this to the same pleasure on a smaller scale experienced by the child during infantile sexuality. In contrast, the satisfaction derived from the more adult form of the sexual act is what he calls "end pleasure" (1905, p. 210). The two are connected, he says, in that the excitation of the erotogenous zones in infantile sexuality makes possible the greater satisfaction in the sex act after puberty. He is saying that the sexually active adult transforms the unpleasure of rising sexual excitation into pleasure due to its association with the satisfaction of sexual orgasm. The pleasure of the erotogenous zones of childhood creates an association with, and expectation of, pleasure in the sexual act of adulthood.

Of interest here is that, in his view, the experiences of infantile sexuality determine the response to the tension of sexual excitement which will take place in adult sexuality (ibid., p. 212). Therefore, if asexual people register no desire to achieve pleasure or satisfaction through sexual acts with another person, this would imply that either the excitation of the erotogenous zones never took place in childhood. Or that it did take place, but the unpleasure associated with the rise in tension caused the infantile or pre-Oedipal subject to transform it in some way. The weight of psychoanalytic theory would favour the latter outcome as being more probable – that is, that excitation of erogenous zones took place in infantile sexuality (ibid., p. 184). Once again, however, Freudian theory reaches a limit in this regard. It does not offer any developed concepts to explain how the theorized and ubiquitous infantile experience of sexuality could undergo a transformation of sexual excitations in infancy into its opposite in adulthood – that is, a distress-free absence of sexual desire.

Asexuality Considered as Narcissism

As mentioned earlier, Freud (1914, p. 69) says narcissism is a necessary inter-mediate stage between the auto-eroticism of infancy and the object-love of early childhood. It is here that he draws a distinction for the first time between ego-libido and object-libido, and states that the more one form of libido is employed, the more the other is depleted. An example of this is when a person is in love and object-love is at its height while ego-libido or narcissism is at its lowest (ibid., p. 76). Attending to what is written and said in asexual discourse, the desire to be in a loving relationship is very much in evidence. An asexual woman respondent in one study says, "I want to have a deep, monogamous relationship with a man, but don't wish to engage in sexual activities with him or anyone else" (Scherrer, 2008).[13]

This suggests that object-libido is functioning and is being directed outwardly at another person. It would equally suggest, if we follow Freud's line of argument, that ego-libido is lowered; that is, narcissism is less in evidence. So in all but the most trenchantly a-romantic and anti-sex asexuals (Carrigan, 2011, p. 468) there should, therefore, be a concomitant decrease in ego-libido or narcissism. If it is the case that a-romantic or anti-sex asexuals are predominantly inclined to nar-cissistic behaviour or traits, then it is not something which current research has found. Using this criterion, it seems reasonable to argue that narcissism might not offer a complete understanding of asexuality.

Looked at another way, if narcissism is the attitude of a person who treats their own body in the same way in which the body of a sexual object is ordinarily treated (Freud, 1914, p. 73), then it also proves inadequate. Asexual testimony suggests that masturbation is commonplace, but it is more often than not carried out without the subject's body being treated as a sexual object. In this light, asexu-ality does not exhibit the primary narcissistic characteristic of having substan-tially greater quantities of ego-libido compared to object-libido. Freud's thinking supports this inference when applied to the question of why some asexuals who do *not* want sexual relationships nevertheless want non-sexual relationships. In his view, if the narcissistic trend – that is, the investment of libido in the ego – exceeds a certain amount, then it must be directed outwardly towards an object. The reason for this is that while a strong ego (i.e., one invested with ego-libido) protects the individual from falling ill, he also believes that "in the last resort", people will fall ill if they are *not* able to love (i.e., direct libido outwardly) (ibid., p. 85). This, for Freud, answers the question of why it is necessary to pass beyond narcissism and attach the libido to objects as other people. It potentially, and indeed speculatively, answers the question as to why asexuals who, like the gen-eral population, may well experience troubling repetitions in their lives, do not appear to fall ill from the direct experience of having no sexual attraction to other people – that is, ego-libido is still, in most cases, being directed outwardly. It also allows for an understanding of the unconscious motive force behind many asexuals' choice to direct their libido outwards to other people but without a sexual aim.

It might also be worth mentioning that the experience for sexually desiring subjects of their libido being directed externally to other people can include the element of sexual overvaluation. This means that the object of desire, as either sexually attractive or as the love-object or both, is free from criticism to a large extent; it is idealized. While the term suggests that the overvaluation is "sexual", Freud says that if sensual impulses are repressed or "set aside", the object can, nevertheless, be "sensually loved" for its spiritual qualities (1921, p. 112). Yet any spiritual qualities the object may represent are only there by virtue of its sensual attraction (ibid.). This implies that, firstly, sexual overvaluation is possible even if sexual attraction is absent and so non-sexual qualities can become the focus of object-love. Secondly, it implies that spiritual love is still based on the sensual qualities of the object – that is, eroticized libido is operating in the background and influencing object-choice. Freud's theory would, therefore, appear to support the possibility that in asexuality, the object can be idealized as a desexualized object due to its sensually imbued qualities. A question which then arises is, to what extent does repression, as it is classically understood, play a role in this desexualization?

Asexuality and Repression

Repression is one of the classical Freudian concepts that produces a form of desexualization whereby an instinctual (drive) impulse meets resistances that can make it inoperative (1915a, p. 146). When this occurs, the instinct (drive) is then said to pass into a state of repression. Freud is aware that repression has a negative tone since it is a preliminary stage of condemnation; in other words, something the ego does not like or want is being kept at bay (ibid.). If, therefore, the sexual drive is subject to repression, this can only suggest that it is experienced negatively or that, as Freud would have it, somehow the drive's aim of seeking satisfaction paradoxically produces unpleasure instead of pleasure. Yet while at this point in his writing he is adamant that there are no such drives because satisfaction of a drive "is always pleasurable" (ibid.), he comes to see this quite differently five years later in "Beyond the Pleasure Principle". If satisfaction of a drive is *not* always pleasurable, then there must be "peculiar circumstances" which lead to the pleasure of satisfaction being changed into unpleasure (ibid.). He now theorizes that not only does the drive *never* achieve satisfaction and instead remains as a persisting tension (1920, p. 42), but also there is a satisfaction which can result not in more pleasure but in its opposite, unpleasure (ibid., pp. 9–10). As this is the foundation of Lacan's concept of *jouissance*, I will be building on this point in further chapters. For the moment, the logic of Freud's theory is that the opposite experience of *no* increase in sexual desire would be more pleasurable. If this is applicable to an understanding of asexuality, then it raises the question as to what process or processes might give rise to this and how they might contribute to the experience of no sexual attraction. I will also be taking up this question in more detail in later chapters, but for now, the question is whether repression as Freud outlined it might be a mechanism capable of bringing this about.

In his understanding, the ego as the reality-facing agency is the most powerful factor in repression. This brings us back to a consideration of a point raised earlier as to whether asexuality represents a repression which the ego ideal requires. Freud believes that the process which detaches the libido from objects and cuts off its return to them is "closely related to the process of repression" (1916–1917, SE XVI, p. 421). However, repression, as it is classically understood, assumes that in the first instance, a sexual drive is being directed towards a sexualized object with the aim of achieving a libidinal satisfaction. Repression, in this scenario, acting on behalf of the ego, can withdraw libido from unsuitable or inappropriate sexualized objects. But this understanding of repression does not take into account the possibility also mentioned earlier, and one that will require more consideration, that there is no sexual drive being directed towards a libidinal object. Also, if the sexual drive and its libidinal excitations are potentially experienced as unpleasurable at the infantile stage, then not only will the ego seek to repress it but, as stated, an ego ideal might potentially be formed which represents a qualitatively different relation to the sexual drive – that is, one for which desexualization becomes the ideal.

If, however, repression is assumed to be the mechanism responsible for making the sexual drive inoperative in asexuality, then Freud's view is that the ideas associated with it should return to the subject in the form of "substitute formations and symptoms" (1915a, p. 154).[14] Since asexuals do not exhibit a symptomatic phenomenology as a result of being asexual, nor indeed does current asexual research contradict this, then asexuality might not necessarily entail repression in its fullest sense. This is not to suggest that asexuality is a particular category which can avoid encountering repression as an ever-present human defence mechanism. Rather, repression might not fully account for the absolute nature of the absence of sexual attraction which asexuals speak about. One survey respondent says this:

> Now I can see that I experienced sexual things, but that doesn't make me sexual. I have no interest in it. So I think to me having an interest in sex is what makes you sexual, and you can be doing sexual things and not really be sexual, I think.
>
> (Prause and Graham, 2007, p. 345)

Another says this:

> I define as asexual because it explains how I can find males attractive without wanting to have sex with them, as well as how that lack of sexual desire for males does not translate to wanting to have sex with females.
>
> (Carrigan, 2011, p. 467)

As it is classically understood, repression is a turning away of something unpleasant and keeping it at a distance from the conscious mind (1915a, p. 147). There are two stages to it, and the first of these is a primal repression in earliest infancy whereby the initial idea that represents the drive is kept from the conscious mind, and so a fixation point is established (1937, p. 227). The second stage involves the repression of all subsequent associative ideas connected with the initial idea that is repressed, which is called "repression proper" (1915a, p. 148). Of particular note here is Freud's elaboration of repression's distinguishing features. While repression obviously triggers a psychical action from the conscious mind to keep an idea repressed, he says there is at the same time a less easily observable *attraction* emanating from the idea onto "everything with which it can establish a connection" (ibid.). In other words, not only does the repressed idea continue to make its presence felt, but it can also build a "power of strength" that it gets from both being dammed up and being influenced by phantasy (ibid., p. 149). This suggests that the repressed idea represents a potentially unpleasurable rising tension in itself. In other words, repression does not merely happen once and bring about a permanent result (ibid., p. 151); it demands a persistent expenditure of energy.

Repression partly explains something of asexuality to the extent that the former's motive force is the avoidance of unpleasure. If the subject experiences infantile sexuality or post-pubertal sexual relations as unpleasurable, then repression would ensure that any idea associated with it remains away from the conscious mind, and asexuals do speak about having an absence of sexual ideation. They also appear to benefit from a split-off quota of affect, what Freud calls the emotional aspect which is split off from the idea. This is the energy of the drives (1915a, p. 152) which becomes the driving force in pursuing non-sexual aims. However, asexual subjects do not describe the persistent experience of keeping sexual impulses at bay or of having to keep sexual ideation out of consciousness. Nor do they describe the presence of sexual fantasies or, indeed, of any internal rising tension from a sexual drive being dammed up. An asexual survey respondent says, "I'm 25 years old and I've never had a crush on or any sexual attraction to anybody and I honestly get confused when people say they're 'horny' because I have no idea how that feels" (Carrigan, 2011, p. 467). Another says this:

> Even though it (sex) is very pleasurable and exciting while I am doing it, I have absolutely no anticipation for it at all. I have no interest or desire that would lead me towards that in the way that I do towards other activities that I enjoy.
>
> (Brotto et al., 2010, p. 610)

Similar to Soler's (2003, p. 86) suggestion that normative heterosexuality may be a symptom, albeit one without clinical or pathological implications, perhaps asexuality may be considered similarly.

Asexuality and Hysteria

The idea of asexuality as a symptom without clinical or pathological symptoms prompts the further question as to whether it has something in common with conversion hysteria, in particular the indifference of the hysteric to their symptom or, as Freud puts it, "the *belle indifférence* of a hysteric" (1895, p. 135 and fn. 1). Both the asexual and the hysteric share a disinterest, in the former, and an aversion, in the latter, to sexual engagement with another person. It is also important to bear in mind that hysteria is a foundational, structural position affecting both men and women, and that it is the sine qua non of obsessional neurosis (1926, p. 113). Of relevance to asexuality, Freud says that hysterics show a number of sex-averse characteristics. These include a degree of sexual repression in excess of what he calls the "normal quantity", an intensification of the resistance against the sexual instinct (drive) and "an instinctive aversion on their part to any intellectual consideration of sexual problems" (1905, p. 164). This is an obvious set of characteristics that asexuality shares with hysteria, including its aversion to having the nature of the asexual orientation explored or examined psychoanalytically because the latter is perceived to be part of heteronormative discourse.[15] The point at which asexuality differs is that classical hysteria includes a further characteristic, and a paradoxical one at that, of the *predominance* of the sexual instinct (drive). In other words, hysteria is indicated by, at one and the same time, an aversion to sexuality and, in equal measure, a strong expression of it. To use Freud's words, it includes the simultaneous existence of an "exaggerated sexual craving and excessive aversion to sexuality" (ibid., p. 165).

While asexuality might fit one of these criteria, it quite obviously does not fit the other and so does not, by this definition, appear to represent a hysterical neurosis. It is, instead, consistently defined as a lifelong absence of sexual attraction for another person which has no subjective distress attaching to it (Brotto et al., 2010, p. 607; Prause and Graham, 2007, p. 350). In conversion hysteria, the process of repression is understood to be completed when the repressed returns with the formation of the hysterical symptom (1915a, p. 154). But there does not appear to be a conversion of repressed libido into symptomatic form in asexuality or at least none that is manifest. As a result, there would seem to be no conversion symptom to be indifferent to, unless it is considered in terms of male sexual impotence or female frigidity which I will consider shortly.[16] Psychoanalytic theory posits that the conditions exist in every subject to be neurotic (i.e., have a symptom) (1916–1917, SE XVI, p. 358), and therefore, a symptom is part of every subject's experience. In this context, it seems reasonable to propose that while the asexual subject, similar to the sexual subject, is not without a symptom, asexuality in itself is not a pathological symptom and does not represent a form of hysteria. In order to further consider asexuality in terms of hysteria, I will revisit this question from the perspective of Lacanian theory in Chapter 5.

Asexuality and Obsessional Neurosis

It also needs to be asked if self-defined asexuality is a form of obsessional neurosis, in which repression brings about a withdrawal of the libido but in a way that makes use not of the symptom but of a reaction formation. This latter is a mechanism of repression which intensifies its opposite whereby the obsessional subject takes a contrary position with regard to the sexual instinct (drive). In other words, an aggressive trend is substituted for an affectionate one, and it is the aggressive trend that is repressed. In the process, the forbidden sexual idea is repressed, but the repression takes place through this uniquely different mechanism (1915a, p. 156).

The presence of affection or positive libido as a first experience, and the substitution of aggression or hostility as a second or follow-on experience, gives obsessional neurosis its ambivalent character. For Freud, this ambivalence not only underpins reaction-formation but is also the point at which the repressed succeeds in returning. He says the "vanished affect" returns in a transformed way, such as anxiety or self-reproaches. The rejected idea is replaced by a substitute idea through the process called "displacement" (ibid.). But once again, a differentiating point emerges between these criteria and asexuality. It could be argued that, like obsessional neurosis, self-defined asexuality includes elements of reaction-formation, where the asexual subject takes a contrary position with regard to the sexual instinct (drive). Asexuality differs from obsessional neurosis, however, in that there do not appear to be the clinical symptoms associated with obsessional neurosis, such as neurotic anxiety, excessive conscientiousness or unlimited self-reproaches.

If, as Freud says, there is no sharply defined normal sexuality (1905, p. 160, 165), then the same conceptualization can be used to include asexuality as a valid sexual orientation. As evidenced with the latency period, an asexual experience is an intrinsic part of human sexuality (1916–1917, SE XVI, p. 326).[17] This opens the possibility for considering asexuality as a unique example of a broken-out, albeit "damped-down" (1905, p. 225), component of the sex drive. As such, there may be no sharp divisions between desiring and non-desiring forms of sexuality since asexuality is quite clearly a stage in every individual's passage to adult sexuality. For this reason, Freud's comment on the facility with which the sexual instinct (drive) diverges from the so-called heterosexual norm is pertinent, and therefore, asexuality may also be "no great rarity", instead forming a previously unrecognized part of what passes for the "normal constitution" (ibid., p. 171).

Asexuality as Inhibition

Inhibition offers a closer explanation, from a Freudian perspective, as to what might be taking place in asexuality. This is because, as Freud puts it, inhibition does not necessarily have a pathological implication, and the inhibition of a function can easily be called a "normal restriction" (1926, p. 87). Here, he is distinguishing inhibition from a symptom which, by comparison, denotes the presence of some pathological process. Although an inhibition may be a symptom as well, his point is that an inhibition simply involves a *lowering* of function. The examples he gives are inhibitions of the sexual function, of eating, of movement (locomotion) and of carrying out of one's professional work (ibid.). Regarding the sexual function, he says that disturbances of it may appear at any point. Referring to men, he says that the chief stages are a turning away of the libido "at the very beginning of the process" of sexual engagement due to an experience of psychical unpleasure, including an absence of erection, a shortening of the experience through premature ejaculation (which could be called a symptom) and a halting of the experience due to the absence of ejaculation (ibid., p. 88). He believes that there is a link between inhibition and anxiety and that the sexual function is avoided because it gives rise to anxiety, which he classes, like the symptom of disgust, under hysteria (ibid.). As stated, Brotto et al. (2010, p. 607) found that rising sexual excitation in adult asexuals correlates positively with rising anxiety. There is a further factor which Freud includes in inhibition, and that is the precautionary measures inherent in obsessional acts, which are of a phobic quality. But, he admits, his enumerative approach to inhibition is not very illuminating, and it is easier to say that inhibitions of the sexual function can be brought about by a "great variety" of means (1926, p. 88). In general, he believes that an inhibition is the expression of an ego-function, which occurs when the physical organs associated with it have become "too strongly eroticized" (ibid., p. 89). This, he believes, is what happens in the case of an inhibition of writing (hands) or walking (legs). Because of this eroticization, the ego renounces these functions so as not to have to undertake fresh repressions, thus avoiding a conflict with the id. He concludes that inhibitions are the "restrictions of the functions of the ego" imposed either as a precaution (to avoid unpleasure) or to prevent an overuse of energy (such as dealing with a "continual flood" of sexual phantasies) (ibid., p. 90). In short, inhibition is a process that takes place within, or acts upon, the ego.

As I mentioned, the concept of inhibition has an obvious affinity with asexuality in its characteristic of not necessarily having a pathological implication. In this way, the sexual function can be inhibited without any symptomatic elements, and so asexuality, with its lack of subjective distress, could be explained in this way. It is also similar to the asexual experience in that, when looked at from a relatively narrow perspective, in some cases, there may be a turning away of the libido "at the very beginning of the process" of sexual engagement due to an experience of psychical unpleasure (ibid., p. 88). As stated, in Freud's understanding of it, these occurrences take place in the context of the ego in an attempt to avoid conflict with the id. In contrast, however, I will be proposing that the aetiology of asexuality is not an ego-driven process, even though it is obviously sustained by an ego position which consciously chooses non-sexual engagement with others. Instead, I will argue that asexuality, like sexuality, has its origins within the unconscious and that, as a result, it is not primarily an ego defence against conflict with the id. Freud's understanding of inhibition has two main characteristics: firstly, there are no pathological implications (except in the case of disgust at sexual activity), a factor which aligns it closely with an asexual position. Secondly, inhibitions are experienced by the subject as an *absence*. In short, the person who is unable to play the piano, walk, write or engage sexually is consciously aware of being unable to carry out these functions. In the case of asexuality, while there is an experience of not wanting to engage sexually with others, there is no experience of this as an absence. The absence of sexual desire is not experienced as such or as a conflict within the ego but as a "natural" or ego-syntonic occurrence. At the risk of generalizing, the asexual does not identify as a subject with a lack of sexual desire but as a subject for whom no desire for sexual activity is a so-called natural state of things. It also has to be borne in mind that the key criterion of an inhibition, for Freud, is that it represents a "restriction of a function" (ibid., p. 87). This implies that a sexual drive seeking satisfaction with an object exists in the first place which must then be restricted in order to qualify as an inhibition. In other words, a sexual function must pre-exist in order for it to become inhibited. In the case of asexuality, there is no pre-existing sexual function or sexual drive in the traditional sense, and so, therefore, there is nothing which is inhibited or on which inhibition can act. For these reasons, inhibition does not appear to fully explain the causation of asexuality. In order to consider this further, I will examine the category into which Freud says most inhibitions of the sexual function are classed together (i.e., psychical impotence) (ibid.).

Asexuality and Impotence/Frigidity

"The sexual function is liable to a great number of disturbances, most of which exhibit the characteristics of simple inhibitions. These are classed together as psychical impotence", according to Freud (ibid.). Therefore, if one chose to consider asexuality as a form of sexual impotence, it seems that inhibition would have an important place in its aetiology. In fact, the closest Freudian theory comes to offering a direct consideration of an asexual disposition is with the concepts of male psychical impotence and female frigidity. Taking male impotence first, Freud says it is a disturbance which affects men who, paradoxically, have "strongly libidinous natures" (1912, p. 179). This supports the suggestion that a manifest sexual drive is a precondition for inhibition to apply. In the case of male psychical impotence, its characteristics include a "refusal" of the genitals to carry out the sex act even though they are capable of doing so (ibid.). For Freud, the origin of this potentially obdurate impotence derives from an incestuous fixation on the male subject's mother or sister, along with any "accidental" or "distressing" experiences during infantile sexual activity. Implicit in this theory is the view that the conditions necessary for psychical impotence to occur are present during the Oedipus complex and that accidental and distressing experiences derive from external events which impinge on the child. Unlike the psychically impotent men in Freud's theory, however, asexuals do not describe having strongly libidinous natures but, rather, describe having no history of sexual attraction or sexual arousal for another person.

A further characteristic of Freud's psychical impotence is that a man can enjoy sex with a woman provided she is not in any way unconsciously associated with the mother or maternal figure. This means, however, that sexual activity can occur only if the woman can be "debased" (i.e., *not* to psychically represent the maternal) in order for the sensual current to find expression (ibid., p. 183).[18] Freud's thinking in this regard is that for men to engage sexually with women who unconsciously represent something of their mothers, both a sensual and affectionate current must combine to allow a "completely normal attitude in love" to take place (ibid., p. 180). As stated, the affectionate current is the older of the two and is present throughout childhood until, at puberty, it is joined by the more powerful "sensual" current. But the sensual current, Freud says, connects to objects (other people) which are chosen on the basis of primary infantile object-choices, only now with far stronger amounts of libido (ibid., p. 181). In essence, the libido of the sensual current is choosing its objects based on the pattern of its infantile experiences (i.e., usually a parent), and this is the unconscious underpinning of the inhibition. Therefore, psychical impotence occurs, in Freud's understanding of it, when affection and sensuality remain split. This split occurs as a result of the strong childhood fixations to the mother as well as the barrier against incest (ibid., p. 184). Sensuality becomes tied to incestuous objects in the unconscious, or fixates on unconscious incestuous phantasies, which prevents the man from performing sexually. As stated, the means by which this can be circumvented is through Freud's concept of the "psychical debasement" of the sexual object. This debasement protects against the overvaluation[19] which idealizes the sexual object in the same way as the incestuous object (ibid., pp. 181–182). In other words, idealization can mean the object-choice becomes unusable as a sexual object, and the only way of reversing this is to put the sexual object at a far remove from any affectionate or incestuous associations. Debasement is the condition which allows sensuality to be freely expressed and for sexual interaction and sexual pleasure to develop, but equally, it is not without the potential for complications in men's relations with women. Noting that the conditions for psychical impotence to occur are universal, he gives a clear indication that difficulty with sex is more common than it appears and that men who cannot redirect their libido towards an object they can debase will remain in this state (ibid., p. 187). However, when Freud refers to male impotence as a refusal, he is pointing to the existence of a primary sexual drive that is secondarily being refused. In other words, the concept of psychical impotence again assumes a sexual drive that is inhibited in its pursuit of satisfaction in the first instance, and this does not appear to be the case with asexuality.

Asexuality and Female Frigidity

Freud believed that the cultural requirement of his time (i.e., for greater abstinence in women rather than in men) was a factor in women becoming frigid

(1908, p. 197). This strict requirement was not, he believed, the best preparation for a full sexual life and was responsible for a suppression of sexuality that could, at its extreme, leave the woman frigid (ibid., p. 198). For Freud, "civilized education" and its antagonism with instinctual life was responsible for this.[20] However, he points out that, unlike men, women showed little sign of the need to debase their sexual object. Instead, he says, the long period of prohibition which they were subjected to, and its influence on their sensuality, had another important consequence for them. It meant they were subsequently often unable to undo the connection between sensual activity and the prohibition on it, and they proved to be frigid when such activity was at last allowed them (1912, p. 186).[21] In other words, the "forbiddenness" in the erotic life of women is what he believed was comparable to men's need to debase their sexual object. Both are the consequences of the long delay, in his era, between sexual maturity and sexual activity, and both resulted from the inability of affectionate and sensual impulses to unite (ibid., p. 187).

While Freud's theory in this area has some obviously dated aspects to it with regard to women, there are still today strong sex-negative messages aimed at women. An example would be the invocation from some sections of the feminist movement that equates women having sex with men as a form of violation.[22] Another example would be religiously motivated messages which depict women's sexuality as shameful or that encourage women to abstain from sexual activity. Abbott et al. (2016, p. 1077) found that as a result of religious influences, women experienced guilt related to their sexual behaviours and were less likely to perceive those behaviours as congruent with their moral standards. Most of their sample identified as Christian, and the authors say, the findings seem convincing given the sex-negative messages often communicated by Christian organizations and authorities. In terms of neurosis, these messages and others of its type within, say, conservative family contexts can provide a similar impetus for symptoms of female frigidity to develop. The point is that while Freud's historical explanations derive from a different time, the conditions for inhibitions in female sexuality are still discernible today albeit in different forms. As Freud moves through his exposition of female frigidity, though, he aligns its aetiology closer to the male experience of impotence by linking it to the Oedipus complex. He says that, because the earliest allocations of libido are both universal and powerful, the earliest infantile wishes in women usually comprise a fixation of the libido on the father or a brother. These wishes were often originally directed towards things other than intercourse or included it only "as a dimly perceived goal" (1918, p. 203). But something of this fixation remains when the woman chooses the man she loves. The husband, in his view, is almost always a substitute for the father (ibid.). The more powerfully the unconscious paternal figure is in a woman's sexual life, the greater the resistance to sexual activity. For Freud, frigidity may then become established as a neurotic inhibition or lead to other neuroses. Psychical impotence and female frigidity assume either a sexual drive that is being impeded or an aversion to satisfying that drive, while their aetiology is theorized to be the result of libidinal fixations during the Oedipus complex.[23] As has been mentioned, this is in contrast to the experience of asexuality where there is no consciously experienced sexual drive being impeded. Fixations of the Oedipus complex contrast with what I will be proposing for asexuality in the following chapters; that is, that pre-Oedipal factors must be taken into account which, in turn, shape the experience of the Oedipus complex. While the incest taboo has a universal application, and undoubtedly has some part to play in asexuality's foreclosure of sexual desire, just as it has for non-asexual subjects, neither impotence nor frigidity appear to provide a full understanding of why no sexual desire is evident in self-defined asexuality. One female asexual survey respondent says, "There's just no desire. I just really have no desire to go and have sex with someone. It's just the furthest thing from my mind. It seems to me to be boring" (Prause and Graham, 2007, p. 345). Even though repression is the main defence system available for dealing with the internal threat of the libido (1919, p. 210), Freud's theory does not extend to a consideration of its potentially formative role in producing a subject who is so successfully repressed that they experience no sexual desire. Of even greater theoretical relevance is the question of whether the dynamics of repression could be sufficient to explain the apparent lack of subjective distress in asexuality (1916–1917, p. 360 and p. 365), given that repression is generally associated with the return of the repressed in symptomatic form. The same can be said for Freud's theory of infantile sexuality which accounts very well for the sources and variations of adult sexuality and for adult psychosexual symptoms but, again, does not extend to a consideration of the almost complete absence of sexual desire for the Other in asexuality. Therefore, while building on Freud's theory of sexuality, it will be necessary to explore Lacanian theory in the chapters that follow in order to access a different range of conceptual psychoanalytic tools with which to approach asexuality's more challenging aspects.

Notes

1   This is particularly apposite when we consider his daughter Anna's concept of "altruistic surrender" mentioned in Chapter 1.
2   He gives two examples of groups which in his view have non-sexual aims, the Church and the Army.
3   Queer theorist Lee Edelman (2004, p. 17) says queerness can never be a seamless identity because identity itself is never complete, based as it is on the signifier as an "alienating and meaningless token of our Symbolic constitution as subjects" (ibid., 8). Also, Weeks (1991, p. 94) believes subjectivity is "always fractured, contradictory, ambiguous, and disrupted", while identity is "not inborn, pregiven or 'natural'".
4   Freud sees this process of introjection also occur in melancholia which involves the perceived loss of the primary loved object.
5   Freud (1915b, p. 195) says a hitherto repressed activity within the unconscious can co-operate with the activity intended by the ego, in this way the unconscious becomes ego-syntonic. See also 1916, p. 316.

6 In footnote 1, Freud (1923, p. 31) says that before a child has arrived at definite knowledge of the difference between the sexes, via the lack of a penis in women, it does not distinguish in value between its father and its mother.

7 Freud says here that the bisexuality he believes is originally present in all children means that the earliest object-choices and identifications are not clear-cut but are more likely ambivalent.

8 One piece of research shows that asexuals have a reduced likelihood of being parents (Greaves et al., 2017, online pagination, p. 5).

9 Here, Freud uses the metaphor of the amoeba to explain the extension of libido on to external objects while a mass of libido remains in the ego. The first article online about asexuality, as stated in the Introduction, was called *My Life as an Amoeba*. Also, the first online asexual community was called Haven for the Human Amoeba (HHA).

10 The term "choice" is used similarly to Dany Nobus's description of it as the "transformative ability of the unconscious to steer a given potential through a multitude of different options" (2017, pp. 349–350). And to what Geneviève Morel describes as "a choice from among the array of figures proposed by the unconscious in response to whatever was imposed on the subject at the beginning (the maternal 'imposed equivocations')" (2019, p. 310). In his later work, Lacan extends the concept of choice to refer to gender. He says, "the sexed being only authorizes himself/herself. It is in this sense . . . that [s]he has the 'choice'". In the margin beside this, his translator has handwritten what appears to be the word "Extraordinary". See Lacan, *Seminar XXI*, 1973–1974, session of 9 April 1974, p. 3.

11 Freud takes up this subject at greater length in *The Economic Problem of Masochism* (1924, pp. 159–161).

12 Here, Freud describes amounts of stimulus that can cause the infant anxiety as "inflowing masses of excitation".

13 See also Brotto et al., 2010, p. 607; Carrigan, 2011, p. 464.

14 See, inter alia, Freud, 1900, pp. 605–606, 1901, p. 80.

15 An example can be found in *Asexuality & Demisexuality: Queer or Anti-Queer,* available at http://loneberry.tumblr.com/post/6413675137/asexuality-demisexuality-queer-or-anti-queer [Accessed 15 November 2021]

16 In the 17th century, frigidity was considered an exclusively male issue, particularly as far as canon law was concerned. See Cryle and Moore, 2011, p. 26.

17 Here, Freud says, "From about the sixth to the eighth year of life onwards, we can observe a halt and retrogression in sexual development, which, in cases where it is most propitious culturally, deserves to be called a period of latency".

18 Heterosexual men can achieve this through sexually engaging with non-maternal figures, such as sex workers, or through extra-marital or extra-relational affairs.

19 Here, Freud writes this: "The greatest intensity of sensual passion will bring with it the highest psychical valuation of the object – this being the normal overvaluation of the sexual object on the part of a man".

20 This is a theme he advocated from the start of his theorizing; see a memorandum to Fliess dated 31 May 1897, *Draft N*, SE I, p. 257, and, inter alia, at the end of *Three Essays on Sexuality* (1905), which appeared three years before the paper, *Civilized Sexual Morality* (1908), cited here.

21 Also, in *Dreams and Telepathy* (1922, p. 214), he cites the case of a woman patient who is manifesting sexual frigidity, and he attributes it to her sexual desires towards her father and death wishes against her mother as factors alongside those just mentioned.

22 "*Violation* is a synonym for intercourse. At the same time, the penetration [*sic*] is taken to be a use, not an abuse; a normal use; it is appropriate to enter her, to push into ('violate') the boundaries of her body" (Dworkin, 1987, p. 154).

23 For some of Freud's views on how sexual inhibitions can arise, see 1912, pp. 184–186, 1918, pp. 201–203, 1905, p. 227, 231.

References

Abbott, D. M., Harris, J. E. and Mollen, D. (2016) 'The impact of religious commitment on women's sexual self-esteem', *Sexuality & Culture*, 20, pp. 1063–1082. Available at: https://link.springer.com/content/pdf/10.1007%2Fs12119-016-9374-x.pdf [Accessed 15 November 2021].

Brotto, L. A., Knudson, G., Inskip, J., Rhodes, K. and Erskine, Y. (2010) 'Asexuality: A mixed-methods approach', *Archives of Sexual Behavior*, 39(3), pp. 599–618.

Carrigan, M. (2011) 'There's more to life than sex? Difference and commonality within the asexual community', *Sexualities*, 14(4), pp. 462–478.

Cryle, P. and Moore, A. (2011) *Frigidity – An intellectual history*. Hampshire: Palgrave Macmillan.

Dworkin, A. (1987) *Intercourse*. New York: Basic Books.

Edelman, L. (2004) *No future – Queer theory and the death drive*. London: Duke University Press.

Freud, S. (1895) With Breuer, J., *Studies on hysteria*, Standard Edition II. London: Vintage/Hogarth.

Freud, S. (1897) 'Extracts from the Fliess papers, draft n', in *Pre-psycho-analytic publications and unpublished drafts (1886–1899)*, Standard Edition I. London: Vintage/Hogarth.

Freud, S. (1900) *The interpretation of dreams*, Standard Editions IV and V. London: Vintage/Hogarth.

Freud, S. (1901) 'Slips of the tongue', in *The psychopathology of everyday life*, Standard Edition VI. London: Vintage/Hogarth.

Freud, S. (1905) 'Three essays on sexuality', in *A case of hysteria, three essays on sexuality and other works*, Standard Edition VII. London: Vintage/Hogarth.

Freud, S. (1908) 'Civilized sexual morality and modern nervous illness', in *Jensen's 'Gradiva' and other works*, Standard Edition IX. London: Vintage/Hogarth.

Freud, S. (1912) 'On the universal tendency to debasement in the sphere of love', in *Five lectures on psycho-analysis, Leonardo da Vinci and other works*, Standard Edition XI. London: Vintage/Hogarth.

Freud, S. (1914) 'On narcissism: An introduction', in *On the history of the psycho-analytic movement, papers on metapsychology and other works*, Standard Edition XIV. London: Vintage/Hogarth.

Freud, S. (1915a) 'Repression', in *On the history of the psycho-analytic movement, papers on metapsychology and other works*, Standard Edition XIV. London: Vintage/Hogarth.

Freud, S. (1915b) 'The unconscious', in *On the history of the psycho-analytic movement, papers on metapsychology and other works*, Standard Edition XIV. London: Vintage/Hogarth.

Freud, S. (1916) 'Some character-types met with in psycho-analytic work', in *On the history of the psycho-analytic movement, papers on metapsychology and other works*, Standard Edition XIV. London: Vintage/Hogarth.

Freud, S. (1916–1917) *Introductory lectures on psycho-analyses*, Standard Editions XV–XVI. London: Vintage/Hogarth.

Freud, S. (1918) 'The taboo of virginity', in *Five lectures on psycho-analysis, Leonardo da Vinci and other works*, Standard Edition XI. London: Vintage/Hogarth.

Freud, S. (1919) 'Psycho-analysis and the war neuroses', in *An infantile neurosis and other works*, Standard Edition XVII. London: Vintage/Hogarth.

Freud, S. (1920) 'Beyond the pleasure principle', in *Beyond the pleasure principle, group psychology and other works*, Standard Edition XVIII. London: Vintage/Hogarth.

Freud, S. (1921) 'Group psychology and the analysis of the ego', in *Beyond the pleasure principle, group psychology and other works*, Standard Edition XVIII. London: Vintage/Hogarth.

Freud, S. (1922) 'Dreams and telepathy', in *Beyond the pleasure principle, group psychology and other works*, Standard Edition XVIII. London: Vintage/Hogarth.

Freud, S. (1923) 'The ego and the id', in *The ego and the id and other works*, Standard Edition XIX. London: Vintage/Hogarth.

Freud, S. (1924) 'The economic problem of masochism', in *The ego and the id and other works*, Standard Edition XIX. London: Vintage/Hogarth.

Freud, S. (1926) 'Inhibitions, symptoms and anxiety', in *An autobiographical study, inhibitions, symptoms and anxiety, lay analysis and other works*. Standard Edition XX. London: Vintage/Hogarth.

Freud, S. (1937) 'Analysis terminable and interminable', in *Moses and monotheism, an outline of psychoanalysis and other works*, Standard Edition XXIII. London: Vintage/Hogarth.

Greaves, L. M., Barlow, F. K., Huang, Y., Stronge, S., Fraser, G. and Sibley, C. G. (2017) 'Asexual identity in a New Zealand national sample: Demographics, well-being, and health', *Archives of Sexual Behavior*, 6, March, pp. 2417–2427. Available at: www.researchgate.net/publication/315733047_Asexual_Identity_in_a_New_Zealand_National_Sample_Demographics_Well-Being_and_Health [Accessed 8 November 2021].

Morel, G. (2019) *The law of the mother: An essay on the sexual sinthome*. New York: Routledge.

Nobus, D. (2017) 'Undoing psychoanalysis: Towards a clinical and conceptual metistopia', in Giffney, N. and Watson, E. (eds.), *Clinical encounters in sexuality – Psychoanalytic practice and queer theory*. New York: Punctum Books, pp. 343–356.

Prause, N. and Graham, C. A. (2007) 'Asexuality: Classification and characterization', *Archives of Sexual Behaviour*, 36(3), pp. 341–355.

Scherrer, K. S. (2008) 'Coming to an asexual identity: Negotiating identity, negotiating desire', *Sexualities,* 11(5, October 1), pp. 621–641.

Soler, C. (2003) 'The paradoxes of the symptom in psychoanalysis', in Rabaté, J.-M. (ed.), *The Cambridge Companion to Lacan*. Cambridge: Cambridge University Press, pp. 86–101.

Weeks, J. (1991) *Against nature – Essays on history, sexuality and identity*. London: Rivers Oram Press.

Chapter 4

Towards a Lacanian Understanding of Asexuality

If the asexual experience consistently records no Other-directed sexual attraction or desire, then any proposed psychoanalytic theory will have to give due respect, and indeed weight, to the absence or nothing which is implicit in this. For this reason, and since it is not included in Freudian theory, it is necessary to turn to Jacques Lacan's formulation of the fundamental phantasy, highlighted in the Introduction, as a way of approaching the concept of the nothing. For Lacan, the fundamental phantasy is the support of desire (2014, p. 100), by which he means it causes the subject to be a desiring subject, and this, as I will contend, is an important consideration for an understanding of asexuality. The fundamental phantasy is written as $ \lozenge a$, which is read as the barred Subject in relation (lozenge) to the *objet petit a*, cause of desire. As cause of desire, then, the *objet petit a* is a central element and this is the "object" which Lacan designates as that which not only causes human desire but also keeps us desiring. It is theorized as the structural support inherent in all human desire and, as such, can take a number of specific but invisible, intangible forms. According to Gallagher (2005, p. 11), these *objets petit a* cause desire by acting directly on the subject without the mediation of language or image. They are, he says, characterized by their relationship to orifices, "or better holes, that enclose nothings in the body" (ibid., p. 11). On this note, and of particular interest to asexuality, is Lacan's inclusion in his list of *objets petit a* one which he terms precisely the "nothing" (2006, p. 693). Just like Lacan's other *objets petit a*, therefore, the nothing in the fundamental phantasy can cause desire even though, in keeping with Freud, human desire is never fulfilled.[1] Lacan works for a long time on various iterations of what would finally become his concept of the *objet petit a*. I will not be going through the many paths he takes, but in *Seminar VII, The Ethics of Psychoanalysis*, he focusses on Freud's concept of *das Ding*. Translated in English as "the Thing", this is conceptually the antecedent of his invention of the *objet petit a*.[2] In his discussion of the transformational effects of *das Ding*, he refers to it as an ineffable and intangible object which mobilizes the subject's desire in an unending but ultimately doomed attempt to refind the lost maternal object. "It is the lost object which must be continually re-found, it is the prehistoric, unforgettable Other" (1992, p. 53). He elaborates on this by saying the Thing is impossible for us to imagine (ibid., p. 125), making of it an

DOI: 10.4324/9781003214946-5

"unknowable x, beyond symbolisation", thus, situating it in the Real. With all the weight of these resonances, the *objet petit a* emerges from 1963, in his *Seminar* on *Anxiety*, where he ties together the *objet petit a* and *das Ding* and describes anxiety as that which may have no cause but is *not* without an object (2014, p. 311).[3] In fact, for him, anxiety's being *not* without an object "very likely designates" the most profound and ultimate object which is the Thing (ibid.).

Viewed in this light, the concept of nothing, as we are going to explore it in asexuality, can now move beyond being a straightforward referent for an absence of sexual attraction as is found in non-psychoanalytic discourses. Nor, indeed, does it have to remain as merely another item on Lacan's list of *objets petit a* (2006, p. 693).[4] Boucher (2005, p. 85) points out that the way Lacan includes it in that "unthinkable" list, which reads "the phoneme, the gaze, the voice . . . the nothing", suggests that the nothing could somehow fundamentally underpin all the other *objets petit a*. In common with these other *objets petit a*, therefore, the nothing can have a pivotal place as cause of desire for the subject operating as it does from its position within the fundamental phantasy.[5] When Lacan introduces his ideas on the mathematical version of the nothing (i.e., zero) in *Seminar XII*, he makes the point that for the emerging human subject during infancy, since there is "an initial zero of the reality of the subject being incarnated in pure lack", there is always something frustrating which escapes language. He says that this something which escapes the nets of language is the residue which manifests where the zero appears. Here, Lacan is describing the very relation of zero to that which subjective experience makes appear in the place of the zero and which he calls the *objet petit a*. In other words, some "thing" is brought in by the subject to cover the fundamental lack within the subject, and this something is the *objet petit a*. As such, it is this intangible "object" which, he says, "inflects the whole possible economy of a libidinal relationship to the object" (*Seminar XII*, session of 3 March 1965, p. 138). In terms of asexuality, this opens up the possibility of a libidinal relationship to the object as the nothing.

I will be considering in more detail later Lacan's mathematically informed theorizing with regard to the concept of zero as representative of the nothing. For now, in his fourth *Seminar*, *The Object Relation*, he is including the nothing when he speaks about the anorectic infant who is not "not eating" but is instead "eating nothing" at the breast. It is worth point out that, for Lacan, nothing is not nothing but "is precisely something that exists on the symbolic plane" (2020, p. 177). He says the child eats *nothing*, which is something other than a negation of activity. In keeping with Lacan's focus, Gherovici (2014, p. 49) says the infant refuses to eat food from the Other to preserve his "appetite for nothing and desire nothing". In this instance, it is a refusal of the oral object as a defence against desire as the desire of the Other. Also on this topic, Fink (2004, p. 60) says, "rather than have us say *that she* [*sic*] *does not eat anything* [emphasis in original], Lacan would have us say that she eats nothing, the nothing as object that causes her desire, keeping her desire alive". Because food reduces desire to pure and simple needs, he says the infant refuses food precisely in order to maintain some space for desire, "some room for desire to subsist in" (ibid.). As we can see, these theorists are positing the nothing in the context of the oral drive as a viable focus and object of human desire. In an obvious contrast to Freudian theory, there are potential resonances here in terms of *not* sexually desiring which offer the possibility that *not* sexually desiring can open onto a hitherto unconsidered form of sexual desire.

It is also interesting from the perspective of asexuality to consider how Lacan is describing the child's response to the earliest experience of the mother as first Other and "primordially all powerful", thus experiencing her presence as an "almightiness" in the context of feeding (2020, pp. 176–177). The same feeding activity takes on an eroticized function in the realm of desire, as Lacan puts it, which is in keeping with Freud's conception of the infantile sexual experience. Furthermore, the mother's omnipotence or "almightiness", not just as the giver or non-giver of the "gift" of sustenance and satisfaction (i.e., the breast) but also as the immense container of "all the primitive phantasmatic objects" (ibid., pp. 177–178), leaves the infant, in this context at least, with only one power against this helplessness: the power to say *no* (ibid., p. 179). So we can read this not literally as a refusal of the breast but as a psychical refusal of dependence on the Other in the face of an overwhelming experience of that Other. The point Lacan is accentuating here, and it can be found with great emphasis in Melanie Klein's theory, which he acknowledges, is that once the breast is understood by the child as belonging to the mother – that is, when the mother becomes a "real being" (ibid., p. 177) – then the almightiness of the maternal object can be experienced as something which "constitutes a virtual field of symbolic annihilation" (ibid., p. 178). In other words, the infant can experience its dependency on the mother as something so powerful that it can threaten to obliterate its very existence. Not only that, for Lacan, this experience of dependency on an "almightiness" is one from which each object to come in the future, understood as others in his or her life, "will in turn drawn their symbolic value" (ibid.). Even though Lacan is highlighting an event that occurs at the oral stage, when we consider its possible relevance in constructing an aetiology of asexuality, it offers some interesting ideas. With this focus, he is giving an example of what is possibly the earliest sexualized experience of dependence for the satisfaction of need, in this case on the mother for food and indeed survival. Also, the dependence for this satisfaction can be potentially overwhelming and, ostensibly, experienced as libidinally infused unpleasure. If so, it allows for the conditions under which a choice to say no can be made and which could, in turn, inform the subject's relations to future objects in their life. In choosing to say no, Lacan theorizes that it is intended to free the child from its "relationship of dependence" on the perceived almightiness of the maternal object (ibid., p. 179). However, he adds some important caveats which are of interest in terms of applying these concepts to asexuality. This freeing itself from a relation of dependence is, in his view, not necessarily going to manifest in a refusal to feed. Nor is it necessarily going to manifest in a direct "negativism" towards the mother. What Lacan is describing is a psychical, unconscious template being laid down for the child at this early stage in which the breast becomes a symbolic object of the subject-Other dialectic – that is, symbolic of the relation of dependence of the child – and which appears under the sign of the nothing (ibid.). By this, we can understand Lacan to mean that in order to deal with the threatening "almightiness" that the mother can represent, the infant must at some level "say no" to the breast's symbolic position in this regard. He says the child puts his dependency on the mother in check by nourishing itself on this nothing, this object with its symbolic contents removed or this object annulled as symbolic (ibid.).[6] Not only that, but he says the child feeding on *nothing* [emphasis in original] is in a position of deriving pleasure from it, underlined by Lacan's description of this feeding on nothing as a "savoured absence" (ibid., p. 177).

From this, he goes on to say that through this operation, the child can bring about a significant reversal in its relation to the demand of, and its own dependence on, the maternal object. He says this:

> It is here that he turns his relation of dependence around, making himself by this means the master of the almightiness that is so eager to keep him alive, he who is initially the dependent one. From this point forward, the almightiness becomes answerable to his desire.
>
> (ibid., p. 179)

The potential for this theorizing to offer some understanding of asexuality now becomes a little clearer. But if it is to be harnessed effectively, and in a way that does not involve pathological associations, then two questions have to be posed. Can such a mechanism have a place in the aetiology of asexuality? If so, and Lacan's theory says that the fundamental phantasy acts as a support for *all* human desire, then what phantasy would support a desire directed at the nothing?

The Emergence of Phantasy

The deployment of conscious fantasy to incite sexual desire for and direct sexual desire towards the Other is absent in asexuality. Nevertheless, the presence of masturbation indicates that an active libido is present even though, again, the Other is not its object. Instead, the repeated experience cited by asexuals is that they do not "feel" sexual desire for the Other and do not imagine the Other as a sexual object (Yule et al., 2014, pp. 92–93). A respondent from one study says this of masturbation: "I can't attach pleasure together with it somehow. Was it physically pleasurable? I don't know. I just can't find the words" (Prause and Graham, 2007, p. 344). A question, therefore, is what does the *unconscious* fundamental phantasy represent for the asexual in the Lacanian sense? In Lacan's writing of the fundamental phantasy as $ \lozenge\ a$, it is the *objet petit a* which is of interest for our purposes. As stated, this is the unattainable lost object that causes desire and drives the subject with the hope of refinding it. Not only is the object perceived as lost, but it was also the object which connected us to the first Other and to their desire and, therefore, remains the object through which we can gain access to the Other's desire (Lacan, 2017, p. 387). The significance of this, as stated in the Introduction, is that for Lacan, man's desire is, therefore, the desire of the Other. For these reasons, the *objet petit a* not only holds out the promise of a complete but unattainable satisfaction of desire but also of total wholeness and, indeed, happiness.

It is important to underline just what the *objet petit a* represents in Lacan's theory, in particular its materially insubstantial nature, something which he went to great lengths to emphasize. It derives from the physical objects which symbolize loss – the breast, the excrement, the phallus and so on – and can associate itself with real objects, but in and of itself, it takes no specular form (1961–1962, session of 27 June 1962, p. 308).[7] In his journey towards the invention of this concept (ibid., session of 28 March 1962, pp. 153–154), Lacan looked to philosopher Immanuel Kant's four nothings and settled on the latter's *nihil negativum* (Le Gaufey, 2020, pp. 29–31, 85) as the object that could represent nothing as an "empty object without a concept".[8] This is the kind of object which he describes as "the very example of the inexistent object and what is more the unthinkable one" (1961–1962, session of 28 February 1962, p. 105), meaning we cannot see it and nor can we think of what it can look like. In the pursuit of such a concept, he had been seeking to situate a "partial" object that is free of a specular unity to any object, one that could become a space holder, empty of content and yet capable of fundamentally transformative effects, particularly in relation to an absence in the form of lack that is essential to mobilizing the desire of the subject. Put simply, if we are not lacking, we do not desire, and if we are without desire, we are, ironically, nothing.

From the point of view of asexuality, the concept of the fundamental phantasy can now include the idea of a desire that can be linked to nothing which, in this reading, is a desire aimed at the object emptied of its libidinous associations. I will be returning to this point later in order to examine further how nothing can become an object cause of desire. For the moment, Lacan's inclusion of the nothing as one of his *objets petit a* allows, on the one hand, a possible theoretical underpinning of asexual desire mobilized through having no sexual attraction for another person. On the other hand, this seemingly paradoxical linking of desire to nothing must be sustained by something capable of providing a consistency between these two apparently contradictory positions. For Lacan, it is the Imaginary register, hence, the importance of phantasy, which puts consistency and meaning on the holes or gaps in the Symbolic order, the latter being the register of culture, language, law and symbolic meaning.[9]

The Fundamental Phantasy and Desexualization

Without a fundamental phantasy which places the divided subject in relation to the *objet petit a* as cause of desire, there is nothing supporting, mobilizing or sustaining desire. This is because it is desire and its correlative lack, represented in the fundamental phantasy by the *objet petit a*, which drives the subject to seek metonymic objects of satisfaction. While the asexual subject appears to have effectively desexualized its relation to the Other, asexual subjects are nevertheless desiring subjects in the broadest sense. This suggests that there is an unconscious fundamental phantasy operating which sustains this position. In particular, it suggests that there must be a unique and possibly desexualized relation within the fundamental phantasy between the barred subject, as asexual, and the *objet petit a*. In current non-psychoanalytic academic research, the desexualized position of the asexual is, in keeping with more general social discourses, viewed as an exceptional position that gives asexuality its unique status in a predominantly sex-normative cultural setting (Chen, 2020, pp. 19–20). While this is undoubtedly the case, the concept of desexualization is one which Freudian-Lacanian theory is familiar with and which it has also traditionally included in its metapsychology of the sexually desiring subject's relation to the world of others.

In *Formulations on the Two Principles of Mental Functioning*, Freud (1911, p. 223) talks about a momentary pleasure deferred in order to gain an assured pleasure at a later time. This is where Freud considers the child at the moment it moves beyond the hallucinatory satisfaction of internal need, such as is found in dreams. When hallucinatory satisfaction does not occur or is not enough, Freud says, it becomes necessary for the "psychical apparatus", as he calls it, to form "a conception of the real circumstances in the external world and to endeavour to make a real alteration in them" (ibid., p. 219). In this way, the second of his two principles of mental functioning is set up: the reality principle. If motor discharge is employed in this "alteration of reality" by being converted into *action*, then it is the process of *thinking* that imposes constraints on carrying out an *action*. "Thinking was endowed with characteristics which made it possible for the mental apparatus to tolerate an increased tension of stimulus while the process of discharge was postponed", he says (ibid., p. 221). In other words, thinking can defer pleasure and, thus, bring about an alteration of reality (i.e., a desexualization).

For Lacan, if Freud contrasts the reality principle with the pleasure principle, it is because of this desexualization of reality (1977, p. 155). However, it is important to bear in mind that in Freud's description, the pleasure principle is in no way deposed but rather safeguarded. The drive towards pleasure and away from unpleasure is constant even if pleasure is deferred. Later on, I will be returning to this idea with an alternative view, but for the moment, the most obvious example within psychoanalytic theory where desexualization of reality can be found is in the Oedipus complex. The child from an early age loves his or her first sexual objects, the primary caregivers or parents, with what Freud describes in *Three Essays on Sexuality* as a "damped-down libido" (1905a, p. 225). In essence, he is describing the subject's earliest deferral of a desire for sexual satisfaction in answer to a cultural demand to render external reality desexualized in service of the incest taboo. He says this:

> Society must defend itself against the danger that the interests which it needs for the establishment of higher social units may be swallowed up by the family; and for this reason, in the case of every individual, but in particular

adolescent boys, it seeks by all means to loosen their connection with their family – a connection which, in their childhood, is the only important one.

(ibid.)

This, however, is a desexualization which is different to what I will be proposing takes place in asexuality. It is certainly theoretically noteworthy that all subjects are considered to have the capacity to desexualize their reality, but in this iteration, it is understood as a desire for sexual satisfaction which is deferred, thus, bringing about the desexualization in question. I will be proposing that in asexuality, by contrast, the desexualization which occurs is not in the order of a deferral but rather a desexualization at the level of the sexual drive itself. In other words, it is not a deferral of libidinal satisfaction until a later time when the conditions within reality are more conducive for achieving that satisfaction. Instead, asexuality from an early stage brings about an annulment of the desire for a sexual desire. I will be returning to elaborate on this point further, but for now, the point of interest is that reality is capable of being "altered" in this way. For sexually desiring subjects, there is the ubiquity of sexuality within the unconscious, and yet, there is the capacity to desexualize reality in order to manage drive tension and defer satisfaction. As Lacan puts it, "the notion that the approach of reality involves a desexualization lies at the very principle of Freud's definition of *Zwei Prinzipien des psychischen Geshehens*, of the two principles into which psychical 'eventiality' is divided" (ibid.). For the purposes of considering asexuality, therefore, psychoanalytic theory holds that even the sexually desiring subject has the capacity to desexualize, through deferral, his or her reality. In terms of the asexual subject and in the context of what Lacanian theory posits as the metonymically, ever-desiring subject, it will be necessary to begin a consideration of how a desire for no sexual desire can come about.

Asexual Phantasy and Desire

Desire, for Lacan, is a disruptive force which is caused by a structural lack that we perpetually seek to, but are ultimately unable to, satisfy or fill. Because no object can ever satisfy its incessant and unrestricted requirements, desire is characterized, therefore, as "paradoxical, deviant, erratic, eccentric, even scandalous" (2006, p. 579). This puts Lacan's desire in similar territory with Freud's concept of the id and, indeed, with philosopher Arthur Schopenhauer's concept of will.[10] For Lacan, desire is not to be satisfied because its purpose is to keep the subject desiring. This is desire's "eccentricity", as he says in *Seminar V*, and it is an eccentricity in relation to "all forms of satisfaction" (2017, p. 318). Not only does desire structure the drives (2006, p. 285), but it also "adjusts to fantasy" in the same way as "the ego adjusts to the body image" (ibid., p. 691). For Lacan, the subject is nothing but *objets petit a*, incorporated as real into the phantasy which supports desire and defends against it at the same time. "It is to this object that cannot be grasped in the mirror that the specular image lends its clothes", he says (ibid., p. 693). The lining of the subject, the "stuff" of the subject, is this object, this "substance caught in the net of shadow" which holds out the "tired lure of the shadow as if it were substance" (ibid.). Therefore, in attempting to answer the question posed earlier as to what kind of fundamental phantasy can support a desire for the nothing, I am proposing that the *objet petit a* which completes the asexual fundamental phantasy *is* the nothing. In this reading of Lacan's theory, the phantasy empties itself of that which makes the subject dependent through demand on the Other. This, paradoxical as it might seem, is the way the *objet petit a* is interpreted by some post-Lacanian theorists. In Žižek's view, the *objet petit a* is not an inaccessible ideal object to which no real object is ever adequate. Rather, he says, the *objet petit a* is "inadequacy itself", a presupposed void in demand which comes to exist as a "pure gap" (2016, p. 37). In my reading, asexual desire adjusts to this fantasy in a way that keeps the asexual subject desiring for this "savoured absence", to use Lacan's term (2020, p. 177), through a *jouissance* that is non-phallic. What this suggests is that, while the encounter with the first Other marks the sexually desiring subject as a subject of lack, by contrast, the asexual's earliest bodily engagements with the Other become primarily associated and overshadowed with unpleasure and *Hilflosligkeit* (helplessness). The result, as mentioned earlier, is that desire goes on to be desexualized and satisfaction derived from a *jouissance* annulled of its sexual element. To borrow a phrase from Lacan, in this context, the "sexual colouring" of libido is "the colour of emptiness" (2006, p. 722).

For the asexual, I am proposing that the encounter with the first Other becomes overshadowed with unpleasure due to the structurally traumatic experience of the component sexual drives in infantile sexuality.[11] In the first instance, this occurs at the oral phase where the erotized activity of feeding enters, as Lacan suggests (2020, p. 176), into a "dialectic of substitution" in which the demand for bodily satisfaction becomes a demand for love. He, thus, points to the inaugural moment when the increase in drive tension in relation to the almightiness of the Other is experienced as unpleasurable (ibid., p. 177). He says that he has located this moment as one in which a reversal can take place within the symbolic dialectic of oral activity which, in turn, reverses the symbolic dependence of the child on the mother into its opposite. He follows this up with a statement which is of particular importance for asexuality when he says that "other types of activity are then seized upon in like fashion" in this libidinal or eroticized dialectic (ibid.). Here, Lacan is essentially pointing to how this mechanism can be considered in subsequent anal and phallic phase activities. This implies that something of the reversal of dependence can carry through from its formative and originary moment at the oral phase to subsequent psychosexual stages. In this way, he is radically opening up a new and potentially fertile interpretation of infantile sexual experiences that can lead to a viable and valid choice to say no.

If desire puts structure on the drives, and if an increase in drive tension *is* unpleasurable, then presumably, desire will adjust to a phantasy aimed at avoiding this. For Lacan, in the repetition of the sexual act, the sexually desiring subject reproduces the initial relation to the Other, which was potentially traumatic (2019, p. 17) and is the very relation which maintains the *objet petit a* (1966–1967, session of 1 March 1967, p. 9). I am proposing that, for the asexual subject, the original rise in drive tension as a result of infantile sexual excitations is potentially unpleasurable, and psychological elaboration is achieved through a "Nirvana principle" response to reduce that tension to zero (Freud, 1920, p. 56). According to Laplanche and Pontalis (1973, pp. 272–273), "the Nirvana principle must be understood as something more than a law of constancy or of homeostasis: it is, rather, the radical tendency to reduce excitation to zero-point, as postulated much earlier by Freud under the 'principle of inertia'. At the same time, the word 'Nirvana' evokes a profound link between pleasure and annihilation, a link that always remained problematic for Freud", they say.[12] The term "Nirvana" in Buddhism means the "extinction" of human desire but in service of a higher goal of tranquillity and self-knowledge.[13] In this reading, then, the *jouissance* of asexual subjects would be similar to that which Lacan considers in *God and Woman's Jouissance* (1999, pp. 76–77) as one which is beyond phallic *jouissance* and one which I will consider later. This would also place it in similar territory to that which Buhle (1998, p. 328) examines in terms of "nonphallic orgasmic joy" which she says has been "configured around pre-Oedipal Oneness" with the maternal figure. In this regard, I am proposing that the *jouissance* which the asexual subject seeks is similarly both "non-phallic" and arises from pre-Oedipal roots.

The Presence of Absence

In asexuality, there would appear to be few, if any, signifiers of sexual desire. There seems to be no struggle to keep unwanted sexual feelings at bay, no repudiation of the sex drive, no recognition that "this is what I want but I am not having it". There appears to be no object that is elevated to the status of the Thing, no un-signifiable *objet petit a* as cause of sexual desire that resides in the Other, no promise of a sexualized lost object being refound, not even as *semblant*, within the fundamental phantasy propping up asexual desire. Equally, there is no desire being consciously acknowledged but suspended, deferred or postponed; no apparent sense of loss, of privation due to the absence of sexual attraction. In fact, in the more obvious sense, there are no observable symptoms or subjective distress as a result. If this is hysteria, then it is hysteria without symptoms. If that sounds enigmatic, then it should be recalled that hysteria itself is, and historically always has been, enigmatic; no answer in and of itself will satisfy the question it represents.[14] I will return to the relation of asexuality to hysteria in Chapter 5, but for now, a desiring subject without any consciously experienced sexual desire suggests something potentially new or different has taken place.

If the asexual's desire is based on the desire of the Other but without sexuality included, then it is reasonable to suggest that the sexual element of two key Lacanian concepts related to sexual desire, the phallus and the *objet petit a*, have been somehow annulled or neutralized. Interestingly, Lacan (2006, p. 580) says that desire itself is founded on annulment, in this case the annulment constituted by the satisfactions which demand brings about in relation to what is sought through need. If every demand is a demand for love, then no object offered in satisfaction of a need will suffice. He says, "demand annuls (*aufhebt*) the particularity of everything" which need requires "by transmuting it into a proof of love" (ibid.). Any satisfactions of need which demand does obtain are, he says, "debased (*sich erniedrigt*) to the point of being no more than the crushing brought on by the demand for love" (ibid.). Something is lost or annulled when need gets articulated in demand, and this is what becomes desire. Yet Lacan posits that man and woman can only enter the field of their own desire, including sexual desire, through the signifier of the phallus (2008, p. 41). He is referring to sexually desiring beings in this instance who take up their sexual desire, and so in order to incorporate asexual subjects, it will be necessary to consider how the phallus operates for them. Can its sexual effects be annulled while the phallus itself still operates as a space holder in the signifying chain, much like the zero in mathematics?[15]

A Consideration of the Nothing as Zero

Lacan spends a good deal of time looking to the generative properties of zero to ask a similar question, particularly in *Seminar XII, Crucial Problems for Psychoanalysis*, and in *Seminar XIII, The Object of Psychoanalysis*.[16] His purpose is to use zero in order to approach the logic of the signifier, basing it on philosopher-mathematician Gottlob Frege's ideas on natural numbers in *The Foundations of Arithmetic* (1884). Two main propositions from Frege's work are of value to any consideration of asexuality, and they are, firstly, his use of logic to include zero not as the absence or lack of some content but as a cardinal number positioned at the start of the number sequence – that is, a number that *exists* before any other number despite the contradiction this implies (1980, pp. 88–93). Secondly, his proposition that zero is the very entity from which all subsequent numbers follow (ibid., p. 96, 118). In each case, we are being presented by Frege with a potency inherent in zero. He says that in the same way that one is the number that follows directly after zero, *all* subsequent numbers follow after zero. In short, everything arithmetically begins with zero, and the lack or absence which it represents *generates* the active progression of all numbers that follow. This metonymy is captured by Frege as $n + 1$ (ibid., p. 93) where n can stand for any natural number that, by definition, includes zero which not only inaugurates but is also entwined with everything that flows from it. My purpose in referring to zero is, therefore, to illustrate the potentially constitutive and potently generative place of the concept and object nothing as a symbol for asexuality's relation to the phallus and, as I will outline later, to the *objet petit a*.[17]

In *Seminar XII*, Lacan says of zero something similar to what he will say in *Seminar XX* of the signifier – that is, the signifier is what represents the subject for another signifier (1999, p. 49). Here, he says that one is what will represent zero for another one (*Seminar XII*, session of 20 January 1965, p. 69), and what this highlights is the central importance of zero in its underpinning of arithmetical progression, a recognition denied it by Greek, Roman, early Christian and Medieval mathematicians (Seife, 2000, pp. 40–61). Jacque-Alain Miller, whom Lacan (1964–1965) invites to speak on Frege's logic in this *Seminar*, relates zero not only to the lack which generates the production of signifiers but also to its role in "the general support for the sequence" (*Seminar XII*, session of 24 February 1965, p. 120).[18] He says one is generated from zero as a number that conjoins both the concept *of* nothing and the object *as* nothing (ibid.). In other words, the nothing can take on a symbolic materiality through verifiable absence which then becomes the placeholder from which sequential numeration as metaphor for desire can emerge. "That is why once you have generated the number zero you finally lay hold of a first object", he says (ibid., p. 119). In this way, the human subject is closely linked to the concept of lack whose number *is* zero (ibid., session of 3 March 1965, p. 128).[19] For the emerging subject of language, therefore, out of a time of no speech (zero) comes speech (one), and unconscious desire represented by the zero in this mathematical consideration is the truth of the subject seeking but never finding full expression through signifiers. From the point of view of asexuality, here we find Miller also theorizing on how absence is a radical presence not only for the generation of numbers but also for the production of the signifying chain which creates the speaking subject. As he says, "It is this decisive proposition that the concept of not-identical-with-itself [nothing] is assigned by the number zero which sutures logical discourse" (1966, p. 5, online pagination). In terms of the word "suture", Miller says that zero's place of lack, and its exclusion from the discourse it internally drives, *is* the suture of the chain of discourse and is, therefore, the logic of the signifier (ibid., p. 7). He reiterates this by posing this question: if the metonymy of zero in the number chain acts as an invisible suturing which moves beneath it, then what is to stop us from seeing in it "the most elementary articulation of the subject's relation to the signifying chain?" (ibid.).

I will be returning to the question of the phallus operating as zero or as space holder in the signifying chain in Chapter 5. For now, this theoretical consideration of zero as more than simply an absence might offer further support in understanding the desire and *jouissance* available to asexuality. If asexuality's definition of not being sexually attracted to another person is the signifier of a desire for no desire, then asexuality's desire remains as paradoxical as desire itself (Lacan, 2019, p. 474). The object that keeps the asexual libidinally desiring would then appear to be one which is emptied of sexual desire for the Other, a paradox which lies at the heart of asexuality as an orientation within the field of human sexuality.[20]

Infantile Reversal of Dependence

As I mentioned earlier, when Lacan is dealing with the oral drive, it is hunger which is the bearer of libido. He is pointing out that even orality is a question of

sexual libido in the strict sense (2020, p. 176). The breast has entered into the dialectic of substitution – that is, the demand for food becomes a demand for love –
within a dialectic of ordinary frustrations whereby the child encounters moments
in which his or her dependence is clearly experienced. In other words, a sexual
relation has become substituted for a feeding relation (*Seminar XIV*, session of
18 January 1967, p. 4) because something more than feeding is taking place. The
child is seeking satisfaction in the demand for love, and so the sucking at the
breast becomes an eroticized activity (2020, p. 176). For Lacan, it is not the object
itself which plays the essential role in this dialectic of frustration. It is rather the
activity which has taken on this eroticized function on the plane of desire – in
this case, the oral function. Nor does the object as breast have to be present for
eroticization to take place; a bottle can substitute for it (ibid.). He goes even further when he says, "it is possible for the same role to be played where there is no
real object at all" (ibid., p. 177). This latter point, small as it might seem, is of
significance when considering asexuality because, in Lacan's view, eroticization
can now take place in relation to absence, a concept that has been unavailable to
non-psychoanalytic researchers in the field of asexuality. We saw an example of
this earlier with Lacan's comment that the subject is not "not eating" but is instead
"eating nothing", a distinct but subtle shift of position from passive to active.
Another point of particular interest for asexuality is the reference Lacan makes to
the mechanism whereby the breast as object is the "annulled object *qua* symbolic
object", and this turns the child's "relation of dependence around" (ibid., p. 179).
This offers an understanding as to how a particular relation to the first Other can
arise in which a subject can experience dependence as a negative and seek to alter
its position in relation to it. It also nuances the theoretical argument, as found
in Freudian concepts such as repression, regression, sublimation and inhibition,
which says the cause of lack of sexual desire is to be found primarily in a retroactive refusal or negation determined by the subject's experience of the Oedipus
complex. Instead, this theoretical point which Lacan is making posits an originary pre-Oedipal experience of a libidinally infused dependence as unpleasurable
which the subject reverses in order to transform it. It is also taking place during
the child's first encounter with the enigma of the Other's unfathomable desire.[21]

Lacan elaborates in *Seminar IV* on how this reversal operates. He says the oral
activity of feeding takes on an eroticized function on the plane of desire which
is "organized" in the symbolic order (2020, pp. 176–177). As stated, it is an eating of nothing which, he says, is precisely a something that exists on the symbolic plane (ibid., p. 177). The child uses this nothing, this "savoured absence",
to make the mother depend on him rather than him depend on the mother, thereby
reversing the relation of dependence. He says, "In virtue of this *nothing*, he makes
her dependent on him" (ibid.). Lacan is outlining the manner in which the infant
can psychically transform a relation of dependence into its opposite because of
a fundamentally unpleasurable experience in relation to the Other. In this regard,
it is worth highlighting the comment he makes immediately after this. He says if
this fundamental process is not taken into account, then we also run the risk of

misunderstanding "other symptoms" (ibid.) which, on the face of it, appears to be an invitation to open out this psychical mechanism to areas beyond his immediate focus. This resonates with his point, mentioned earlier, that "other types of activity are then seized upon in like fashion", by which he means this reversal can appear in subsequent psychosexual stages within the libidinized dialectic between the child and the mother (ibid.). In this context, the reversal of dependence is being moved away from a sole focus on the oral stage, and his point about "other symptoms" refers to the potential ubiquity of this mechanism of reversal to have a determining role across different symptom categories. It might be necessary here to point out that this focus on symptoms is not intended to obliquely pathologize asexuality. As mentioned in Chapter 3, psychoanalytic theory from Freud onwards believes that the conditions exist for neurosis in every subject, sexual or asexual (i.e., to have a symptom) (1916–1917, SE XVI, p. 358). It is also worth repeating Colette Soler's (2003, p. 86) point mentioned in the Introduction that heterosexuality might also be considered a symptom.

In terms of the reversal of dependence, then, Lacan is suggesting it takes place because the child has understood something of the omnipotence or almightiness which the mother wields in relation to it.[22] He says the drive to reverse the relation of dependence is due to a realization for the child that this real being as the mother is omnipotent, and it is this real being on whom "the gift or the non-gift depends, absolutely and with no recourse" (2020, p. 177). He says, "I'm telling you that the mother is primordially all-powerful, and that this cannot be eliminated from this dialectic if we are to understand anything worthwhile" (ibid.). At this point, he overlays a Kleinian interpretation and says that the depressive position of Melanie Klein[23] is connected to the same maternal omnipotence he is examining. In order for a "real omnipotence" to bring about a depressive state, the child must have reached a stage of being able to reflect on the contrast of the mother with its own powerlessness (ibid., p. 179). He situates this point at around the sixth month, the same time as his Mirror Stage can take place. He says this:

> When he finds himself in the presence of this totality in the form of the maternal body, he is forced to observe that it doesn't obey him. Therefore, it is in so far as the reflected specular structure of the mirror stage comes into play that we can conceive of maternal almightiness as being reflected upon solely from a distinctly depressive position, namely the child's sense of powerlessness.
>
> (ibid.)

He further emphasizes that the power the child employs to defend against the omnipotence of the mother is not negativism but rather the "annulled object *qua* symbolic" (ibid.). In this way, he says, the child puts its dependency in check, precisely by "feeding on nothing", and it is here that it reverses its relation of dependence on the mother (ibid.). If, by extending Lacan's theory, this operation is potentially available to the child in terms of phallic sexuality as opposed to orality, then it has relevance for any consideration of asexuality. Furthermore, it might lay a theoretical foundation on which to further theorize how, post-Oedipally, the Symbolic phallus as sexualized signifier might be taken up by the asexual. The question which Lacan makes possible is whether the asexual reverses the relation of dependence with regard to the libidinized or eroticized relation to the Other in a manner that goes beyond an unadorned refusal. In the following chapters, I will examine the implications of this.

For the moment, Lacan's theorizing allows for the possibility that the subject, beginning in infancy, can unconsciously protect itself from the libidinal unpleasure experienced via the omnipotence of the first Other and, by extension, from the perceived omnipotent desire of subsequent others. Therefore, rather than assuming that asexuality is a refusal of sexual desire or a desire for an unsatisfied desire, it could instead be considered a desire for no desire, in which context, the question of a satisfied or an unsatisfied sexual desire becomes moot. The infant is making himself or herself master of the almightiness of the mother, and from there on, the mother's almightiness depends upon the child's desire and, indeed, is at the mercy of the child's almightiness (ibid.). On this model, while asexuality might engage a similar psychical mechanism, it could be understood as distinct from, say, a refusal of food and, instead, viewed in terms of sexually desiring nothing. In this scenario, desire forms itself around a vacuole just as we find with the origin of all desire and, indeed, with language. But it occurs in a way that does not involve symptoms or subjective distress and precludes the demand of the Other as sexually desirable or sexually desiring. If this represents an emptying of the drives, then as Moncayo (2017, p. 20) puts it, "emptiness can also be revealed as a still and serene presence that constitutes the opposite of anxiety".

The male asexual subject interviewed in a newspaper article titled "We're married, we just don't have sex" (O'Donnell, 2008) describes his desire for the asexual woman he married. But his desire is not based on sexual need, and therefore, in Lacanian terms, it is not available to be articulated in demand. If there is no seeking of satisfaction through demand, it would suggest that the asexual subject's dependence on the Other is considerably different from a dependence that *is*. The supposition arising from this is that the asexual subject is uniquely different in terms of their relation to sexual need and demand. In asexuality, generally, a prominent characteristic is the manner in which the sexual demand of the Other is assiduously circumscribed. I have proposed so far that the child's experience of the omnipotence of the first Other and the helplessness which ensues represent motive forces for need, demand and desire to be voided of sexual content. In the sections which follow, I will be adding the potential for the sexual drive to be experienced as traumatic in this context also. But for the moment, if sexuality is determined through the interplay of castration, the phallic signifier, the phantasy and the Other, then asexuality fits within this broad range of human experience. However, emanating from a cultural milieu which overdetermines sexualization (Verhaeghe, 2005, p. 33), asexuality appears to have found a way of perpetuating desire through having no sexual desire and through deriving *jouissance* from the savoured absence of this. Viewed in this way, asexuality becomes an active, driven form of sexuality that, just like conventional forms, emanates from a dialectic of substitution, which takes place within a dialectic of frustration (Lacan, 2020, pp. 172–177).

The reported experience of asexuals is that, in general, they are not aware of any sexual desire directed externally to objects (Carrigan et al., 2014, p. 35). In keeping with Freudian-Lacanian theory, however, even if no conscious experience of sexuality exists, sexuality is present in the unconscious of every subject. Also, if asexuality were simply a case of a libido that was passive, which I have suggested is not the case, Lacan reminds us that libido has active effects in every instance, even in the passive position, because activity is necessary in order to adopt the passive position (2020, p. 37). So again, psychoanalytic theory emphasizes that libido is always present, irrespective of the conscious experience of the subject, and that the drive is a permanence within the subject's unconscious (Lacan, 1977, p. 165).[24] Extending this logic would imply that the assumption mentioned in the Introduction is still valid – that is, the lack of evidence of libido in the asexual subject is not evidence of its absence. In other words, while asexuality manifestly has no sexual attraction for another person, nevertheless, it is, of itself, a form of *latent* sexuality that has a unique relation to sexual desire. But if, as Lacan proposes, the very reality of the unconscious is a sexual reality (ibid., p. 150), how is asexuality's experience of the absence of Other-directed sexual desire to be understood?

The Role of Transference and Repetition

To answer this question, it is necessary to consider Lacan's theory in terms of the aetiology of the sexually desiring subject's relation to the Other. This, in turn, can be usefully approached by examining his exposition of the place of both transference and repetition in the unconscious of the subject in relation to the desire of the Other. For Lacan, and indeed Freud, transference[25] is a challenge for psychoanalysis in particular and for the human subject's relation to the Other in general. It is so because transference is a closing of the unconscious that combines a structural trauma experienced by all subjects with both sexuality and the Real. Lacan says that this view is in contrast to other schools of psychoanalysis who classically understand it as an opening up that renders the unconscious accessible. "Far from being the handing over of powers to the unconscious, transference is, on the contrary, its closing up", he says (ibid., p. 130). In making this claim, he is following a path travelled by Freud who variously describes transference as the worst obstacle to treatment, the strongest weapon of the resistance and the thing that can completely annul the analytic situation.[26]

Referring to Freud's psychoanalysis of Dora, Lacan talks about her transference to Freud in terms of such a closure of the unconscious and describes its various iterations as "the permanent modes according to which she constitutes her objects" (2006, p. 184). The word "permanent" here denotes fixity and, indeed, repetition (ibid.). Four years on, Lacan is saying that transference as closure is in the imaginary in *The Purloined Letter*, and he outlines the dialectic of intersubjectivity, which is transference, in his Schema L (ibid., pp. 39–40). In that schema, he represents two people as a couple who are involved in a reciprocal imaginary objectification with the terms *a* and *a' (prime)*, a theme he has already brought out in his 1949 paper, "The Mirror Stage" (ibid., pp. 75–81). In this scenario, transference is the product of the Imaginary as the ego, itself an imaginary construct, of one party engages dialectically with the ego of the other. But in *Seminar XI*, his idea of transference changes significantly. While it still represents a closure of the unconscious, now it is not due to the Imaginary but is the enactment of the sexual reality of the unconscious, and it is this latter concept which requires asexuality to be considered within an inherently sexual context. This is because it gives rise to the following question: if transference is the enactment of the sexual reality of the unconscious, why does its enactment bring about a closure of the unconscious? Lacan argues that it is due to the very nature of what sexual represents, and this is what becomes of central importance in considering asexuality. Transference, as the primordially ordered relation to the Other, is dependent on repetition compulsion to ensure that the relation to the Other occurs again and again. Therefore, as stated, this is why it is necessary in approaching his line of reasoning in this regard to go back and include what he says about repetition compulsion and its relation to transference.

In the 1955 *Seminar* on *The Purloined Letter*, the symbolic order is constitutive of the subject (2006, p. 7), and this is the realm of the signifier, the pure signifier, which, just like the titular purloined letter, drives repetition (ibid., p. 10). It is an insistence driven by a determinism which, "is unable to satisfy itself except by *refinding an object that has been fundamentally lost* [emphasis in original]" (ibid., p. 34). In *Seminar XI*, this changes radically when repetition, while still trying to refind something that is fundamentally lost, is grounded not in the Symbolic but in the first encounter with the Real and, what is more, with a Real that is originally unwelcome (1977, pp. 53–55). The Real, not the Symbolic, is central now, and the thing that is getting repeated is always a chance encounter with the Real which is traumatic – and here he uses Aristotle's word *tuché* (ibid., p. 69). He says that the function of *tuché*, of the Real as chance encounter, is essentially the missed encounter which first presented itself in psychoanalysis in the form of trauma (ibid., p. 55).

> Is it not remarkable that, at the origin of the analytic experience, the real should have presented itself in the form of that which is *unassimilable* in it – in the form of the trauma, determining all that follows, and imposing on it an apparently accidental origin?
>
> (ibid.)

At the very heart of the primary processes, he says there is the insistence of the trauma arising from this first encounter (ibid.), an insistence that is now of the Real not the Symbolic. He points out that it is necessary to ground this repetition first of all in the very split that occurs in the subject in relation to this encounter. The split gives us a glimpse of the dialectical effects of this Real as something "originally unwelcome" (ibid., p. 69), with the word "dialectical" signalling the necessity of the Other. Then he comes to the primal scene as the *perceptual* experience of the sexuality of the Other which is also traumatic. He wonders why this is so (ibid., p. 70) and asks why as an experience it always occurs too early or too late. Why does the subject take either too much pleasure in it, as in obsessional neurosis, or too little, as in hysteria? He also asks why it does not sexually arouse the subject immediately, if we all are truly sexual beings. Instead, the encounter is *dustuchia (a misfortune)*. He says in his reply to Francoise Dolto, "The central bad encounter is at the level of the sexual" (ibid., p. 64). Here, Lacan is positing a primary sexual encounter with the Real which is experienced as trauma. This parallels his view in *Seminar IV* that I have been considering, which is that a trauma in the Real brings about a reversal of the child's relation of dependence on the Other. In *Seminar XI*, however, he is referencing an Oedipal and, therefore, phallic stage experience which, nevertheless, also has pre-Oedipal roots in the first encounter with the Real of the Other but which, this time, has a more direct sexual or phallic context. In *Seminar IV*, in contrast, he is referencing an oral, but no less sexual, pre-Oedipal experience.

Sexual Reality and Its Relation to Trauma

Thus far, Lacan has theorized the occurrence of an original but chance moment that grounds repetition. It is one that is not only unwelcome but also sexual and traumatizing because it is unassimilable to the signifier. In *Seminar XI*, when considering the repetition of the *Fort-Da* game, the wooden reel is the *objet petit a* that is used to symbolize the mother's departure as cause of a traumatic *Spaltung*, or split, in the child (ibid., pp. 63–64). In this way, a prototypical representative of the fantasy object is used by the child to put meaning on a part of the Real that resists the Symbolic. But this endless repetition is not necessarily about mastery. Rather, Lacan says it is a repeated attempt to accommodate an alienation that unsteadies the subject (ibid., p. 239), with the *objet petit a* holding out the promise and, indeed, the means of achieving that accommodation. Therefore, his view is that repetition holds the key to unlocking the meaning of transference which, in turn, unlocks the apparent conundrum of why transference brings about a closure rather than an opening of the sexual reality of the unconscious.

The originally unwelcome and traumatizing Real is sexual. Therefore, transference as the enactment of the sexual reality of the unconscious has to include traumatism, similar to the way repetition is considered. Or to put it another way, at some level, every encounter with the Other of desire must include something of this originary traumatism. Repetition seeks to have an encounter that it repeatedly misses, driven by the unrealized hope of finally mastering the original trauma. But transference, Lacan says, has an unusual ambiguity. In *The Dynamics of Transference*, Freud (1912, p. 108) says that transference phenomena are essential for making the patient's hidden and forgotten erotic impulses immediate and manifest because it is impossible to destroy anything *in absentia* or *in effigie*. So even though these phenomena of transference are played out on the screen of the analyst's or the other's person, they are originally based on something Real – that is, beyond symbolization through language. Lacan, for his part, says that this ambiguity of the Real being given in the transference is one that can be unravelled by understanding the Real in repetition (1977, p. 54). As stated earlier, in repetition, what gets repeated always occurs as if by chance, *tuché*, but despite this accidental character, it is the original trauma that repeats (ibid., p. 55). In transference, therefore, the trauma returns, and its resistance to signification is the reason there are limits to memory for Lacan. As Freud says, what cannot be remembered is repeated in behaviour (1914, p. 150).

In this way, then, a post-Oedipal, desexualized reality becomes sexualized through the transferential relationship to the Other. In the transference, something of the trauma returns, and this is why, for Lacan, the transference is the means by which the unconscious closes up again. Repetition, he says, continuously seeks to make the appointment with the *objet petit a* but misses it, while transference holds out the promise of providing an Other with whom the appointment can be made. Each in their way are determined by a traumatism which is brought about by an original encounter with a sexual Real. I will be proposing that this experience of structural trauma which every subject undergoes brings about a particular outcome for the asexual subject, and in the following chapters, I will be theorizing as to how this might potentially occur.

Sexuality and Unpleasure

In the context of the primordial and ambivalent effects of the sexual Real which I have just been considering, the question posed in 1896 by Freud about sexuality takes on a particular significance. "In my opinion", he says, "there must be an independent source for the release of unpleasure in sexual life: once that source is present, it can activate sensations of disgust, lend force to morality, and so on" (p. 222). Verhaeghe suggests that even before any conscious or external sexual trauma might take place, the internal structural trauma of the drive itself involves an internal rise in excitation that threatens to overwhelm the ego (1998, p. 93). He proposes that "every" person experiences an infantile sexual trauma "because of the structural relationship between the drive and our psychological apparatus" (2001, p. 51). He makes the point that there is a strong analogy between drive and trauma in terms of their effects on the psyche. In fact, his view is that human sexuality contains potentially the same effect for the subject as an external trauma (1998, p. 96), and relating it back to Freud's question, this allows for an understanding of how sensations of disgust and the release of unpleasure in sexual life might come about. It might also allow for a clearer consideration as to why a subject might choose an asexual position, with "choice" being used again in the sense defined in Chapter 3. It might also be worth including here that when discussing the related area of Lacanian "sexuation", a concept close to but not the same as gendered identity, Morel (2019, p. 206) believes that the choice of sex also has to be situated at a level where an unconscious decision is made based on a contingent or chance encounter with the Real. Furthermore, she suggests that this choice occurs at a more fundamental level than that of the Name-of-the-Father and phallic signification – that is, at the primary level of the maternal discourse (ibid., p. 310). These are topics which I will also be returning to a little later.

For now, and drawing on Lacan's ideas in *Seminar XI*, the unpleasure of sexual life is based on an originally unwelcoming Real and is implicitly determined by the trauma caused by the first encounter with this Real, similar to what he has been pointing to in *Seminar IV*. In turn, this posits asexuality as a distinct sexual orientation in response to the potentially traumatizing libidinal effects of the drive in relation to the Other, just as occurs for sexually desiring subjects but with a different outcome in terms of *jouissance*. The sexual subject is driven by a libidinal impulse to return to the site of the trauma – that is, to the sexualized presence of the Other (Verhaeghe, 2001, pp. 13–15). The asexual has, as I have been outlining, made a different but equally valid choice. Yet even for sexually desiring subjects, Lacan consistently says there is no such thing as the sexual relationship. For him, all notions of binarity and complementarity between the sexes are erroneous, and the idea of unity is merely a suture provided by the Imaginary. The hegemony of sexual harmony which he is seeking to disrupt with his "no sexual relationship" can be traced back to Plato's work in *The Symposium*. In it, Aristophanes explains how Zeus, father of the Gods and men, originally cut men in two and how, forever after, they have desired to be reunited with their "other half".[27] It puts a particular context on the historical belief in and attraction towards a theory of symmetry and reciprocity in which a natural and harmonious relationship exists or once existed between the sexes. In his theorizing, Lacan, in contrast to religious and classical discourses, embraces the contrary. For him, unity between the sexes is an impossibility, the sexual relationship does not exist and asymmetry better represents the relation between them. As early as *Seminar II*, he is saying that genital love, or the sexual act, is "absolutely unassimilable to a unity", one that does not secure anything (1991b, p. 263). Twelve years later, in *Seminar XIV, The Logic of Phantasy*, referring to what he terms the central concern of psychoanalysis, he says that everything turns around not "being" but the difficulty inherent in the sexual act, and the word "act" here means sexual relationship (session of 22 July 1967, p. 2). During the same period, and yet developing another idea that first occurs in *Seminar II*, he says that there is no sexual act weighty enough to affirm in the subject the certainty that it is of a particular sex (Gallagher, 1999, p. 4). What is at stake, rather, is the "incommensurability" of the *objet petit a* to any unity of beings of opposite sexes (ibid., p. 5). In *Seminar XVIII*, he states bluntly that "There is no sexual act" (again, "act" meaning "relationship") (session of 20 January 1971, pp. 12–13). After this, there is what he terms the "no sexual relationship" of *Seminar XX* (1999, p. 12), and in *Seminar XXII*, the concept is repeated in different forms; one such example being "there cannot be established a relationship between the sexed" (session of 17 December 1974, p. 31). In the latter *Seminar*, Lacan asks this: what does "there is no sexual relationship" mean, particularly when the very concept of the sexual relationship is to be found spoken about on every street corner? He makes the comment that this is the Real of the knot[28] – that is, that while sexuality and its gendered manifestations might be obvious and observable, they are beyond symbolization in language, despite being what people have spoken about for all time. For him, no elaboration of the sexual relation is possible which is logical or mathematical, and so as far as the sexual relationship is concerned, it is strictly impossible to write "x in relation (R) to y" (session of 18 March 1975, pp. 125–126). In other words, there is no neat encapsulating of the sexual relationship between sexed beings in any full or final meaning. The object cause of desire, *objet petit a*, mobilizes the desire of each subject differently to the desire of any other subject, and therefore, it does not bring two subjects closer to a manifest combinatory that clarifies their sexual identity. The approach taken by Lacanian psychoanalysis, therefore, highlights the impossibility or *impasse* at the core of sexuality and, in turn, the very relationship model which society tends to aggrandize as an exemplar of sexual normativity. In short, the sexual relationship is unsatisfactory both in terms of providing the subject with certainty of its subjective sexual identity and by way of providing a binary complementarity in relation to the Other. Against this theoretical background, I will explore in Chapter 5 how the asexual subject deals with the challenge of libido in bringing about an annulment of sexual desire.

Notes

1 For Lacan, desire is the metonymy of the subject as want-to-be – that is, the subject as always lacking and, therefore, always desiring and always in the act of becoming (Lacan, 2006, p. 520). Also, while lack, understood as a universal and structural cause of human desire, is central to how desire is mobilized, it has to be distinguished from Lacan's concept of lack of lack. Lack of lack leaves the subject without lack to mobilize desire and is, instead, a state of undesiring helplessness which produces anxiety. See Lacan, 2014, p. 42, 65, and also Lacan, 1977, p. xli.

2 "The world of our experience, the Freudian world, assumes that it is this object, *das Ding*, as the absolute Other of the subject, that one is supposed to find again. It is to be found at the most as something missed. One doesn't find it, but only its pleasurable associations" (Lacan, 1992, p. 52).

3 This, as stated, is in contrast to Freud for whom anxiety *is* without an object (1926, p. 165).

4 Here, Lacan lists his other *objets petit a*: the breast, the faeces, the phallus (as imaginary object) and the urinary flow. He later includes the gaze as an *objet petit a* (1977, pp. 67–119).

5 Žižek reminds us that when we try to see the *objet petit a* in everyday life, irrespective of any "form" it might take, it dissipates because "in itself it is nothing at all" (2008, p. 192).

6 The word "annul" derives from the Latin *annullare*, to make to nothing.

7 "Small o is being in so far as it is essentially missing in the text of the world. And that is why around little o there can slide everything that is called the return of the repressed,

namely that here there is betrayed the true truth which interests us and which is always the object of desire, in so far as the whole of humanity, the whole of humanism is constructed to make us miss it" (Lacan, *Seminar IX*, 1961–1962, session of 27 June 1962, p. 308 – mis-dated in manuscript translation as February).

8 Le Gaufey traces Lacan's search from Freud's *das Ding* to Plato's concept of *agalma* and Kant's *nihil negativum* until his invention of the *objet petit a*.

9 Along with the Imaginary and the Symbolic, the third register of human experience for Lacan is the Real, a random and traumatic register that is unassimilable to language but which insists on breaking through.

10 "It (the will) is manifest in every force of nature that operates blindly" (1995, p. 42). "No attained object of desire can give lasting satisfaction, but merely a fleeting gratification" (ibid., p. 119).

11 According to neuroscientist David Eagleman (2015, p. 6), the human brain is born "remarkably unfinished" and is "shaped by the details of life experience" which leads to "long periods of helplessness" as "the young brain slowly molds to its environment".

12 Freud credits borrowing the term from British psychoanalyst Barbara Low.

13 Again, something similar can be found in Schopenhauer's philosophy (1995, pp. 261–262).

14 "We'll give the name of hysteric to this object which cannot be mastered by knowledge and therefore remains outside of history, even outside its own. This disjunction (//) can be expressed in the following way: if hysteria is a set of statements about the hysteric, then the hysteric is what eludes those statements, escapes this knowledge" (Wajcman, 2003, online pagination, p. 1).

15 "This is the zero of the place-holder notation, having no value itself but giving value by its presence to other numerals" (Kaplan, 1999, pp. 59–60).

16 He also considers the role of zero in *Seminar IX, Identification*, when working on concepts related to topological surfaces and when discussing the issue of negation.

17 André Green picks up on this relation between zero and Lacan's (1965–1966) *objet petit a* in his presentation in *Seminar XIII* (session of 22 December 1965, p. 31). He says it is not legitimate to count the number zero as nothing, thereby also acknowledging a presence in its apparent emptiness (ibid., p. 32). Lacan, for his part, enlarges its role when he says he "regards the function of zero as suturing the agency of the subject and of articulating the relationship of the subject to desire and also to castration" (ibid., session of 1 June, 1966, p. 260).

18 These ideas, first presented by Miller in Lacan's *Seminar XII*, were subsequently published separately as *La Suture (Éléments de la logique du signifiant)*, CpA 1.3 (January 1966), pp. 37–49. The English translation by Jacqueline Rose first appeared in Screen 18:4 (Winter 1977–1978), pp. 24–34.

19 This interchangeability of the terms "zero" and "nothing" is contained within Frege's definition (1980, p. 87): since "nothing" is "not identical with itself", then zero is the number that belongs to this concept. Zero designates nothing because nothing is the only thing that cannot be identical with itself.

20 Rather than being intimidated by the presence of such paradoxes, Fink suggests that psychoanalysis should avoid covering them over in order to prove that its theory is not lacking. Instead, he invites us to "take such contradictions and paradoxes as far as they can go" (1995, p. 135).

21 Cox Cameron (2021, p. 13) says the unanswerable question of the Other's desire is a terrifying moment for the child which, for Lacan, is the moment of original trauma.

22 Leader (2021, p. 17) points out how rising amounts of excitation are relational and are felt by the infant, "as indexes of the Other's presence and absence" due to the Other's role in calming or reducing the infant's bodily tension.

23 See Klein, 1998a, pp. 306–343; Klein, 1998b, pp. 344–369.

24 Here, Lacan says, "The first thing Freud says about the drive is, if I may put it this way, that it has no day or night, no spring or autumn, no rise and fall. It is a constant force".

25 The transferring of unconscious ideas and affects onto the analyst in the treatment. Lacan broadens it to human relations generally when he says, "Each time a man speaks to another in an authentic and full manner, there is, in the true sense, transference" (Lacan, 1991a, p. 109).

26 This path is evident in Freud's work from *Studies on Hysteria* (1895), p. 301; to the Dora case (1905b), p. 116; and in *The Dynamics of Transference* (1912), p. 104; and *Observations on Transference Love* (1915), p. 168; up to *Analysis Terminable and Interminable* (1937), p. 239.

27 "He spoke and cut men in two, like a sorb-apple which is halved for pickling. . . . After the division the two parts of man, each desiring his other half, came together, and throwing their arms about one another, entwined in mutual embraces, longing to grow into one" (Jowett, 1953, pp. 520–525).

28 The knot here is Lacan's Borromean knot, three interconnecting registers, depicted as rings, in his topology of human experience. They are the Symbolic, Real, Imaginary, all sharing in the centre a common link to the *objet petit a*. If one ring is broken, they all come apart. See his *Seminar XXII, RSI* (1974–1975) for a fuller exposition on this.

References

Boucher, G. (2005) 'One hand clapping: The phoneme and the nothing', *Filozofski vestnik*, 26(2), Zalozba Z R C, Ljubljana, Slovenia, pp. 83–93.

Buhle, M. J. (1998) *Feminism and its discontents – A century of struggle with psychoanalysis*. Cambridge, MA: Harvard University Press.

Carrigan, M., Gupta, K. and Morrison, T. G. (2014) *Asexuality and sexual normativity: An anthology*. New York: Routledge.

Chen, A. (2020) *ACE – What asexuality reveals about desire, society and the meaning of sex*. Boston: Beacon Press.

Cox Cameron, O. (2021) (with Owens, C.), *Studying Lacan's seminar VI: Dream, symptom, and the collapse of subjectivity*. Oxford: Routledge.

Eagleman, D. (2015) *The brain: The story of you*. Edinburgh: Canongate Books.

Fink, B. (1995) *The Lacanian subject – Between language and jouissance*. Princeton, NJ: Princeton University Press.

Fink, B. (2004) *Lacan to the letter, reading écrits closely*. Minneapolis: University of Minnesota Press.

Frege, G. (1980 [1884]) *The foundations of arithmetic* (Austin, J. L., trans). 2nd revised edition. Evanston, IL: Northwestern University Press.

Freud, S. (1895) With Breuer, J., *Studies on hysteria*, Standard Edition II. London: Vintage/Hogarth.

Freud, S. (1896) 'Extracts from the Fliess papers, draft k', in *Pre-psycho-analytic publications and unpublished drafts (1886–1899)*, Standard Edition I. London: Vintage/Hogarth.

Freud, S. (1905a) 'Three essays on sexuality', in *A case of hysteria, three essays on sexuality and other works*, Standard Edition VII. London: Vintage/Hogarth.

Freud, S. (1905b) 'Fragment of an analysis of a case of hysteria', in *A case of hysteria, three essays on sexuality and other works*, Standard Edition VII. London: Vintage/Hogarth.

Freud, S. (1911) 'Formulations on the two principles of mental functioning', in *Case history of Schreber, papers on technique and other works*, Standard Edition XII. London: Vintage/Hogarth.

Freud, S. (1912) 'The dynamics of transference', in *Case history of Schreber, papers on technique and other works*, Standard Edition XII. London: Vintage/Hogarth.

Freud, S. (1914) 'Remembering, repeating and working-through', in *Case history of Schreber, papers on technique and other works*, Standard Edition XII. London: Vintage/Hogarth.

Freud, S. (1915) 'Observations on transference-love', in *Case history of Schreber, papers on technique and other works*, Standard Edition XII. London: Vintage/Hogarth.

Freud, S. (1916–1917) *Introductory lectures on psycho-analyses*, Standard Editions XV–XVI. London: Vintage/Hogarth.

Freud, S. (1920) 'Beyond the pleasure principle', in *Beyond the pleasure principle, group psychology and other works*, Standard Edition XVIII. London: Vintage/Hogarth.

Freud, S. (1926) 'Inhibitions, symptoms and anxiety', in *An autobiographical study, inhibitions, symptoms and anxiety, lay analysis and other works*. Standard Edition XX. London: Vintage/Hogarth.

Freud, S. (1937) 'Analysis terminable and interminable', in *Moses and monotheism, an outline of psychoanalysis and other works*, Standard Edition XXIII. London: Vintage/Hogarth.

Gallagher, C. (1999) 'Jacques Lacan's summary of the seminar of 1966–1967 (Year book of the Ecole Pratique des Hautes Etudes)', *The Letter*, Irish Journal for Lacanian Psychoanalysis, 15, Spring, The School of Psychotherapy, St. Vincent's University Hospital, Elm Park, Dublin 4, Ireland, pp. 1–7.

Gallagher, C. (2005) 'Nets to knots: The odyssey to a beyond of barbarism', *The Letter*, Irish Journal for Lacanian Psychoanalysis, Autumn, [International Joyce-Lacan conference], The School of Psychotherapy, St. Vincent's University Hospital, Elm Park, Dublin 4, Ireland, pp. 1–18.

Gherovici, P. (2014) 'Where have the hysterics gone? Lacan's reinvention of hysteria', *ESC*, 40(1), March, pp. 47–70. Available at: ojsadmin,+Journal+manager,+ESC+40.1+Gherovici (6).pdf [Accessed 29 November 2021].

Jowett, B. (1953) *Collected works of Plato*. 4th edition. Oxford: Oxford University Press.

Kaplan, R. (1999) *The nothing that is: A natural history of zero*. Oxford: Oxford University Press.

Klein, M. (1998a [1935]) 'A contribution to the psychogenesis of manic-depressive states', in *Love, guilt and reparation and other works, 1921–1945*. London: Vintage.

Klein, M. (1998b [1940]) 'Mourning and its relation to manic-depressive states', in *Love, guilt and reparation and other works, 1921–1945*. London: Vintage.

Lacan, J. (1961–1962) *Identification*, Seminar IX, unpublished (Gallagher, C., trans). Available at: www.lacaninireland.com/web/wp-content/uploads/2010/06/Seminar-IX-Amended-Iby-MCL-7.NOV_.20111.pdf [Accessed 18 November 2021].

Lacan, J. (1964–1965) *Crucial problems for psychoanalysis*, Seminar XII, unpublished (Gallagher, C., trans). Available at: www.lacaninireland.com [Accessed 21 November 2021].

Lacan, J. (1965–1966) *The object of psychoanalysis*, Seminar XIII, unpublished (Gallagher, C., trans). Available at: www.lacaninireland.com [Accessed 21 November 2021].

Lacan, J. (1966–1967) *The logic of phantasy*, Seminar XIV, unpublished (Gallagher, C., trans). Available at: www.lacaninireland.com [Accessed 21 November 2021].

Lacan, J. (1970–1971) *On a discourse that might not be a semblance*, Seminar XVIII, unpublished (Gallagher, C., trans). Available at: www.lacaninireland.com [Accessed 22 November 2021].

Lacan, J. (1974–1975) *RSI*, Seminar XXII, unpublished (Gallagher, C., trans). Available at: www.lacaninireland.com [Accessed 6 December 2021].

Lacan, J. (1977 [1964]) *The four fundamental concepts of psycho-analysis*, Seminar XI (Miller, J-A., ed.) (Sheridan, A., trans). London: Penguin.

Lacan, J. (1991a [1953–1954]) *Freud's papers on technique*, Seminar I (Miller, J.-A., ed.) (Forrester, J. and Tomaselli, S., trans). New York: Norton.

Lacan, J. (1991b [1954–1955]) *The ego in Freud's theory and in the technique of psychoanalysis*, Seminar II (Miller, J.-A., ed.) (Tomaselli, S., trans). New York: Norton.

Lacan, J. (1992 [1959–1960]) *The ethics of psychoanalysis*, Seminar VII (Miller, J.-A., ed.) (Porter, D., trans). London: Routledge.

Lacan, J. (1999 [1972–1973]) *Encore*. Seminar XX (Miller, J.-A., ed.) (Fink, B., trans). New York: Norton.

Lacan, J. (2006 [1966]) *Écrits – The first complete English edition* (Fink, B., trans). New York: W. W. Norton.

Lacan, J. (2008 [1967]) *My teaching* (Macey, D., trans). London: Verso.

Lacan, J. (2014 [1962–1963]) *Anxiety*, Seminar X (Miller, J.-A. ed.) (Price, A. R., trans). Cambridge: Polity Press.

Lacan, J. (2017 [1957–1958]) *Formations of the unconscious*, Seminar V (Miller, J.-A., ed.) (Grigg, R., trans). Cambridge: Polity Press.

Lacan, J. (2019 [1958–1959]) *Desire and its interpretation*, Seminar VI (Miller, J.-A., ed.) (Fink, B., trans). Cambridge: Polity Press.

Lacan, J. (2020 [1956–1957]) *The object relation*, Seminar IV (Miller, J.-A. ed.) (Price, A. R., trans). Cambridge: Polity Press.

Laplanche, J. and Pontalis, J. B. (1973) *The language of psycho-analysis* (Nicholson-Smith, D., trans). London: Hogarth Press/Institute of Psycho-Analysis.

Le Gaufey, G. (2020 [2006]) *Lacan and the formulae of sexuation – Exploring logical consistency and clinical consequences* (Gallagher, C., trans). Oxfordshire: Routledge.

Leader, D. (2021) *Jouissance – Sexuality, suffering and satisfaction*. Cambridge: Polity.

Miller, J.-A. (1966) *Suture (Elements of the logic of the signifier)*. Available at: http://cahiers.kingston.ac.uk/pdf/cpa1.3.miller.translation.pdf [Accessed 21 November 2021].

Moncayo, R. (2017) *Lalangue, sinthome, jouissance and nomination*. London: Karnac.

Morel, G. (2019) *The law of the mother: An essay on the sexual sinthome*. New York: Routledge.

O'Donnell, B. (2008) 'We're married, we just don't have sex', *The Guardian*, 8 September. Available at: www.guardian.co.uk/lifeandstyle/2008/sep/08/ relationships. healthandwellbeing [Accessed 4 November 2021].

Prause, N. and Graham, C. A. (2007) 'Asexuality: Classification and characterization', *Archives of Sexual Behaviour*, 36(3), pp. 341–355.

Schopenhauer, A. (1995 [1819]) (Berman, D., ed.) *The world as will and idea: Abridged in one volume*. London: Everyman.

Seife, C. (2000) *Zero: The biography of a dangerous idea*. London: The Souvenir Press.

Soler, C. (2003) 'The paradoxes of the symptom in psychoanalysis', in Rabaté, J.-M. (ed.), *The Cambridge Companion to Lacan*. Cambridge: Cambridge University Press, pp. 86–101.

Verhaeghe, P. (1998) 'Trauma and hysteria within Freud and Lacan', *The Letter*, Irish Journal for Lacanian Psychoanalysis, 14 (Autumn), The School of Psychotherapy, St. Vincent's University Hospital, Elm Park, Dublin 4, Ireland, pp. 87–105.

Verhaeghe, P. (2001) *Beyond gender – From subject to drive*. New York: Other Press.

Verhaeghe, P. (2005) 'Sexuality in the formation of the subject', *Psychoanalyse. Aesthetik. Kulturkritik.*, 25, Heft 3/05, Passagen Verlag, Wien, pp. 33–53.

Wajcman, G. (2003) 'The hysteric's discourse', *The Symptom* (4), Spring. Available at: www.lacan.com/hystericdiscf.htm [Accessed 19 November 2021].

Yule, M. A., Brotto, L. A. and Gorzalka, B. B. (2014) 'Sexual fantasy and masturbation among asexual individuals', *The Canadian Journal of Human Sexuality*, 23(2), pp. 89–95.

Žižek, S. (2008 [1989]) *The sublime object of ideology*. London: Verso.

Žižek, S. (2016) 'Events through imaginary, symbolic and real', in Cerda-Rueda, A. (ed.), *Sex and nothing – Bridges from psychoanalysis to philosophy*. London: Karnac.

Chapter 5

The Challenge of Libido and the Annulment of Sexual Desire

Up to now, I have conceptualized asexuality's absence of sexual desire as something distinct from an absence of wanting to desire. This is on the basis that the asexual lived experience, and indeed, the working definition of self-defined asexuality make no claim or reference to an absence of "wanting". Instead, if considered as an embodied rendering of the "no sexual relation", asexual desire clearly signals that no sexual attraction for another person is experienced.[1] This apparent conundrum can be approached by taking into account Lacan's view that rather than a case of "not wanting to desire", it is instead a "wanting not to desire" (1977b, p. 235). Or as I have been referring to it, a desire for no sexual desire. This would allow for the possibility that asexuality is not a passive absence of sexual desire but is instead an active desire *not* to sexually desire. In this reading, the desire for no sexual desire *becomes* the desire. If asexuality's definition of no sexual attraction for another person signifies a void which can cause a desire for no sexual desire, then it now becomes necessary to ask how such a desire might operate.

If we begin by considering what Lacan has to say about sexuality, he makes the point that whether it is approached intra-subjectively in terms of the subject of lack produced by castration, or inter-subjectively in terms of the non-relation between the sexes, sexuality is not amenable to understanding through language. Sexual reality escapes any final meaning available to us, and yet meaning is the only thing which might make our sexual reality manageable or understandable.[2] For Lacan, not only is language unable to provide meaning, but he also includes thinking as radically inadequate to dealing with sexual reality (1966–1967, session of 18 January 1967. p. 11). In this light, sexuality itself has, much as we saw with Freud, the intrinsic capacity to cause trauma, defined as any experience which threatens to overwhelm the ego because it is incapable of being symbolized through language. Yet it is around language, and its inadequacy to provide meaning as to what is involved in sexual reality, that the function of the *objet petit a* is defined (ibid., p. 12). The *objet petit a* is an eroticized object which the sexually desiring subject will at certain vanishing points in relation to the Other's desire use as support via phantasy (ibid.).[3] Lacan says that in sublimation, the so-called object of the genital drive can "without any inconvenience" for the

DOI: 10.4324/9781003214946-6

sexually desiring subject be extracted from the sexual drive and that this can be done "without it losing anything of its capacity" in terms of satisfaction (ibid., p. 6). This supports the premise that in asexuality, the *objet petit a* can be situated in phantasy as the nothing as cause of desire because, on this basis, the genital drive can aim at a void without losing its capacity for satisfaction. This could then be considered an unconscious annulment of phallic *jouissance*. As mentioned in Chapter 4, in Lacan's view, the infant's oral refusal of food as the symbolic object is the pivot on which the reversal of dependence on the Other turns. With asexuality, I will be proposing that the process involves the annulment of the phallus as the pivotal signifier of sexual desire on which this reversal turns and that this is a valid and non-pathological direction which the sexual drive can take.

Asexuality, as I have been proposing, begins in the first experiences of the child in its relation to the first Other and annuls the phallic signifier and any associated phallicization of the *objet petit a*. Put another way, it annuls not just the signifier but also phallic *jouissance* accessed through it with the aim of allowing the subject remain independent of the Other. An encounter that every subject experiences in the primordial relation with the first Other has, in asexuality, a unique and contingent effect which brings about a desexualization of phantasy, desire and phallic *jouissance* in relation to the Other. This is, essentially, the sexual orientation of asexuality. In response to the fear of being engulfed, the *objet petit a* undergoes signifying substitution as the nothing, as the desired object of lack located in the gap between subject and Other which can, nonetheless, provide a *jouissance* through absence.[4] For the asexual subject, just as with sexually desiring subjects, the manner in which the first Other is experienced uniquely shapes their subjectivity (ibid., session of 16 November 1966, p. 4). Perhaps unsurprisingly, masturbatory activity which does not require the Other is frequently reported in studies of asexuality (Brotto et al., 2010, p. 607). But even where there is self-directed masturbation, the conscious fantasy accompanying it takes the form of no sexual desire for the Other. This is articulated by one asexual as follows:

> I did masturbate. It wasn't a sexual urge for me, I didn't fantasise, it was just something my body decided to do. People say about asexuals: "But if they masturbate doesn't that make them sexual?" It's hard to explain, but if you're asexual you don't necessarily feel an explicit connection between masturbation and sexual orientation. It's just part of having a human body – a physical, biological process.
>
> (O'Donnell, 2008, p. 1)

The Challenge of Libido

For Lacan, psychoanalysis rests entirely on the notion of libido, on the energy of desire (2019, p. 4), and for him, libido is the effective presence and indicator of desire at the level of the primary process (1977b, p. 153). Taking this as the traditional position of psychoanalysis, it would appear that asexuality represents a paradoxical challenge. If libido is an unavoidable bodily and psychical reality for all subjects, then how can asexuality claim to experience nothing of this? Before addressing this question, it is important to restate a number of theoretical psychoanalytic constructs relating to the paradoxical nature of both desire and, in turn, libido. Even non-asexual subjects who experience sexual desire will defend themselves against it because, as stated, it represents the threat of engulfment from the desire of the Other (Verhaeghe, 2001, p. 14).[5] Lacan also points out that the very term "sexual desire" seems to offer openness and plenitude, but given the unpredictable nature of desire, it can be distinct from love in that it is possible to love one person and desire another (2019, p. 450). He also distinguishes between desire and need because, while the latter seeks satisfaction through demand, the former does not and instead has, as stated earlier, a "paradoxical, deviant, erratic, eccentric and even scandalous nature" (2006, p. 579). Even if desire does bring a certain amount of love the subject's way, he points out that very often it is a love which is not "owned" by the subject and often "refuses to be owned" (2019, p. 5). He is establishing that even in the realm of recognized libidinal desire among sexually desiring subjects contradiction and disavowal can occur.

In contrast, I am proposing that asexuals remain desiring subjects because, as I hope to show, not only is a desire emptied of phallic *jouissance* tenable, but also, as Lacan indicates in *The Direction of the Treatment*, absence is just as much a presence on the symbolic plane (2006, p. 497). The point of interest for asexuality is in relation to Lacan's view on the provenance of desire. Desire is not something that man or woman is simply possessed by or invested with. He says the subject has to find this desire (2019, p. 257). In this sense, he is pointing towards the subjective particularity of desire, its absence of pre-determinism in terms of its object and its capacity to remain veiled from the subject until it is revealed. He says it is not something organized or put together in a preformed harmony between "desire and the way the world works" (ibid., p. 359). Rather, he says, the history of desire is organized in a discourse which develops in "the realm of the nonsensical" which is what the unconscious is (ibid.).

As stated, supporting desire by causing it to be both mobilized and sustained is the role of the fundamental phantasy which includes in its terms the ineffable, intangible and unattainable *objet petit a*. As is the case for all subjects, the *objet petit a* as a semblance or a substitute object ensures *das Ding*, as the primordial experience of Otherness and in its role of substituting for the original lost object, is never too close and never too much for the subject to bear. As semblance, therefore, the *objet petit a* has greater appeal because of its very quality as imitation which structurally posits a gap between it and the real thing. I am proposing that in asexuality, a similar gap allows the subject remain defended not only against the loss *of* the original object by providing a compensatory *jouissance* but also, in contrast to sexually desiring subjects, against being lost *in* the omnipotence or almightiness of the original object. Once again, using the term "vanishing", this time in regard to the risk of the subject disappearing, Lacan says, "Let us say that, in its fundamental use, fantasy is the means by which the subject maintains himself at the level of his vanishing desire, vanishing inasmuch as the very sat-isfaction of demand deprives him of his object" (2006, p. 532). By this he means that every object which satisfies demand is, by definition, a semblant and not *the* object of desire, which remains and must remain elusive. Therefore, phan-tasy continues to support and cause our desire with the promise that a final and complete, but ultimately unattainable, satisfaction of desire could yet occur. I am proposing that asexuality operates similarly and that the asexual phantasy, with *objet petit a* as the nothing, maintains the subject from vanishing in the face of the omnipotent Other's originally traumatizing desire. But if the *objet petit a* as cause of desire in asexuality is voided of its libidinal elements, what are the implications of this for the Lacanian signifier of desire, the phallus?

The Place of the Phallus in Asexual Desire

In Lacanian theory, the phallus is not an imaginary or real object, nor is it a bod-ily organ; it is the signifier which "designates meaning effects as a whole" (ibid., p. 579). As such, it is the signifier of desire (ibid., p. 523), and in particular, the signifier that can unlock meaning around the desire of the Other (ibid., p. 583). While it is a signifier, it is a very particular one in that it is missing from the sig-nifying chain and, for this reason, is both involved in every relation to the Other and is also the metonymy of the being of the subject (2019, p. 23). Lacan makes the phallus as signifier an essential element for understanding and negotiating the networks of desire in relation to the Other with, again, the goal of desire always understood as one of becoming the desire of the Other. The paradox of desire, however, is that it is central as a life force, or *élan*, which drives the subject, and yet it is located in the desire of the Other and so represents a signifying *Spaltung* or split for the subject (2006, p. 582). This is why Lacan says that, in the sense of Spinoza, desire really is the essence of man (2019, p. 474). But desire is not a simple *élan* because, as stated, it presents itself as more problematic, dispersed, polymorphous and contradictory, or far from an "oriented coaptation", as he puts it (ibid.). The phallus as the signifier of the desire of the Other also plays a spe-cific role at the level of the object because the "essential object" or *objet petit a* takes the place of that which the subject is symbolically deprived (i.e., the phal-lus) (ibid., p. 312). Therefore, to link back to the question asked at the end of the previous section, if the *objet petit a* which takes the place of the phallus is being theorized as the nothing, what does this imply for the phallus?

The logical sense of castration as the place where something is lost is based on the view that any meanings around it, and any signifier that might make it manageable or understandable, are lacking. This is what Lacan terms the "having or not having the phallic connotation" (1966–1967, session of 18 January 1967, p. 11). There is a lack in terms of language at the heart of the emergence of sexual-ity, whereby the subject can neither symbolize the experience of their own sexual-ity nor the antagonistic enigma of sexual difference (ibid.). This something which is perceived to have been lost at castration, for both asexual and non-asexual subjects, becomes the phallus as signifier which, in turn, allows the subject to a greater or lesser extent put some meaning on the question of the desire of the Other. For asexual subjects, however, I am proposing that the phallus becomes the signifier of a desire for no sexual desire *for* the Other and *of* the Other. Lacan says this:

> in the articulation of fantasy, the object takes the place of what the subject is deprived of – namely, the phallus. It is owing to this that the object assumes the function it has in fantasy, and that desire is constituted with fantasy as its prop.
>
> (2019, p. 312)

In short, the *objet petit a* which is essential to the phantasy is the "effect of castration" which takes the place of what is lost – that is, the phallus as the "object of castration" (ibid., p. 368). In order to fully explore the concept of castration and loss for asexuality, I will revisit Lacan's ideas on the phallus in order to establish the point of difference that it can represent for asexuality.

For sexually desiring subjects, Lacan associates the phallus, in terms of either being it (woman) or having it (man), with a power which the subject must preserve at any cost (ibid., p. 205). But he equally places its importance in a realm that goes beyond sexuality and into the realm of being. He says that human subjects:

> cannot help but consider themselves to be nothing more than beings who are, in the end, missing something. Whether they are male or female, they are castrated beings. This is why, in our experience of the One, the phallus is essentially related to the dialectic of Being.
>
> (ibid., pp. 218–219)

A phallically underpinned relationship to being is an essential element in the dialectic that takes place in the unconscious development of different stages of identification, from the first relationship with the mother, through the Oedipus complex and on to the operation of the law (ibid., p. 213). But it would appear that asexuality takes up a different and unique position to the signifier phallus as a result of its trajectory through this domain. Taking the infant's first position with regard to the Imaginary phallus, Lacan cites Melanie Klein's idea that the child comes to understand "from the outset" that the mother "contains" the phallus (2006, p. 582). But this phallus as a third term in the mother-child dyad is something enigmatic and veiled. It is a point beyond the child towards which the mother's desire and, thus, her lack, is aimed (Hook, 2006, p. 70).[6] For Lacan, the child must, therefore, become this Imaginary phallus in order to become the thing that the mother desires. This is how the first identification begins, and he says, "If the mother's desire *is* for the phallus, the child wants to be the phallus in order to satisfy her desire" (2006, p. 582). The generally understood implication of this statement is that this is so for all subjects,[7] despite it being an "original passive traumatic" encounter with the "threatening enjoyment of the Other from which the subject flees" (Verhaeghe, 2001, p. 13). Yet much of what Lacan has written in *Seminar IV*, mentioned earlier, suggests that a subject position is equally possible in which becoming the Imaginary phallus for the mother is *not* inevitable and can even be rejected, particularly with regard to his concept of the reversal of dependence on the Other. In *The Direction of the Treatment*, he is also questioning the universality of this idea of becoming the Imaginary phallus. There, he says, "Ultimately, by refusing the mother's demand, isn't the child requiring the mother to have a desire outside of him, because that is the pathway toward desire that he lacks?" (2006, p. 524) This opens up the possibility that, with regard to asexuality, the subject, rather than choosing to become the Imaginary phallus for the mother, might opt instead *not* to do so.[8]

As outlined in Chapter 4, the almightiness of the mother represents a traumatic encounter which causes the infant to reverse its relation of dependence on her. Indeed, Lacan identifies a moment when this reversal might conceivably take place, and it is when the child reaches an awareness that the breast is the possession of the mother, not of the child (2019, p. 219). The child's awareness now extends to the new possibility of being deprived of the desired object since the object's presence is at the apparent whim of the mother. Lacan equates this time with the onset of the Kleinian depressive position "when the mother as totality" is realized (ibid.). I am proposing that in asexuality, this has implications for the child's relation to the Imaginary phallus and, post-Oedipally, to the Symbolic phallus, its second iteration, as inter alia signifier of the desire of the Other. In this context, it seems reasonable to propose that Lacan's "test of desire" which takes place in the phallic phase may have a qualitatively different effect for asexuality. Lacan theorizes that the absence of the penis in the mother has symptomatic consequences for the child who has taken up the position of becoming the Imaginary phallus for her (2006, p. 582). If the asexual position is one in which the child does *not* choose to become the Imaginary phallus for the mother, the discovery of the absence of the mother's real phallus should in theory have far less symptomatic consequences. As I am proposing that this is the context from which the emerging asexual subject approaches the Oedipus complex, a closer examination of this is necessary.

From Imaginary Phallus to Symbolic Phallus

The transition from Imaginary phallus to Symbolic phallus as signifier is a necessary one for every subject to make. Without it, the child risks remaining in the position as Imaginary phallus for the mother – that is, fixed in a position of attempting to be the thing that fulfils her desire. Hook (2006, p. 76) says the child gradually comes to realize it cannot incarnate the Imaginary phallus for the mother, and so the child must make the momentous step of giving up being the Imaginary phallus. This is the point of the castration complex when the child is required to take up a relation to the Symbolic phallus, and only when this has taken place can the Oedipus complex be dissolved. But before this, the important transition from Imaginary to Symbolic must take place. Lacan's "test of desire" (2006, p. 582), therefore, is essential since it effectively marks the threshold between Imaginary phallus and Symbolic phallus and is the moment when, as stated, every subject learns that the mother does not have a real phallus. This test, in Lacan's view, is one without which symptomatic or structural consequences related to the castration complex cannot take effect (ibid.). Should the subject accept the mother has no penis, this ultimately dispels the Imaginary concept of the phallic mother and dissipates the desire of the child to identify with and try to become this Imaginary object.[9]

The test is, for Lacan, the foundational experience that ties desire and castration together in a way that will allow for a relation with the Symbolic phallus (ibid.). But this recognition that the mother does not have a real phallus, in turn, still has to undergo what Lacan calls "the law introduced by the father in this sequence" (ibid.). I am proposing that the law of the father which prohibits the mother as object of desire is also experienced differently for the asexual. It is different because the projected separation of the child from the mother which is brought about by the father has, for all intents and purposes, already been put into effect by the child and to the same end as the prohibition to be brought about by the no of the Father.[10] For sexually desiring subjects, once Lacan's test has been passed, the child is able to transition from Imaginary phallus to Symbolic phallus via the paternal metaphor, and so the Oedipus complex comes to an end. From this point on, the child takes up a relation to the phallus as signifier – a position in relation to Symbolic authority and the law – and so the phallus becomes a symbolic function rather than "an instrument of Imaginary kinds of identification" (Hook, 2006, p. 76).

> The Oedipus complex is dissolved at the point that the child realises it can no longer directly materialise the phallus for the mother; it must now give up the idea of the phallus as an Imaginary object and position itself in a relation to the phallus in its Symbolic dimension as the phallic signifier that will determine sexual identity.
>
> (ibid.)

I am proposing that the asexual subject undergoes the castration complex in a qualitatively different way to the sexual subject. Because the asexual subject has annulled the Imaginary phallus, he or she will unconsciously bring about an alteration in the relation to the Symbolic phallus, whereby the latter's sexual element is also annulled. In this reading, therefore, instead of designating meaning effects as a whole within a phallic context, or becoming "the bar with which the demon's hand strikes the signified" (Lacan, 2006, p. 581), the desexualized signifier phallus allows the post-Oedipal child to sustain its reversal of a phallicized relation of dependence on the Other while still remaining a desiring subject (Lacan, 2020, p. 179). To use Lacan's point in a different way, this is not simply about saying no, taking an action of refusal or a form of a negativism per se. Instead, it is about the taking of an active position in relation to the object which, he says, "has appeared to us under the sign of the nothing" (ibid.). The symbolic order then becomes the very place in which these first imaginary relationships are played out and, of relevance to asexuality, in such a way that a different subjective position can be taken up (ibid.).

The Post-Oedipal Asexual Subject

For the post-Oedipal asexual subject, the implications of either being or having the signifier phallus are also different. The Symbolic phallus as signifier does not operate in the same way in asexuality – that is, it does not designate sexually infused meaning effects in relation to the desire of the Other. As one female asexual puts it, "I don't have sex and don't understand why people would want to have sex" (Scherrer, 2008, p. 626). Similarly, a male asexual says, "Well, I've always been this way. Even my friends knew I was different – they even avoided topics about how 'cute' someone is with me because they were aware I couldn't understand" (ibid., p. 628). The phallus as signifier does not function to illuminate the *Umwelt*, or outside world, of the asexual speaking subject with a phallicized meaning that mediates between his or her *Innenwelt*, or inner world,[11] and the desire of the Other.[12] It is in sharp contrast to the experience Lacan describes for the sexually desiring subject when he says, "the part of this being that is alive in the *urverdrangt* [primally repressed] finds its signifier by receiving the mark of the phallus's *Verdrangung* [repression] (owing to which the unconscious is language)" (2006, p. 581). The fact that the phallus is a signifier requires that the subject can access it only if it is in "the place of the Other" (ibid.). For sexually desiring subjects, it is in the place of the Other only in "veiled" form and as "ratio" or measure of the Other's desire because the Other's desire is what "the subject is required to recognize" (ibid., p. 582). I am proposing that due to experiences which begin at the oral stage, and for the reasons I have outlined so far, the asexual subject does *not* recognize the libidinized desire of the Other and yet remains a desiring subject. Lacan has argued that through a process of signifying substitution, from breast to faeces and so on, the phallus becomes a signifying element and that this substitution is, in his view, the mainspring of symbolic progress (2019, p. 220). I am proposing, in contrast, that this "signifying substitution" has occurred differently in the case of asexual subjects so that the phallus does *not* become the signifying element of an all-pervasive libidinization of subjective reality.

In *The Direction of the Treatment*, Lacan gives an example from one of his own analysands in which the signifier phallus remains situated in the latter's female partner and so the sexually impotent analysand cannot bring the phallus into play (2006, p. 527). The analysand's mistress has a dream in which she has a real phallus, and on hearing this, the analysand's sexual powers are restored (ibid., p. 527). According to Lacan, this was a case of refusal of castration, which is first and foremost a refusal of the mother's and, in turn, the Other's castration (ibid., p. 528). In other words, this is a result of a refusal or inability to give up the Imaginary phallus in return for the Symbolic phallus. The change that took place for Lacan's analysand was due to the woman's desire yielding to the patient's desire "by showing him what she does not have" – that is, that she is castrated (ibid.). The dream of his wife having a phallus highlighted what she does not have in reality, that she is lacking and that he no longer needs to *be* the Imaginary phallus and could, instead, find a use for his real phallus (ibid.). A similar encounter with the Imaginary phallus takes place in Lacan's account of Ella Sharpe's analysis of her analysand's dream of a trip with his wife around the world (2019, p. 143). They are on a road in Czechoslovakia, and he is having "sexual play" with a woman in front of his wife. Lacan points out that the man is far from being able to recognize that the other is castrated, let alone that he is castrated (ibid., p. 159), which places him at the stage of the Imaginary phallus also. Because the Symbolic phallus is not something that can be demanded when it is most needed, the subject finds himself "broken down" (ibid., p. 226). As Lacan puts it, "he must consent to perceive that the woman is castrated" (ibid.).

In both of these examples, it is possible to see the power of an incompletely renounced Imaginary phallus to create symptomatic effects in sexually desiring subjects. In the latter example, the analysand has taken up a position where the female Other contains the phallus just as the mother once did. Lacan himself says that this analysand does not want to give up "his queen, like those bad chess players" who equate it with losing the game. "This is what the subject absolutely does not want to do. Why? Because for him the phallic signifier is identical to everything that transpired in his relationship with his mother" (ibid., p. 205). This situates the analysand in the position of an identifying regression as the infant who has not yet been brought to accept that the mother does *not* have the phallus. It illustrates what Lacan was referring to when he said that "what makes people most neurotic" is not the fear of losing the phallus or of being castrated. Rather, he says, "The thoroughly fundamental mainspring of neurosis is not to want the Other to be castrated" (ibid., p. 229). If the Other is castrated, then the Other does not have the phallus, and the significance of this is traced back to the fact that the original place of the phallus was the place of the I, the place of what Lacan calls primitive identification to the mother (ibid., pp. 233–234). Therefore, given the centrality and importance of the phallus in Lacanian theory, what are the implications if, as signifier of the desire of the Other and the signifier which designates meaning effects as a whole, it is annulled in asexuality?

The Phallus Annulled

Because there is no signifier that guarantees or authenticates the signifying chain, Lacan points clearly to the manner in which the sexual subject brings in something "for help in sustaining his desire" and in "dealing with the Other's desire" for the purpose of "constituting himself as desiring" (ibid., p. 428). He says, "His very desire is a defence and can be nothing else. This is what the subject does not perceive" (ibid.). Lacan is pointing to the paradox at the heart of this dialectic of desire, whereby the subject must constitute himself or herself as desiring in relation to the Other's desire and, at the same time, must defend himself or herself from this desire of the Other. I am proposing that the asexual subject similarly constitutes himself or herself. Hook (2006, p. 80) says it follows from Lacan's maxim (i.e., man's desire is the desire the Other) that taking on a relation to desire is always "*a taking on of how one will be desired by another*" [emphasis in original]. In this regard, the self-defined asexual's relation to sexual desire is, first and foremost, a relation in which the phallic dependence on the Other and the phallic demand of the Other are annulled. As mentioned earlier, Lacan says that the sexually desiring subject "must always call on something that presents itself in a tertiary position for help in dealing with the Other's desire" (2019, p. 428). This something is the phallus, and it is a support for the "vanishing relation of $ when faced with *a* to be tenable" (ibid., p. 429). I am proposing that the asexual subject supports himself or herself similarly. The "role of this thing" (i.e., the phallus) is to allow both the sexual and asexual subject the capability "to symbolize" their situation in relation to the Other so that, as Lacan argues, the subject can sustain and continue to "be recognized and satisfied as a subject" despite the "paradoxical" and "contorted" effects of the symptom (ibid.). The differences between sexual and asexual positions, however, are twofold in that, firstly, the phallus for the asexual is annulled in the manner which I have been proposing. Secondly, the *objet petit a* as the nothing and as cause of desire which comes to take the place of the phallus (ibid., p. 312) supports a desire that is non-phallic[13] and directs the asexual subject towards a *jouissance* that is equally so.

Lacan's theory says that it is the relationship of the desire of the subject to the desire of the Other that constitutes an essential structure, not only of neurosis but every "analytically defined structure" (ibid., p. 425). The phantasy is used to sustain this desire of the subject in the face of this desire of the Other. Lacan's theory states that in every case, the subject summons the help of the phallus in a "third position" with respect to the desire of the Other. But as the signifier is linked in the unconscious to the law (ibid., p. 430), he also believes the notion of distance from desire might be essential in order to maintain, sustain and even preserve desire (ibid., p. 439). In essence, a similar paradoxical relation to desire for sexually desiring subjects could also be applied to asexual subjects. Distance from sexual desire is, after all, the psychical template on which asexuality is based. I am proposing that the difference between sexually and asexually desiring subjects is that in asexuality, this concept of distance is instated from the pre-Oedipal stages, beginning at the oral, through the anal and into the phallic stage. For the sexual subject, in contrast, the libidinized desire which drives them towards the Other for satisfaction must be defended against and kept distant as a result of Oedipally installed prohibitions and, indeed, the scandalous nature of sexualized desire itself. For the asexual, as a result of this distance being unconsciously instated from infancy, the position of being the Imaginary phallus for the mother is marked by a desire *not* to be it. In turn, the transition to Symbolic phallus is qualitatively different and leads instead to a reversal of desire which can bring about the annulment of the phallic signifier since to annul the Imaginary phallus would, theoretically at least, have to lead inexorably to an annulled, desexualized Symbolic phallus. Lacan discounts the possibility of a desexualized libido, and in my proposition, this position still holds (1977b, p. 155). The concept of a desexualized phallus is not intended to give rise to the assumption that libido as the energy of desire in asexuality is equally desexualized. As I have argued, the desire for no sexual desire in asexuality *is* the desire which keeps the asexual subject desiring.[14] In this way, an Other-directed delibidinized phallic signifier maintains the libidinally underpinned but non-phallic *jouissance* of asexuality.

Lacan's Non-Phallic *Jouissance*

Similar to how Freud's sexual theory includes an asexual phase as part of every subject's experience, Lacan's sexual theory also incorporates the concept of an asexual pleasure or non-phallic *jouissance* at the heart of it.[15] In the latter's *Formulae of Sexuation*,[16] where he sets out to logically map an understanding of sexual difference in sexually desiring subjects (i.e., those seeking phallic *jouissance*), he includes a form of *jouissance* which is non-phallic or asexual. This is to be found on the woman side of the *Formulae*. The woman position, like the man position, is defined not by biology but rather by its relation to the phallus as sexualized signifier of desire.[17] But while "all men" are fully subject to the phallic function,[18] women are not completely so and, instead, have access not only to phallic *jouissance* but also to a second or Other *jouissance* which is asexual and supplementary or additional to phallic *jouissance*.

Woman, therefore, has only a partial relation to the phallus, and this supports not only the concept of a phallus which can be annulled, here at least partially, but also the presence of a non-phallic *jouissance* at the heart of a phallically structured theory of sexual enjoyment. Because this Other or Feminine *jouissance* is partial, Lacan terms it the Not-All of woman, by which he means that she is able to participate in, but is not fully covered by, phallic *jouissance* (1999, p. 76). In the *Formulae*, this Not-All is written as $\overline{\forall}x\,\phi x$ and reads "not all of woman is subject to the phallic function". This Other *jouissance* is, in Lacan's view, "the path of love" (Barnard, 2002, p. 172), a place he associates with divine love, religious love, mystical love, ecstasy and so on (Fink, 1995, p. 197).[19] Lacan references the orgasmic expression on the face of St. Theresa in Gian Lorenzo Bernini's statue of her in Rome (1999, p. 76). It is, however, not simply a question of withheld or denied orgasm because Feminine *jouissance* is on the path of ex-sistence; Lacan's way of saying that something is in the Real, outside of language (Fink, 1995, p. 25). He is pointing to something other that accounts for it; an inexpressible Other *jouissance* is attained that is both sublimated (Lacan, 1999, p. 121)[20] and desexualized or asexual (Žižek, 1996, p. 1. online pagination).[21]

Lacan agrees with Freud that sublimation is a sexual activity that is desexualized, and Lacan believes it can be defined as "the very form into which desire flows" because it can "empty itself of the sexual drive" (2019, p. 484). For him, this emptying itself of the sexual drive is a "notorious notion" (ibid.) which is hard to conceptualize given that the drive no longer includes a source, an aim or an object, instead comprising just the very nature of the libido that is invested.[22] Later in his writing, though, he advances his idea of sublimation in a way which pivots on a finely nuanced point. Accepting the premise that full satisfaction is an impossibility,[23] he nevertheless proposes an equivalence between sexual and sublimated satisfactions which takes the latter concept into terrain of particular relevance to asexuality. Describing sublimation as a satisfaction of the drive without repression, he tells his audience at the École Normale Supérieure the following:

> In other words – for the moment, I am not fucking, I am talking to you. Well! I can have exactly the same satisfaction as if I were fucking. That's what it means. Indeed it raises the question of whether in fact I am not fucking at this moment.
>
> (1977b, pp. 165–166)

The point here is that now, sublimation is being considered capable of providing a satisfaction which, for Lacan, is not a *substitute for* but *equivalent to* sexual satisfaction, dissatisfactions included, presumably, even though there is no direct sexual activity. From the perspective of asexuality, therefore, it now appears that sublimation is capable of offering a potential array of *equivalent* satisfactions from activities which are not directly sexual, including the act of thinking. Zupančič (2017, p. 1) picks up on Lacan's comments and elaborates on the paradox in his treatment of this idea. Her approach is not to explain the satisfaction he derives from talking at the École Normale Supérieure by referring to its sexual origin, which most understandings of sublimation tend to do. Rather, the satisfaction in talking is *itself* sexual, and she says we should start thinking in terms of how this satisfaction in talking, as one example of sublimation, "contains a key to sexual satisfaction" and not the other way around (ibid.).[24] To restate then, this reading moves sublimation on from a consideration of being a substitute satisfaction for an underlying desire for sexual satisfaction to, instead, being a directly sexual satisfaction for a subject who does not experience Other-directed sexual desire. This broadens both an understanding of what might constitute the sexual and also the libidinal satisfactions available to asexuality as a sexual orientation. This approach allows asexuality, as I have been theorizing it, greater scope on the Woman's side of Lacan's *Formulae* where sublimation, now understood as equivalence, might allow a subject who has annulled the phallus access to an asexual *jouissance*.

Asexuality and the Place of the Exception

On the Man side of the *Formulae*, the traditional reading of Lacan's theory is that non-phallic *jouissance* is nowhere to be found. There are only two positions here, as with the Woman's side, that of "all men" who are phallically enjoying subjects but symbolically castrated and, therefore, subject to the incest taboo and the law of the Father. This ensures that their sexual desire is exogenous (i.e., directed outside the family of origin). The only other position is that of the exception which founds the general rule of castration for all men, and here, the same rules do not apply because he is, in contrast, capable of sexually (i.e., phallically) enjoying *all* women with no restrictions whatsoever.[25] Yet some theorists have suggested that this might not be the case and that, potentially, a *not* all-enjoying figure could occupy the place of exception. For example, when Fink (2002, p. 38) alternates the usual wording for this position in Lacan's *Formulae* from "there is at least one who is not subject to the phallic function" to allow it to read, instead, as "there is one who believes in a jouissance that could never come up short, a belief in another jouissance",[26] it introduces a number of things. It shifts the perspective further away from a Freudian view of castration with its threatened loss of a real object to a Lacanian one, whereby castration is a now a real operation brought about by language (Grigg, 2006, p. 58). More crucially, it disrupts the fixed correlation between the place of the exception and access to unbridled phallic pleasure and moves it to a question of whether some uniquely different pleasure is possible. In short, it introduces the possibility that the mythical Father might derive *jouissance* from something other than limitless sexual gratification of all the women.

In this regard, we find Le Gaufey pointing out that the position logically equivalent on the Man side of the *Formulae* to the asexual Feminine or Other *jouissance* on the Woman side is, in fact, this very place of the "exception" (2020, pp. 49–51, 54).[27] The latter position is formally written as $\exists x \bar{\phi} x$ and, as stated, is read as "there is at least one who is not subject to the phallic function". In Lacan's theory, this is the place where supposedly no one inhabits other than Freud's mythical figure of the Father of the primal horde, the unrestricted enjoyer of all the women, the one whose un-failing *jouissance* fills the imagination of all men who are castrated. He is the exception who grounds the rule of castration for all men. But like Fink earlier, Le Gaufey also offers an alternative perspective because in his reading of Lacan's "at-least-one", this is a figure who, in diachronic fashion, can be imagined by "all men" in different ways and at different times in history rather than as a monolithic "totemic father choosing at will from his fish pond of women" (ibid., p. 58). In fact, Le Gaufey goes on to give this position on the man's side a religious tone, which is an interesting perspective given the quasi-religious tone Lacan gives to Feminine *jouissance* on the woman side and, indeed, the religious status of Freud's King Kukulu.[28] Le Gaufey suggests that Jesus, the central figure of Christianity, could be an example of "exception-in-chief" (ibid.), and this could well be the first time an asexual presence has been associated with this position.

Considering it further, Lacan himself has a different idea of this exception to Freud and says the original father, in his reworking of the latter's primal myth through the Master discourse, is from the beginning castrated (2007, p. 101) – that is, subject to the phallic function. Drawing on Lacan's work in *L'étourdit*, Price (2015, p. 143) says the phallic function can be "flatly negated" in the position of the exception on the male side but that the "saying no" to it is a "contained act". In keeping with Lacan's view that the exception is a castrated figure, an asexual reading of this would then offer the possibility that the containment in question involves a flat rejection of the phallic signifier but an acceptance of castration via the paternal metaphor. In other words, the "at-least-one" can accommodate an exception who is castrated but not bound by a purely phallic or sexual *jouissance*. I will come back to this later, but for now, while concurring that the primal father is a castrated figure, Verhaeghe (1995, p. 90) further elaborates by saying that if we compare the Freudian primal father with the Lacanian Master signifier, S1, the difference is very clear: with Freud's version, everybody sees a sexually enjoying "elderly greybeard roving between his females". But he says, "It is very difficult to imagine this greybeard using the S1 . . . which precisely opens up *the possibility of other interpretations* of this very important function [emphasis added]" (ibid., p. 79). So while maintaining an allegiance to Freud in basing the "at least one" on the primal father, Lacan's own theory appears to offer room for a crucial digression from the Freudian reading in that, to paraphrase the former, it is in a beyond of the phallicized fantasy, in a place where it renounces the object, that a certain love can emerge (1977b, p. 276). This would require castration because any viable relating of one sex to another – the non-rapport notwithstanding – requires the intervention of the paternal metaphor (ibid.). Or as Verhaeghe (1995, p. 90) puts it, the hidden truth of the Master is that even he is divided. Rather than despotic, therefore, Lacan says the father of the myth is an idealized father (2007, pp. 100–101, 114), and as soon as he enters the field of the Master's discourse, "he is, from the origins, castrated" (ibid.).

The possibility of a non-phallically enjoying occupier of the place of the exception offers a perspective on a further paradox of this concept. Grigg, for instance, questions how, in Freud's version, the sons institute a prohibition on incest and murder due to their *love* for the primal father, the same Father who is motivated by "jealousy" and "intolerance" (2006, p. 65). How does love become their motivation after his murder? In *Seminar XXIII*, Lacan addresses the same paradox and acknowledges its "mind-boggling" aspect. He says, "The sons love the father to the very extent that they are deprived of women" (2016, p. 130). This would appear to suggest the equal possibility of a benign, asexual Father driving the maddening prohibition just as much as a malign, sexually unbounded one. Earlier, in *Seminar XVII*, we find Lacan pointing to this loving identification to a primal father who *is* love (2007, p. 100). He admits that this idea is a strange one to come out of or "survive" from Freud's myth. In his view, Freud believed that the prohibiting, jealous, despotic, all-enjoying Father would make religion evaporate, but in fact, his "strangely composed myth" (ibid., p. 101) produces the very father that ensures it will survive. It is out of the love for, and quite possibly love from, this father that a subsequent structural order evolves. Behind these contradictions, Lacan finds it "strange" that Freud preserves, without realizing it, an all-loving father (ibid.). Grigg (2006, p. 66) probes further when he says the "forced abstinence" of the sons produces an emotional tie with the father that runs counter to what we should expect. His explanation links the father of the myth to obsessional neurosis so that we get an all-depriving but equally all-loving father, an object of *hainamoration*, Lacan's term for Freudian ambivalence in which love is partnered with hate (ibid.). But if we take into account the various questions already raised, then another possible explanation is that a non-phallically enjoying Father of the horde deprived the sons of the women for an entirely different set of reasons. So in the same way that we considered an alternative possibility of an asexual in the place of exception, we can also consider the possibility of an asexual Father of the primal horde. Whatever the implications for Freud's myth, or for Lacan's *Formulae*, it nevertheless allows for a different interpretation of the "at-least-one" and opens the possibility of a non-pathological asexuality available to both sexuated positions of man and woman. Any addition to the man side, such as the one proposed, still supports the concept of exception which is necessary to ground the rule for "all men" to phallically enjoy. It also suggests that at the centre of Lacanian sexual theory, there is potential for asexuality to be represented.

Revisiting Asexuality and Hysteria

The question of whether asexuality is a form of hysteria was considered earlier, but it is important to revisit this question from a Lacanian perspective because, since Freud, ordinary hysteria is now considered to have no symptoms (Wajcman, 2003, p. 5).[29] It is not the hysteria of Lacan's period up to the late 1950s where it was considered as imaginary inversion, the paradigmatic example of which was Dora's masculine identifications in Freud's (1905) case study. But rather, it is the hysteria Lacan spoke about from 1960 onward, after the introduction of the *objet petit a* and the phantasy (Palomera, 2012, online pagination, p. 7). The hysteric's position, whether man or woman, is to refuse phallic *jouissance*, particularly the Other's, and yet at the same time to be the cause of the desire of the Other. We find this, for example, in some sexual-with-asexual marriages whereby the asexual partner encourages the non-asexual partner to engage sexually with a substitute (De Paulo, 2011, see note 3). What is involved in hysteria is, "to be the lack of desire, to be the nothing of desire", as Palomera puts it (2012, p. 9), and this, it could also be argued, is similar to the asexual position in relation to the Other. But while hysteria's identification with the lack of desire resonates with asexuality, the self-defined asexual does not transform this lack or void into the hysteric's question of "Am I a man or a woman?" I am proposing that this is because the symbolic register has provided self-defined asexuality with an answer in the form of the signifier "asexual", thereby producing a qualitatively different relation to lack.

Hysteria, as Lacanian theory understands it, refuses the Master or the Master signifier, written as S1, which can be read as anything the Master's discourse designates as an answer to hysteria's question. Self-defined asexuality, in contrast, embraces its Master signifier of "non-sexually desiring", and its S1 is clearly denoting "no sexual desire". As Guéguen (1992, p. 72) points out, phantasy in its role as support for desire "shows up whenever the unfolding of the signifying chain comes to a dead end, comes to a kind of breach in its development". The signifying chain, historically, has not provided asexuality with a signifier to cover the gap in cultural discourse until relatively recently. As Decker (2014, p. 92) puts it, "If people are confused by asexuality, it's unlikely that it's because of the word". By this I understand her to mean that behind the relatively new signifier "asexuality", there is the *concept* asexuality which is capable of evoking an estranged and destabilizing response among sexually desiring subjects. It could be argued, therefore, that the destabilizing and newly emerged signifier "asexual" has arrived at a moment in history when the signifying chain had reached a dead end for asexual subjects. From another perspective, Vanheule (2016, p. 3) says that hysteria, as the active formulation of complaints, involves the search for an Other who is presumed to have an answer. Asexuality is not characterized by the active formulation of complaints, aside from its quest for discursive inclusion and societal recognition. Furthermore, if its antipathy to psychoanalysis indicates anything,[30] it not only signals a mistrust and scepticism for a Master discourse but also suggests that, once self-identification has taken place, it is not in search of an Other who is presumed to have an answer. Therefore, if we accept that in the sphere of social relations "discourse unfolds when someone forges a position in relation to another" (ibid., p. 4), then asexuality has created a discourse with society at large by announcing its presence, by forming online and offline communities and, subjectively, by having a direct engagement with the absence of sexual attraction at the heart of its orientation. Is there a case to be made that this approaches similar territory to that which Lacan once designated for himself when he said, "When all is said and done, I am a perfect hysteric, namely, symptomless"? (1976–1977, session of 14 December 1976, p. 16). If the notion of perfection is too parodic to be applicable in terms of either Lacan or asexuality, then his view that the hysterics of old are gone and have instead been subsumed into the social framework might be more apt (1977c, p. 5).

The symptoms of hysteria, if they are manifest, speak to the Other and demand answers in the form of knowledge, but at the same time, hysteria is a riddle, and no answer will ever be sufficient. Self-defined asexuality, in contrast, by-passes the Other and provides an answer to the question of "who or what am I?" It subjectifies the lack rather than objectifies it and, once self-definition has taken place, states that "this (version of lack) is what I am", as opposed to the hysteric's metonymic question of "what (version of lack) am I?"[31] Asexuality, like hysteria, *does* have questions about its lack which are "located at the level of the Other" (Lacan, 1993, p. 170), particularly in the stages before self-definition takes place (Carrigan, 2011, p. 471). However, I will propose in Chapter 6 that asexuals do not

find their place in a pre-existing and "preformed symbolic apparatus that insti-
tutes the law in sexuality" in the same way as sexually desiring subjects do, as
Lacan suggests, but instead realize their sexuality by creating something new "on
the symbolic plane" (1993, p. 170). In a sense, asexuality could be considered a
veiled response to the enigmatic but ultimately dependent position of hysteria
down the centuries which, similarly, has a "radically ambiguous relationship with
the other", whereby hysteria supports the Other "while constantly interpellating
it" (Gherovici, 2014, p. 66). In this regard, it is often asked why asexuality has
made its appearance at this particular time in history. It would be convenient to
view asexuality as a newly evolved version of hysteria which forecloses on the
sexual demand of the small other while, at the same time, questioning the master
position of a big Other whose understanding of it is impeded by hegemonic eroto-
normative discourses. If hysteria is a demand directed to the Other for answers
that are metonymically inadequate, asexuality is only tangentially so because it
directs this demand to itself and provides its own answer. The answer is not sought
in the Other or in psychoanalysis, and this, I am proposing, generates a very different position compared to hysteria in terms of both asexual desire and the phantasy which supports it.

For Gherovici (ibid., p. 63), if the hysteric is defined as someone who cannot
determine his or her *objet petit a* and who is always questioning whom she or
he is loving, then hysteria "unveils the very structure of human sexuality". I am
proposing that asexuality should also be considered an element of the structure
of human sexuality but one where an *objet petit a* is established, where desire is
possible and where *jouissance* is derived from a "savoured absence". Gherovici
points out that Lacan in *Seminar V* works with a definition of hysteria that takes
on an extended social sense which exceeds the confines of neurosis, to include a
dimension that is latent in all speaking beings as long as they question their desire.
"That desire can be a source of perpetual questioning is the natural consequence
of the alienation introduced by speech – the speech of hysterics and non-hysterics
alike", she says (ibid., p. 62). This is particularly so in relation to the limits of
speech in signifying the enigma and trauma of the Real of human sexuality. As
Salecl (2000, p. 2) puts it, sexual difference is the name of a deadlock, a trauma
that resists every attempt at its symbolization. Hysteria, according to Soler (1992,
p. 30), is "tempted by sacrifice" in order to keep desire unsatisfied and, in this
way, the subject's desire as the desire of the Other is sustained. Asexuality, in
contrast, subjectivizes lack in order that a desire for no sexual desire of the Other
is sustained. Rather than a form of hysteria, I am proposing that asexuality can be
represented in the various structures of neurosis, psychosis and perversion, just
as sexuality can and which, for Lacan, can also carry "symptomatic sediments"
(1966–1967, sessions of 22 February 1967, p. 7., and 10 May 1967, p. 10). Non-
asexual forms of sexuality only fall under the different diagnostic structures once
their symptomatology in relation to castration and the organization of *jouissance*
is determined. If structure does not define sexuality, then it does not define asexuality since, like heterosexual and LGBTQIA+ orientations, asexuality, while it

may also have symptomatic sediments, is a unique positioning of the subject in relation to castration, *jouissance* and the Real of the drive.

Asexuality's Distinct Desire

Asexuality's desire is distinct from hysteria's desire for an unsatisfied desire, as seen in Freud's case study of Dora, in his interpretation of the dream of the Witty Butcher's Wife and in Lacan's writing about medieval Courtly Love. In the case of the Witty Butcher's Wife, she desires for an indefinitely deferred thing (1900, pp. 147–148). This, in turn, is based on a hysterical identification with her female friend who desires salmon but does not allow herself to have it (Soler, 1992, p. 19). Both the desire for salmon and the unfulfilled desire for caviar indicate the desire for an unsatisfied desire (ibid.). Her desire for caviar in real life is the thing that is absent in her dream, and as Lacan says, the signifier of her unsatisfied desire *is* her desire for caviar (1977a, p. 285). Dora was also, at some level, aware that a desire was being kept at bay. According to Voruz (1999, online pagination, p. 4), her phantasy is one in which she can see herself as the object of desire, a desire she sustains as unsatisfied. It is a position that is essentially beyond demand and sexual satisfaction (ibid.). According to Lacan, "the problem of her condition is fundamentally that of accepting herself as the object of desire for the man, and this is for Dora the mystery which motivates her idolatry for Frau K" (1982, p. 68). But when Herr K in the scene by the lake punctures the phantasy by alluding to Dora as a sexual object, everything changes. She no longer sees herself as identified with the object cause of desire but instead as the object of *jouissance* for Herr K and as an object of exchange between him and her father. In contrast to asexuality, Dora is refusing something that is ever-present for her; she reads books about it; she keeps out of the way of it when Frau K and her father are together; she is daily reminded of it by the flowers and gifts Herr K sends her. In this sense, Dora is libidinally orientated. She is in a position of desiring, and of being desired, while remaining protected from the threat of desire ever being satisfied; a classic hysterical position. Dora's symptoms, in Freud's terms, are a communication of the conflict between a repudiation of her sexuality and its attempt at recognition (1905, p. 88). Even if her desire was not for the person Freud thought, she has an active, if unsatisfied, sexually orientated desire.

In Lacan's reflections on Courtly Love, we see something similar. This was a practice in the Middle Ages across Europe which allowed ladies of the court, especially those in loveless, pre-arranged marriages, to engage in romantic relationships with honourable knights, provided that strict rules of fidelity and chastity were observed. It had an unusual aspect to it in the sense that, in Lacan's reading of the poets of the time, the Lady was an intimidating object, often cold, terrifying and inhuman. From a psychoanalytic point of view, the Lady is both the object of desire and the obstacle to its fulfilment. Like Dora, but perhaps even more obviously, Courtly Love's relation to sexual desire is clearly visible through the techniques of "holding back, suspension, and *amor interuptus*" which belong, as Lacan says, to the sphere of foreplay (1992, p. 152). They signify a desiring intent behind the postponement. A heightened desire is operating around the Lady whose function as vacuole, or empty space, is the very object around which the detour of desire is organized. That is Lacan's point, mentioned earlier, when he says that in sublimation, the object is raised to the "dignity of the Thing" (ibid., p. 112).

These examples which Lacan highlights in various parts of his theory illustrate the existence of a sexual desire which must be refused and/or repressed, a desire manifest in the signifiers that come to represent it and a desire which must remain unsatisfied as a prerequisite for desire itself. In Chapter 6, I will be proposing that asexuality is a distinct sexual orientation which differs markedly from this. The asexual subject, like the non-asexual subject, is libidinally desiring but functioning in a qualitatively different way. Lacan in *Seminar V* refers to the "hysteria latent in every kind of human being in the world" (2017, p. 441). He says this is because all speaking subjects are constituted by the desire of the Other's desire. But while hysterics led Freud to develop psychoanalysis, they were simultaneously seeking to prove the inadequacy of his knowledge. As such, they posed a limit to the very knowledge from which they were at the same time demanding answers, in a dialectic in which absolute knowledge would always remain elusive. Again, it could be argued that asexuality occupies a similar but not identical position in that, like hysteria, it confounds existing knowledge. Fink (1995, p. 134) references the Heisenberg uncertainty principle in quantum mechanics which states that there is a fundamental limit to the precision with which physical properties of a particle can be known.[32] In 1927, he points out, this shocked the physics world because it posits something that cannot be known and is impossible to know. In terms of Lacanian theory, impossibility is related to the Real, and it is the *objet petit a* (ibid.). In Lacan's writing of the hysteric's discourse, the *objet petit a* is in the position of truth in the Real which means it is outside of language. In essence, it is a truth that is governed "by that which does not work, by that which does not fit" (ibid., p. 135). The point here for asexuality is that its desire is also supported by a phantasy whose *objet petit a* is in the Real and is beyond the signifying chain. It is so because it originates in a primal, erogenous experience of the first Other as omnipotent and traumatic. This traumatic inflection associated with the infantile sexual Real in relation to the first Other transfigures the dyadic foundations of the dialectic of need, demand and desire. It becomes, as can be found in mathematics, a unary operation of annulment with only one operand or single input which, I am proposing, becomes the dominant tendency in the libidinal relation to the symbolic object starting at the oral phase. If this proposition holds, then, sexual desire for the asexual is potentially delimited from its very beginning by the elision of the libidinal element of the part-objects that come to represent the relation of subject to Other. This, then, leads to the question of what psychical mechanism could bring about such an elision of the libidinal element.

A Consideration of Annulment

For Lacan, the main purpose of refusal at the oral stage and the subsequent reversal of dependence is about the object as symbolic object of the subject-Other dialectic which appears, as he says clearly, under the sign of the nothing (2020, p. 179). As mentioned in Chapter 4, he identifies the mechanism which brings this refusal about when he says that it is with regard to the "annulled object *qua* symbolic" that the child puts his dependency on the mother in check by feeding on nothing (ibid.). This mechanism of annulment during infantile sexuality, therefore, offers scope in approaching the foundations of asexuality's lack of sexual attraction to the Other. Lacan uses Freud's term, *Versagung*, when discussing annulment, and he is cognisant of the word's meaning as frustration, not simply from being denied satisfaction but also from denying oneself something. Lacan describes it as "the notion of reneging, in the sense one says *to renege a treaty* [emphasis in original], to withdraw from an engagement" (ibid., p. 172). Freud, for his part, writes about *Versagung* as a prohibition of one kind or another which brings about frustration which then leads to privation or the experience of being without the object of satisfaction (1927, p. 10). Offering a possible link between the two perspectives, Laplanche and Pontalis point out that Freud's conception of *Versagung* includes a refusal as much by the child as by the mother, and they point out that *Versagung* as frustration not only designates an empirical fact but also designates a "relation implying refusal . . . on the part of the agent". They see *Versagung*, then, as a frustration that includes an *active* sense, and they define the word as a "condition of the subject who is denied, *or who denies himself*, the satisfaction of an instinctual demand" [emphasis added]. While the translation as "frustration" implies the subject is "passively" frustrated, *Versagung* "in no way lays down *who* does the refusing" [emphasis in original] (1973, p. 175). Lacan, for his part, makes the following observation:

> I'm saying that any satisfaction that is in question in frustration arises there against the backdrop of the fundamentally disappointing character of the symbolic order. Here, satisfaction is a mere substitute, a compensation. The child quashes, as it were, the disappointing aspect of this symbolic interplay by orally seizing the object of satisfaction, the breast in this instance.
>
> (2020, p. 175)

At about this time, Lacan in his writing also refers to a crushing, this time of the satisfactions of bodily need which are achieved through the child's demand (2006, p. 580). He explains that this crushing takes place because the satisfactions which the infant's demand obtains do not satisfy the "proof of love" into which the demand for satisfaction has been "transmuted" (ibid.). This idea of the child crushing what is disappointing is coterminous with the conception of *Versagung* under consideration. It can be seen, therefore, that refusal is thinkable on both sides of the mother-child dyad but that the contingent, often accidental delay which is perceived as refusal on the mother's side to offer the gift of the breast at the precise moment it is demanded might be considered a primary refusal. The frustration that this gives rise to in the child then produces a secondary refusal whereby the gift of the breast is refused, in the sense of the child crushing what is disappointing in the experience (i.e., it did not satisfy the "proof of love"). In this sense, then, frustration is not just the refusal of an object of satisfaction but is also the refusal of a gift. According to Lacan (2020, p. 174):

> The gift arises from a zone that lies beyond the object relation, precisely because it presupposes behind it the full order of exchange that the child has entered, and it can arise from this beyond-zone only with the character that constitutes it as specifically symbolic.

The refusal of the gift for the child is the experience of frustration thinkable only as the perceived refusal by the mother to provide the gift as symbol of love (2020, p. 173). It is at this point in Lacan's account that the nothing enters in the context of the gift – that is, mother's reply to its call when the object of satisfaction is *not* there (ibid., p. 175). When it *is* there, the object appears "only as the sign of the gift" and, as the object of satisfaction, is nothing. "It is there precisely to be pushed away in so far as it is this nothing", he says (ibid.). He will go on to say that against this "background of revocation", the gift as sign of love is given or not given in reply to the call (ibid., p. 174). This "symbolic game" has a fundamentally disappointing character but is, nevertheless, the manner in which he believes satisfaction takes on its meaning (ibid., p. 175). I am proposing that the pre-Oedipal choice of *Versagung* or annulment as it arises in the fundamentally disappointing symbolic game theorized for all subjects is formative in designating the asexual subject position with regard to a foundational desexualization that then transmits through subsequent phases of libidinal engagement with the Other. It is a choice to say no to a libidinally infused experience which has been encountered as frustrating, disappointing and traumatic. This choice is one which essentially responds to a negatively experienced encounter and seeks to turn it into a positive one. It is taking place at the level of the unconscious and is being theorized as a legitimate choice in response to unpleasurable libidinal excitations experienced in relation to the Other. As Leader (2012, pp. 79–81) says, without refusal, there is assimilation to the Other's demand which effectively negates the subject. So if this mechanism of annulment is taken into account, it allows for a further consideration of what kind of *jouissance* is available to a subject who makes this choice. In Chapter 6, I will address this question by outlining how the asexual can potentially derive a *jouissance* that is both non-phallic and asymptomatic.

Notes

1 A survey respondent says, "I am not at all interested in sex. It doesn't disgust me or bother me . . . it just doesn't register". Another says, "I identify as asexual because

I do not get the urge to have sex. If I do have sex, I only like it for the first minute or so, and then I am satisfied and would like to stop. Basically, sex is not necessary in my life and I could live without it. There are other things I would rather do" (Carrigan, 2011, p. 467).

2 Philosopher and Lacanian theorist Joan Copjec writes that sex and the sexual serve no other purpose than to remove the subject from, inter alia, "the realm of pure understanding". She says, "sex, in opposing itself to sense, is also, by definition, opposed to relation, to communication" (2015, p. 207). See also Alenka Zupančič (2017, p. 22) who says, "there is no doubt sex exists" but what seems to be missing is the "idea of sex, its essence". She says the sexual, therefore, is an "absence" which curves and defines the space of the sexual with consequences for the field structured around it.

3 These vanishing points occur when the experience of the Other's desire is either overwhelming, puzzling, enigmatic or unpleasurable, requiring the subject to rely for support as to how they can position themselves in relation to this desire through unconscious phantasy.

4 The concept of an asexual *jouissance* is one that Lacan's theory includes when he discusses Feminine *Jouissance*, and I will explore this later. Yet when he refers to Kierkegaard's giving up of physical love for his paramour Regine Schegel (née Olsen) in return for a religious life of spiritual/mystical love, rather than positing the *objet petit a* as a void which causes a desire for no sexual desire, he refers to Kierkegaard's new desire as a desire for a good, "that is not caused by a little a" (Lacan, 1999, p. 77).

5 Here, Verhaeghe says the fear of disappearing in the enjoyment of the Other, and the anxiety which accompanies it, is the original threat which emanates from the mother as "the first great Other".

6 Here, Hook says, "At this bodily and egocentric stage of life, the most important focus of pleasure and identity . . . is that which psychoanalysts refer to as *the phallus*. What this means, therefore, is that the child both wishes to have and possess – and here we are looking forward to what Lacan will add to the theory – and to *be* the phallus for her. This is the child's unconscious fantasy: that it will be the phallus which epitomises the mother's desire" (ibid., p. 55).

7 For an example, see Verhaeghe, 2005, pp. 8–9, online pagination.

8 Leader (2021, pp. 79–81) links refusal *of* the Other with an attempt at separation *from* the Other.

9 "In his relation to his mother (Little) Hans sees the phallus as being at the centre of her desire, and he takes up different positions in order to attract and captivate this desire. He tries to imagine himself as she imagines him and guesses at her imagined world in order to become perfectly identified with her object. Correlatively, she is for him a phallic mother" (Gallagher, 1998, p. 121).

10 The Father's no of the incest taboo.

11 Lacan's uses these terms in his 1949 paper on The Mirror Stage (2006, p. 78).

12 Przybylo (2019, p. 22) theorizes a form of substantive asexual intimacy "that is not reliant only on sex or sexuality for meaning".

13 In this regard, Lacan's original matheme for the fundamental phantasy of sexually desiring subjects could be written for asexuality as $ \$ \lozenge a^0 $, the barred Subject in relation to the *objet petit a* as cause of desire for no sexual desire.

14 Within asexual writing, we can find a similar concept. Przybylo (2014, p. 230) says, "to understand oneself as inhabiting a sexual identity category of asexuality is to understand an absence of sexual interest as integral to the self. In other words, not being interested in sex or having no sexual attraction or sexual desire becomes sedimented into a *sexual identity* in a way it never has before historically".

15 For Fink (1995, p. 120), Lacan's other *jouissance* is an "asexual jouissance" (i.e., the carrier of libido while at the same time deriving pleasure from non-sexual activity).

16 "Sexuation" is Lacan's term by which man and woman identify themselves as sexed beings on the basis of their respective modes of *jouissance* (See Lacan's *Formulae*, 1999, p. 78; Fink, 2002, p. 36 ff.; Soler, 2000, p. 41).

17 The concept that defines man's or woman's sexuation is not biology or society but rather his or her relation to the phallus as signifier and to the *objet petit a* as object cause of desire. Men are wholly under the phallic function apart from one mythic exception, and their *jouissance* aims at the *objet petit a* as it is represented in a partner. Women are not wholly under the phallic function and can also experience a *jouissance* that is non-phallic or asexual.

18 Men pursue a phallic or sexual *jouissance* through the *objet petit a* located in their partner by way of compensating for the lack installed at castration. This male phallic position is written as $\forall x \phi x$ and is read as "all men are subject to the phallic function".

19 "And why not interpret one face of the Other, the God face, as based on feminine jouis-sance?" (Lacan, 1999, p. 77).

20 This is the same *Seminar* in which he questions the "very existence of frigidity" (Morel, 2002, p. 83), calling it "putative" and "notorious" in reference to its historical antecedents (Lacan, 1999, pp. 74–75).

21 Žižek says, "love is here no longer merely a narcissistic (mis)recognition to be opposed to desire as the subject's 'truth' but a unique case of direct asexual sublimation (inte-gration into the order of the signifier) of drives, of their jouissance, in the guise of the asexual Thing (music, religion, etc.) experienced in the ecstatic surrender".

22 Laplanche and Pontalis (1973, p. 433) are of the view that Freud left the theory of sub-limation in such a primitive state that "the dividing-lines" between it and the pro-cesses, such as reaction-formation, aim-inhibition, idealization and repression, remain vague. In Freud's own conception of sublimation, it is a limited solution, as outlined in Chapter 2.

23 Fink (1995, p. 115) sees sublimation as offering a *real* non-phallic satisfaction, but he says that full satisfaction of a sublimated sexual drive might be an impossibility. Here, sublimation is theorized in the Freudian sense of a substitute, albeit real, satisfaction for the sexual drive.

24 This perspective resonates with the "asexual erotics" concept of Ela Przybylo which I will elaborate on later.

25 The fictional libertine Don Juan and the historical adventurer and womaniser Giacomo Casanova are relatively modern examples of this concept which has its roots in Freud's theory of the primal horde (1913 [1912–1913], pp. 141–146).

26 For Lacan, phallic *jouissance* as sexual *jouissance* of the organ is a *jouissance* that fails (1999, pp. 58–59), one that is never enough and that keeps man, in particular, tied to his *objet petit a* rather than their real partner (ibid., p. 80, 86).

27 A view that Fink (1995) shares, see p. 113 and note 3, p. 194.

28 In *Totem and Taboo*, Freud cites an example of a tribal king in Lower Guinea, West Africa, who lives alone in a wood, celibate and removed from contact with the women of his tribe because of the dangerous exalted power he represents. King Kukulu is not just a chief or king, he is also a priest as well as an exception but, significantly, not one who enjoys all the women (1913, p. 45, 125).

29 Wajcman says, "Normal hysteria has no symptoms and is an essential characteristic of the speaking subject" (ibid.).

30 For examples of this, see the comments in the online discussion forum at www.asexuality.org/en/topic/56290-what-would-freud-make-of-asexuals-and-asexuality/ [Accessed 29 November 2021].

31 Edelman (2004, pp. 113–115) uses the neologism "sinthomosexual" to link Lacan's *jouissance* with a homosexuality that figures the lack in Symbolic meaning-production around Other-directed sexuality. The sinthomosexual, he says, affirms this lack/loss and maintains it as an empty space, vacuole, at the heart of the Symbolic.

32 If a particle's position is known, its momentum cannot be known at the same time and vice versa. Nor can this be subject to observable verification.

References

Barnard, S. (2002) 'Tongues of angels: Feminine structure and other jouissance', in Barnard, S. and Fink, B. (eds.), *Reading seminar XX, Lacan's major work on love, knowledge, and feminine sexuality*. Albany: State University of New York Press, pp. 171–185.

Brotto, L. A., Knudson, G., Inskip, J., Rhodes, K. and Erskine, Y. (2010) 'Asexuality: A mixed-methods approach', *Archives of Sexual Behavior*, 39(3), pp. 599–618.

Carrigan, M. (2011) 'There's more to life than sex? Difference and commonality within the asexual community', *Sexualities*, 14(4), pp. 462–478.

Copjec, J. (2015) *Read my desire: Lacan against the historicists*. New York: Verso.

De Paulo, B. (2011) 'Keeping marriage alive with affairs, asexuality, polyamory, and living apart', *Psychology Today Blog*, 2 June. Available at: www.psychologytoday.com/blog/living-single/201106/keeping-marriage-alive-affairs-asexuality-polyamory-and-living-apart [Accessed 29 November 2021].

Decker, J. S. (2014) *The invisible orientation, An introduction to asexuality*. New York: Skyhorse Publishing.

Edelman, L. (2004) *No future – Queer theory and the death drive*. London: Duke University Press.

Fink, B. (1995) *The Lacanian subject – Between language and jouissance*. Princeton, NJ: Princeton University Press.

Fink, B. (2002) 'Knowledge and jouissance', in Barnard, S. and Fink, B. (eds.), *Reading seminar XX, Lacan's major work on love, knowledge and feminine sexuality*. Albany: State University of New York Press, pp. 21–45.

Freud, S. (1900) *The interpretation of dreams*, Standard Editions IV and V. London: Vintage/Hogarth.

Freud, S. (1905) 'Fragment of an analysis of a case of hysteria', in *A case of hysteria, three essays on sexuality and other works*, Standard Edition VII. London: Vintage/Hogarth.

Freud, S. (1913 [1912–1913]) 'Totem and taboo', in *Totem and taboo and other works*, Standard Edition XIII. London: Vintage/Hogarth.

Freud, S. (1927) 'The future of an illusion', in *The future of an illusion, civilization and its discontents and other works*, Standard Edition XXI. London: Vintage/Hogarth.

Gallagher, C. (1998) 'Lacan for beginners, Dora and Little Hans', *The Letter*, Irish Journal for Lacanian Psychoanalysis, 13, Summer, The School of Psychotherapy, St. Vincent's University Hospital, Elm Park, Dublin 4, Ireland, pp. 117–124.

Gherovici, P. (2014) 'Where have the hysterics gone? Lacan's reinvention of hysteria', *ESC*, 40(1), March, pp. 47–70. Available at: ojsadmin,+Journal+manager,+ESC+40.1+Gherovici (6).pdf [Accessed 29 November 2021].

Grigg, R. (2006) 'Beyond the Oedipus complex', in Clemens, J. and Grigg, R. (eds.), *Jacques Lacan and the other side of psychoanalysis: Reflections on Seminar XVII*. Durham, NC: Duke University Press, pp. 50–68.

Guéguen, P.-G. (1992) 'On fantasy: Lacan and Klein', *The Newsletter of the Freudian Field (NFF)*, 6(1 & 2), Spring/Fall, pp. 67–75.

Hook, D. (2006) 'Lacan, the meaning of the phallus and the 'sexed' subject', in Shefer, T., Boonzaier, F. and Kiguwa, P. (eds.), *The gender of psychology*. Lansdowne, South Africa: Juta Academic Publishing, pp. 49–84.

Lacan, J. (1966–1967) *The logic of phantasy*, Seminar XIV, unpublished (Gallagher, C., trans). Available at: www.lacaninireland.com [Accessed 21 November 2021].

Lacan, J. (1976–1977) *L'insu que sait de l'une-bévue s'aile à mourre*, Seminar XXIV, unpublished (Gallagher, C., trans). Available at: www.lacaninireland.com [Accessed 29 November 2021].

Lacan, J. (1977a [1953]) *Écrits: A selection* (Sheridan, A., trans). London: Tavistock Publications.

Lacan, J. (1977b [1964]) *The four fundamental concepts of psycho-analysis*, Seminar XI (Miller, J-A., ed.) (Sheridan, A., trans). London: Penguin.

Lacan, J. (1977c) 'Propos sur l'hysterie' ('Remarks on hysteria [Lacan in Brussels]'), *Quarto*, 2, pp. 5–10.

Lacan, J. (1982 [1951]) 'Intervention on transference', in Mitchell, J. and Rose, J. (eds.), *Feminine sexuality*. New York: Norton.

Lacan, J. (1992 [1959–1960]) *The ethics of psychoanalysis*, Seminar VII (Miller, J.-A., ed.) (Porter, D., trans). London: Routledge.

Lacan, J. (1993 [1955–1956]) *The psychoses*, Seminar III (Miller, J.-A., ed.) (Grigg, R., trans). New York: Norton.

Lacan, J. (1999 [1972–1973]) *Encore*. Seminar XX (Miller, J.-A., ed.) (Fink, B., trans). New York: Norton.

Lacan, J. (2006 [1966]) *Écrits – The first complete English edition* (Fink, B., trans). New York: W. W. Norton.

Lacan, J. (2007 [1969–1970]) *The other side of psychoanalysis*, Seminar XVII (Miller, J.-A., ed.) (Grigg, R., trans). New York: Norton.

Lacan, J. (2017 [1957–1958]) *Formations of the unconscious*, Seminar V (Miller, J.-A., ed.) (Grigg, R., trans). Cambridge: Polity Press.

Lacan, J. (2019 [1958–1959]) *Desire and its interpretation*, Seminar VI (Miller, J.-A., ed.) (Fink, B., trans). Cambridge: Polity Press.

Lacan, J. (2020 [1956–1957]) *The object relation*, Seminar IV (Miller, J.-A. ed.) (Price, A. R., trans). Cambridge: Polity Press.

Laplanche, J. and Pontalis, J. B. (1973) *The language of psycho-analysis* (Nicholson-Smith, D., trans). London: Hogarth Press/Institute of Psycho-Analysis.

Leader, D. (2012) *What is madness*. London: Penguin.

Le Gaufey, G. (2020 [2006]) *Lacan and the formulae of sexuation – Exploring logical consistency and clinical consequences* (Gallagher, C., trans). Oxfordshire: Routledge.

Morel, G. (2002) 'Feminine conditions of jouissance', in Barnard, S. and Fink, B. (eds.), *Reading seminar XX: Lacan's major work on love, knowledge and feminine sexuality*. Albany, NY: Suny Press, pp. 77–92.

O'Donnell, B. (2008) 'We're married, we just don't have sex', *The Guardian*, 8 September. Available at: www.guardian.co.uk/lifeandstyle/2008/sep/08/relationships.healthand wellbeing [Accessed 4 November 2021].

Palomera, V. (2012) 'The ethics of hysteria & psychoanalysis', *The Symptom*, Summer, 13. Available at: www.lacan.com/symptom13/the-ethics.html [Accessed 29 November 2021].

Price, A. R. (2015) 'I start off from the limit', *Lacunae*, APPI International Journal for Lacanian Psychoanalysis (11), November 2015, pp. 131–164.

Przybylo, E. (2014) 'Masculine doubt and sexual wonder: Asexually-identified men talk about their (a)sexualities', in Cerankowski, K. J. and Milks, M. (eds.), *Asexualities – Feminist and queer perspectives*. New York: Routledge, pp. 225–224.

Przybylo, E. (2019) *Asexual erotics: Intimate readings of compulsory sexuality*. Columbus, OH: Ohio State University Press.

Salecl, R. (2000) 'Introduction', in Salecl, R. (ed.), *Sexuation*, SIC Vol. 3. London: Duke University Press, pp. 1–9.

Scherrer, K. S. (2008) 'Coming to an asexual identity: Negotiating identity, negotiating desire', *Sexualities*, 11(5), 1 October, pp. 621–641.

Soler, C. (1992) 'History and hysteria: The witty butcher's wife', *Newsletter of the Freudian Field (NFF)*, 6(1 & 2), Spring/Fall, pp. 16–33.

Soler, C. (2000) 'The curse on sex', in Salecl, R. (ed.), *Sexuation*, SIC Vol. 3. London: Duke University Press, pp. 39–53.

Vanheule, S. (2016) 'Capitalist discourse, subjectivity and Lacanian psychoanalysis', *Frontiers in Psychology*, 7, December, Article 1948, pp. 1–14 online pagination.

Verhaeghe, P. (1995) 'From impossibility to inability: Lacan's theory on the four discourses', *The Letter*, Irish Journal for Lacanian Psychoanalysis, 3 (Spring), pp. 76–99.

Verhaeghe, P. (2001) *Beyond gender – From subject to drive*. New York: Other Press.

Verhaeghe, P. (2005) 'Sexuality in the formation of the subject', *Psychoanalyse. Aesthetik. Kulturkritik.*, 25, Heft 3/05, Passagen Verlag, Wien, pp. 33–53.

Voruz, V. (1999) 'The scene by the lake: When desire fails as defence', *Psychoanalytical Notebooks*, 3, London Society of the New Lacanian School. Available at: Voruz-Veronique_The-Scene-by-the-Lake.pdf (londonsociety-nls.org.uk) [Accessed 30 November 2021].

Wajcman, G. (2003) 'The hysteric's discourse', *The Symptom* (4), Spring. Available at: www.lacan.com/hystericdiscf.htm [Accessed 19 November 2021].

Žižek, S. (1996) *Love beyond law*. Available at: www.lacan.com/zizlola.htm [Accessed 17 November 2021].

Zupančič, A. (2017) *What is sex?* Cambridge, MA: MIT Press.

Chapter 6

Asexual *Jouissance* and the Lacanian *Sinthome*

Up to now, I have used the term "annulment" to build an understanding of the aetiology of this unqualified lack of sexual desire, in keeping with Lacan's use of the term from *Seminar IV*. However, the absolute nature of the unconscious elision of sexual desire in asexuality, even among asexuals who engage sexually with a partner, suggests that something unconditional is taking place. On this basis, it is necessary to consider the possibility that the term "foreclosure" may be more appropriate to describe the mechanism responsible for what happens when the position of Imaginary phallus is rejected. In considering the term "foreclosure", which is the translation of *Verwerfung* that Lacan suggests,[1] it might also be useful to bear in mind his earliest translation of *Verwerfung* as a "rejecting intention",[2] given that the hypothesized foreclosure in question is taking place at a pre-Oedipal stage.[3]

When the term "foreclosure" is introduced into a consideration of the aetiology of asexuality, it raises the question of psychosis. It has been a long-held precept of Lacanian theory that psychotic structure is determined by the foreclosure of the signifier of the Name-of-the-Father as agent of castration. As Grigg (2017, p. 48) points out, Lacan introduces the term "foreclosure" to explain the massive and global differences between neurosis and psychosis. This use of foreclosure in designating psychosis refers to the Name-of-the-Father which acts to symbolically castrate/negate the subject as Imaginary phallus of the mother and, in turn, castrates the Imaginary phallus that the child represents for the mother (Moncayo, 2017, pp. 5–6). Lacanian theory proposes that without this, separation psychosis ensues, and Fink (1999, p. 76) encapsulates this when he says, "foreclosure is the cause of psychosis. It is not simply associated with psychosis; it is constitutive of psychosis".

A consequence of foreclosure of the Name-of-the-Father is that metaphoric processes that determine the subject remain fundamentally unstable (Vanheule, 2011, p. 79). This symbiotic relation of foreclosure and psychosis stems from Lacan's early position in *Seminar III* and in his paper of the same period, *On a question prior to any possible treatment of psychosis*. In *Seminar III*, for example, his view is that everything that takes place in psychosis is a question of the subject's access to this signifier, or rather "the impossibility of that access" (Lacan,

DOI: 10.4324/9781003214946-7

1993, p. 321). "It can thus happen that something primordial regarding the subject's being does not enter into symbolization and is not repressed, but rejected", he says (ibid., p. 81). The Name-of-the-Father is the essential signifier on which he centres his theory of psychosis (Lacan, 2017, p. 133). In foreclosure or *Verwerfung*, "whatever is refused in the symbolic order", as the Name-of-the-Father is, then "reappears in the real", in the form of paranoia or psychotic hallucination (Lacan, 1993, p. 13). It is the void which foreclosure of the Name-of-the-Father opens up in terms of the subject's initial introduction to fundamental signifiers which has the most significant implications in terms of psychosis (ibid., p. 252, 321). But I am proposing that asexuality forecloses not the Name-of-the-Father but an earlier imaginary object of desire, the Imaginary phallus. For this reason, I would suggest it is a foreclosure that does not produce psychosis.

Foreclosure without Psychosis

Lacan (ibid., p. 150) says if there are things the subject "wants to know nothing about", then foreclosure is the mechanism because what is at issue in *Verwerfung* is the "rejection of a primordial signifier into the outer shadows". Or as Grigg (2017, p. 29) puts it, what is foreclosed is not the possibility of an event coming to pass but the very signifier that makes expression of it possible in the first place. In short, foreclosure ensures the subject lacks the very linguistic means for making a statement at all. It is also worth pointing out that, in Evans's definition (1996, p. 142), the Imaginary phallus (φ) represents "phallic signification" which positions it as a primary signifier in terms of sexuality. As stated, I am proposing that in asexuality, it is not a foreclosure of the Name-of-the-Father because the subject has already brought about a foreclosure of the Imaginary phallus, thus effecting a separation from the mother in the form of a reversal in the relation of dependence. I am further proposing that this theorized foreclosure of the Imaginary phallus may not be so radical.

For the non-asexual subject, the choice of taking up the position of the Imaginary phallus represents a challenge. Lacan says that the mother will "equip" herself with the phallus, and reciprocally, the child "generously grants it" to her, but this does not result in a perfectly harmonized symmetry (1993, p. 319). "Now, the couple finds itself on the contrary in a situation of conflict, even of respective internal alienation", he says (ibid.). The reason for this is that the phallus is with the father who is "supposed to be" its vehicle (ibid.). In *Seminar XVII*, he says the mother's desire in this regard "will always wreak havoc" (2007, p. 112). On the side of the child, there are also potential negative consequences if the Imaginary phallus is "ingested" too fully. In *Seminar VII*, he points out that a relationship that is "entirely governed by the imaginary" leads either to psychosis or perversion (1992, p. 301). I am proposing that the foreclosure of the Imaginary phallus in asexuality makes the movement to the father and away from the mother a more tranquil transition. In this sense, asexuality represents what Lacan terms a *père-version* (2016, p. 11) or a turning towards the father. However, unlike perversion which does *not* give up the Imaginary phallus for the Symbolic phallus, the asexual forecloses the Imaginary phallus and with it the *jouissance* of being the "instrument of the Other's jouissance" (Swales, 2012, p. 61).

Furthermore, as Lacan suggests on more than one occasion in *Seminar XXIII*, foreclosure's unequivocal link with psychosis may not necessarily be intractable. On one occasion (2016, p. 42), he says that the *sinthome*, as the created and additional support for what is foreclosed, stands out, not as psychotic but as "something neurotic". Moncayo (2017, p. 48) offers the view that here, Lacan seems to "collapse the distinction between psychotic structure and a psychotic symptom within a neurotic structure". Later in the same *Seminar*, Lacan points to a foreclosure that takes place in terms of the Real foreclosing meaning (*sens*). This is not the foreclosure of the Name-of the Father but rather a consequence of the "orientation of the real" that does so (Lacan, 2016, p. 102). Foreclosure is now being associated with the Real, rather than solely with the fundamental signifier of the Name-of-the-Father whose absence, as stated, has always been the cause of psychosis.[4] He explains his enlargement of the term "foreclosure" thus:

> I'm saying this because yesterday I was asked whether there are other types of foreclosure besides the one that results from the foreclosure of the Name-of-the-Father. It's quite certain that foreclosure has something radical about it. In the end, the Name-of-the-Father is something slight.
>
> (ibid.)

Also, the "de facto *Verwerfung*" that Lacan describes in James Joyce (ibid., p. 72) does not, for instance, put Joyce in the position of a psychotic, at least not to the extent that Lacan ever names him as such. The traditional argument would contend that this is consistent with the Lacanian concept of the *sinthome*, which I examine later, acting as the new signifier which protects the subject from psychosis, and in Joyce's case, his writing is his *sinthome*. However, Harari argues that the theorizing of the final Lacan, with its emphasis on the *sinthome*'s stabilizing role in knotting the three registers of the Symbolic, Real and Imaginary for *all* subjects, posits an effective "psychotic" kernel in *every* individual. Conceding that the accepted understanding of foreclosure is that it is "a properly psychotic mechanism" (1995, p. 144), he, too, argues for a broader conception of the term. In his view, *Verwerfung* now becomes what he calls "the mechanism of an unavoidable dimension of the psyche, that of the constitution of the subject", one which takes up "the role of a constitutive hole" (ibid.). This implies that something is irreparably lacking which, Harari says, Lacan writes as SA, the signifier of the lacking Other. This, he believes:

> indicates that what we find at the place of the signifier is what is absent by definition. We can thus say that the signifier is foreclosed. Here, we are

dealing with a "normal" foreclosure, so to speak, a foreclosure that is constitutive, irreducible, bearing on the very condition of being a speaker.

(ibid.)

The implication of this is that Lacan is introducing, particularly in the last sessions of the *Seminar*, the possibility of other types of foreclosure other than that which produces psychosis (ibid., p. 247). Harari considers these alternative foreclosures are already evident in Lacan's work, and they include various Lacanian formulas containing *il n'y a pas* or *il n'existe pas;* Lacan's famous aphorisms that there is no sexual relation or the Woman does not exist (ibid., p. 291). Equally, Harari argues that the Symbolic is also based on a foreclosure that does not allow a signifier to represent itself; the S_1 must turn towards another signifier, the S_2 (ibid., p. 286). Furthermore, there is the foreclosure of language itself whereby there will always remain "something final or primal that is unsayable" and that this "amounts to a primordial feature of foreclosure" (ibid., p. 287). "In this sense, we find – for we have looked for them – foreclosures in neurotics", he says (ibid., p. 291). Grigg concurs with this view when he says that there appears to be nothing to rule out the possibility that foreclosure "is a normal psychic process" (2017, p. 54). He says that Lacan's work in *Seminar XXIII* "effectively generalizes the concept of foreclosure" and that psychosis is only *one* response to it while "the symptom-metaphor of neurosis is another" (ibid., pp. 65–66).

A Different Form of Foreclosure

If the application of foreclosure solely to psychotic structure is no longer absolute, this opens up new possibilities. In particular, it allows that asexuality might represent an alternative foreclosure that has not, so far, been considered within Lacanian theory. In this sense, as I am proposing, it could represent the foreclosure of the Imaginary phallus. Again, it is important to highlight that this is a very different position to perversion which, Lacan says, sees the child's relationship to the mother "constituted" by its "dependence on her love" (2006, pp. 462–463). In either identifying with the Imaginary phallus (perversion) or becoming the Imaginary phallus (neurosis), for Lacan, there is a "phallocentrism produced by this dialectic" between mother and child which is due to an "intrusion" of the phallic signifier into the child's psyche. Underlining its centrality, he views the imaginary function of the phallus as the "pivotal point in the symbolic process" for both sexes (ibid.).

On this basis, a foreclosed Imaginary phallus is, by extension, going to bring about, if not a foreclosure of, then, at the very least, a consequent diminution of the signifying status of the Symbolic phallus. This would permit desire as the desire of the Other to be foreclosed of its sexual content. Lacan clearly refers to the role of the *sinthome* in making up for what is missing in the context of James Joyce when he says that Joyce's "art is the guarantor of his phallus" (2016, p. 7). Morel interprets this as Lacan stating that the Joycean *sinthome* stands in for not just the foreclosed Name-of-the-Father but also the "foreclosed phallus" (2019, p. 135). I am proposing that in asexuality, the foreclosure of the Imaginary phallus and, by extension, the Symbolic phallus *is* the foreclosure of sexual desire. This foreclosure does not, however, disrupt the subject's relation to either language or its metaphoric processes as can be found in the foreclosure of the Name-of-the-Father.[5]

As I outlined, for Lacan, foreclosure is the mechanism that brings about the rejection of a primordial signifier into the outer shadows. In an asexual context, while the primordial signifier that is being rejected is the Imaginary phallus, the Name-of-the-Father, as agent of castration and separation, is nevertheless still experienced and acknowledged, no matter how "slight" it happens to be (2016, p. 102). If, therefore, the Imaginary and, by extension, the Symbolic phallus are foreclosed while the Name-of-the-Father is not, this implies that the phallus, as object of castration, is separate to, while at the same time being coextensive with, the Name-of-the-Father as agent of castration. In Lacan's theorizing 20 years before *Seminar XXIII*, in his formula for the Name-of-the-Father, the latter is intrinsically linked with the Phallus, along with the mother's desire in *On a question prior to any possible treatment of psychosis* (2006, p. 465). In his I Schema in this paper (ibid., p. 476), he provides a distortion of his R Schema (ibid., p. 462) in order to offer a didactic mapping of psychosis. In the I Schema, he clearly places the foreclosed Name-of-the-Father (P_0) in the Symbolic with a foreclosed Phallus (Φ_0) in the Imaginary. In this writing, it would appear impossible to conceive of one being foreclosed without the other being foreclosed also.

However, if I am proposing that in asexuality the Name-of-the-Father is *not* foreclosed because the subject has already brought about a foreclosure of the Imaginary phallus, effectively a pre-Oedipal form of separation from the mother, then this theorization presupposes a possible separation of the two. This would come about because the motive force necessary to foreclose the phallus is present in asexuality, but the motive force necessary to foreclose the Name-of-the-Father and cast it into the outer shadows is absent. As such, my proposition sees a dividing of the Name-of-the-Father from the Phallus so that, as stated, the latter is foreclosed while the former is not. In support of this proposition, we find Morel highlighting a case study of Hector which includes this very configuration – that is, it involves phallic foreclosure (Φ_0) without the Name-of-the-Father (P_0) being foreclosed (2019, p. 300, fn. 16). She says this represented a "new case of castration anxiety" but one which was no longer phobic. In contrast, it involved a confrontation with the law but without any acceptance of phallic castration. The Name-of-the-Father was certainly recognized, in that Hector feared his father, but phallic signification or castration were not recognized, the latter being associated with the Name-of-the-Father in the paternal metaphor. "For Hector, the phallus remained maternal", Morel says (ibid., p. 286), signalling it as a case of male perversion. She adds that while Lacan envisaged a disjunction between these two foreclosures, he did not believe one would exist without the other; hence, she claims her case study is a counter-example. I am proposing that asexuality is also an example of an explicit disjunction that can potentially occur between the two.

A further question which arises from this proposition regarding foreclosure of the Imaginary phallus is how the asexual subject sustains itself as a result of this. As I have indicated, the emergence of asexuality as a sexual identity has allowed many contemporary asexuals to self-identify and to benefit from the stabilizing effect which this can have. However, before asexuality became an emergent identity, it is reasonable to assume that asexuals existed and functioned well in their lives. It is also a reasonable assumption that not every contemporary non-sexually desiring subject identifies as asexual and yet functions, to all intents and purposes, as an asexual. The question, therefore, is how an asexual subject can sustain their position in the absence of both the phallus *and* identificatory supports.

A *Jouissance* of Absence

If the asexual subject experiences no sexual attraction and does so without subjective distress, this would suggest a unique and hitherto unconsidered form of *jouissance*. To quote Freud (1916–1917, p. 345), albeit from a different context, asexuality would appear to offer "a mode of satisfaction which alone the subject desires". If we also take into account Lacan's idea of a *jouissance* that ultimately derives from the child's quashing of what is disappointing in the Symbolic interplay (2020, p. 175), this offers a potential frame with which to view a prototypical asexual *jouissance*. In *Seminar IV*, Lacan is focussed on what are, essentially, oral-stage effects, and he outlines what happens when the satisfaction of need is substituted for a symbolic satisfaction. The fact of substitution means there is a transformation of the real object (the breast) into, as he puts it, a sign in the demand for love, or a symbolic request. This is how, for him, orality comes into being, and as an instinctual form of hunger, it is the bearer of a libido that is vital for preservation. But it goes beyond this to become a sexual libido once it has entered the dialectic of substituting bodily satisfaction for the demand for love, and so becoming an eroticized activity. He says, "It is libido in the strict sense, and it is sexual libido" (ibid., p. 176). This is the link, he says, between frustration on the one hand and the permanence of desire on the other. In other words, frustration has nothing to do with bodily need that can be satisfied because it is not the refusing of an object of bodily satisfaction (ibid., p. 173). In this context, his premise concerning Freud's *Versagung*, whereby the child quashes what is disappointing in the symbolic and quashes "the fundamental unfulfillment of this relationship" (ibid., p. 175), holds out the theoretical prospect of an unconscious, prototypical refusal of the eroticization of the first part-object. This is my interpretation of Lacan's view, mentioned earlier:

> Freud never speaks of frustration. He speaks of *Versagung*, which falls more adequately in line with the notion of reneging, in the sense one says *to renege a* treaty, to withdraw from an engagement. This is so true that one can even on

occasion place *Versagung* on the opposite side, because the word can mean both *pledge* and *the breaking of a pledge.*

(ibid., p. 172)

Part of the theoretical approach I am proposing also assumes that this "breaking of a pledge" or annulment of libidinal desire must, in some way, carry through as a persistent rejecting intention in the subject's various stages of formation. In *Seminar VI, Desire and Its Interpretation*, Lacan elaborates on how a transmission of *Versagung* might occur through oral, anal and phallic phases. What he terms a "code of demand" or "vocabulary" (2019, p. 120) passes through a certain number of relationships via food, excrement and so on. These relationships involve the same process of substitution by way of an interchangeable object that he defines as food for the oral relationship and excrement for the anal relationship. If, therefore, this "code" can encompass the *Versagung* as Lacan speaks about it, then the stamp of a renunciation, or an annulling of the object as symbolic in the demand for love, would appear to be distinctly possible, carrying through from the first relation to the breast as object in the dialectic of substitution. When it comes to the phallic phase, Lacan says that it is by a type of "continuation of the subject's signifying fragmentation in relations involving demand" that the signifier phallus of the genital stage comes to appear, albeit in what he calls a "morbid way, including all its symptomatic forms of impact" (ibid.). It is because the phallus is quite obviously not a detachable object like the breast or the faeces that it only becomes one by "shifting to the status of a signifier", he says (ibid.).

This hypothesized movement of an annulling *Versagung* through subsequent psychosexual stages amounts to a divergent trajectory when set against one which, for example, Verhaeghe outlines in terms of sexually desiring subjects. In keeping with the theorized position for sexually desiring subjects, he says that the sexual drive "colonizes basic somatic needs" which is synonymous with the transition from need to desire (2005, pp. 2–3, online pagination). In contrast, I am proposing that Lacan's theorizing allows for a consideration of *Versagung* as an alternative choice which is capable of bringing about an unconscious and prototypical renunciation of eroticization at the oral stage which egresses or moves forward through subsequent psychosexual stages. As a result of this "continuation" of the "code of demand" passing through the oral, anal and into the phallic phase, the Imaginary phallus is foreclosed and the Symbolic phallus also. In other words, as a consequence of the foreclosure of the Imaginary phallus, the Symbolic phallus becomes variously stripped of some or all its signifying effects. But because the Name-of-the-Father has brought about castration,[6] the phallus continues to operate as a place holder in the signifying chain, analogously to how zero operates in mathematics, as outlined in Chapter 4. For sexually desiring subjects, the Name-of-the-Father, as structuring metaphor, allows the child to separate from the mother and find its objects of desire in the external world by installing a prohibition on the child's desire for the mother, and vice versa.[7] It is symbolization mediated through the Name-of-the-Father that leads to the emergence of the

Symbolic phallus which is not only located in the place of the Other but is also the measure (ratio) by which the sexually desiring subject can recognize the Other's desire (2006, pp. 581–582). For asexuality, however, when Lacan distinguishes the refusal of the oral object as something other than a negation of activity, it is an important distinction and an important illustration of a no that can bring about a psychical separation. This is because he is not referring to a drive that is negated or repressed but a drive that gains *jouissance* from a "savoured absence" (2020, p. 177). In other words, in my interpretation, he is pointing to a no which is a positive and which has the potential to be constitutive of the subject.[8] As such, I am proposing that this psychical mechanism might inaugurate the formation of the asexual subject. In *The Direction of the Treatment and the Principles of its Power*, his paper one year after *Seminar IV*, he examines, inter alia, Ernst Kris's "fresh brains" case, and here, again, he is considering the idea of a desire for nothing. This time, however, he moves it beyond an exclusive association with orality, even though the case study offers up its meanings through the analysand's reference to physical hunger for a plate of fresh brains. For Lacan, Kris's case study is about absence rather than about the presence of the *idea* of being a plagiarist. What he draws out from it is the very notion that this patient's fear of becoming a plagiarist functions as a form of stealing nothing (2006, p. 502). Here, it is not an oral drive but is instead of the "mental realm" and, as Lacan puts it, is about "the desire on which the idea lives" (ibid.). This, I would argue, supports the theorizing of asexuality as a phenomenon that concerns desire for no sexual desire, and in this paradoxical way, desire is supported and a productive functioning maintained.

The Support of the Fundamental Phantasy

I am proposing that asexual desire is supported through a fundamental phantasy which has its roots in the desire to be independent of the almightiness or omnipotence of the Other. Lacan is clear that the relation of the *objet petit a* to the Other is based on the fact that the subjective structure of the child depends on the imaginary of the mother (1966–1967, session of 16 November 1966, p. 4). As stated, thinking is radically inadequate for dealing with sexuality (ibid., session of 18 January 1967, p. 4) and so, too, is language when it emerges (ibid., p. 12). Therefore, this is the lack around which the function of the *objet petit a* is defined for both sexual and asexual subjects (ibid.). It is the place where the central object as nothing of the asexual phantasy begins, as a paradoxical eroticized piece of the Real that cannot be assimilated into language, at the place where the Symbolic emerges but where this *objet petit a*, as not only a remainder but also an eroticized object, escapes symbolization (ibid., session of 25 January 1967, p. 9). For Lacan, it is with regard to the object, under the sign of nothing, that "resistance to almightiness in the relationship of dependence" is elaborated (2020, p. 179).

At one and the same time as being the originary place of lack, this is also the place of inaugural helplessness (*Hilflosigkeit*) for the subject. As Lacan says in his *Seminar* on *Desire*, in the primitive presence of the opaque and obscure desire of the Other, the subject is without recourse. "He is hilfloss, *Hilflosigkeit*", and this is the "foundation" of the "traumatic experience" (2019, p. 17). The cause of this trauma of helplessness, he says, cannot be defined in any other way than having no recourse in the face of "the Other's desire" (ibid., p. 425). For him, this drama is an essential constituent of every analytically defined structure. If so, the trauma associated with the desire of the Other allows for a fresh perspective on the aetiology of an asexual desire for no sexual desire. Lacan returns to this idea in *Seminar XIV, The Logic of Phantasy*, when he considers refusal of the oral object as a way "to save oneself from being engulfed by the maternal partner" (session of 10 May 1967, p. 4). In *Seminar IV*, the unavoidable reality or *Wirklichkeit* for the child is, similarly, that of the omnipotence of the mother as the "primordially all-powerful" figure (2020, p. 177).

Asexuality is not a refusal of the oral object but is a foreclosure of the phallus as imaginary (object) and symbolic (signifier) to allow the formation of a subject voided of sexual desire for the Other beginning in the first experiences with the first Other. In other words, an encounter that every subject experiences with regard to the primordial Other produces a unique and contingent effect for the asexual subject. This, ultimately, results in a desexualization of desire, phantasy and *jouissance* in relation to the Other which, in essence, is the manifest sexual orientation of asexuality. The lack of sexual desire is potentially based on an originally unwelcoming Real experienced through an unpleasurable increase in drive tension, implicitly determined by the early encounter(s) with this Real. The psychological elaboration of this trauma for sexual subjects who reach so-called genital maturity[9] is to seek discharge for the unpleasurable rise in tension through a repetitive engagement in the sexual act which, as stated, can also be considered to have symptomatic sediments. In the repetition of the sexual act, the sexually desiring subject reproduces the initial relation to the Other, which was potentially traumatic and is, as stated in Chapter 4, the very relation which maintains the *objet petit a* (1966–1967, session of 1 March 1967, p. 9). For the asexual subject, in contrast, the rise in drive tension and its related dependence for discharge of this tension on an omnipotent Other is unpleasurable. In this case, psychological elaboration is achieved through the support of a fundamental phantasy aimed at the *objet petit a* as the nothing – that is, *not* aimed at another person.

While this might lead to an assumption that the death drive (*Thanatos*) is dominant within asexuality (i.e., a Nirvana-like reduction of drive tension to zero), there are other considerations that need to be taken into account. The phenomenology of asexuality indicates that a persisting tension exists due to its counter-cultural stance in relation to sex-normative discourses; on one interpretation, at least, this is an indicator of the death drive.[10] "Death drive means precisely that the most radical tendency of a living organism is to maintain a state of tension, to avoid a final 'relaxation' in obtaining a state of full homeostasis", according to Žižek (2012, p. 21). Interweaving with this research and the testimony of asexuals show that many form loving relationships with both asexual and non-asexual partners which indicates a counter-balancing presence of *Eros*. Therefore, despite any hypothesized unconscious intention to reduce excitation to zero, the conscious lived experience of asexuals can also prove to be unsettling for many asexual subjects, most particularly until a further support is encountered in the form of identification, which I will consider next.

The Support of Identification

A recurring theme within the experiences of asexual subjects is the stabilizing effect that occurs when the designation "asexual" is discovered at a particular moment in their lives. It appears to provide a subjective anchoring for what had often been, up to that point, a confusing and alienating sense of their sexuality. Research by Carrigan (2011, p. 471) shows that before self-identifying as asexual, most assume a pathological cause for their sexual orientation. The following quote is representative of this experience:

> I finally identified myself as asexual, and coming out to myself and the world was one of the most liberating experiences I've ever encountered. . . . I'm comfortable with it. I'm relieved by it. . . . It makes all the sense that nothing made before and I'm glad to not spend countless hours worrying about why I am broken anymore.

> (ibid., p. 474)

Asexuals, in the period when they have not yet defined their sexuality in terms of an absence of sexual attraction for another person, and who do not yet have access to this "signifying formulation" (Thurston, 1996, p. 189), experience varying degrees of distress. Carrigan shows that while specific biographical details vary greatly among individuals, there is a typical pattern to the experience of asexual subjects before they transform their intrapsychic experience into a symbolically assimilated identification as asexual.[11] The pattern which Carrigan identifies begins with a sense of being different from their peer group. This is then followed by a period of self-questioning which leads, in general, to an assumption of pathology – that is, the idea that to experience no sexual desire must be a disordered condition. The assumption of pathology can endure until self-clarification is obtained through the acquisition of the identity "asexual" via a communal authentication (ibid., 2011, p. 471). Similarly, research by Scherrer (2008, p. 631) suggests that it was only after "encountering the language of asexuality" that asexuals respond to that identity. In this sense, then, it would appear that asexuals who do not have access to "asexuality" as an identity can experience challenges in their ability to function in a productive manner. One asexual man puts it this way in another Scherrer study:

> Before I knew asexuality existed, I did consider asking a doctor why I am like I am. I never did because I knew I wouldn't want to be "cured". So a doctor

wasn't the person to ask. I would have found it extremely difficult to talk about because at that time I felt it almost made me not a real person.

(Foster and Scherrer, 2014, p. 426)

Asexuality and the *Sinthome*

In the era before asexuality was available as an identity category, asexual subjects who had undergone this theorized foreclosure of the phallus could access an alternative supporting concept. As briefly mentioned earlier, Lacan called it the *sinthome*, and it is, in fact, available to all subjects, whether sexual or asexual. Access to the *sinthome* would also be available to those contemporary subjects living as asexuals who do not, or cannot, self-identify as asexual. In his later teaching, Lacan introduces the *sinthome* as a subject-specific act of artifice whereby a unique and particular creation such as an artistic or personal construction constitutes a fourth ring which ties together the Borromean knot of Real, Symbolic and Imaginary, thus anchoring the subject (2016, p. 131). Morel says the *sinthome* is a "knowing way of dealing with repetition" because it constitutes a "response to the equivocal naming of the child's jouissance by the mother" and, as a mode of separation, "entails the invention of a new relation to the Other" (2019, p. 5). In other words, it is a "creation" which allows the non-identified asexual subject create *something* within their lives which sustains them. Through the *sinthome*, they can unconsciously support a desire for no sexual desire which allows for a productive engagement with desire. I am proposing that non-identified asexuals, not only through the creation of a *sinthome* but also, as Gherovici (2010, p. 247) suggests in relation to transgender subjects, through identifying with it, can function without the phallic signifier, thus representing a creative reinvention of their sexuality.

If we consider some of the examples I mentioned earlier, we can see how this might operate. T. E. Lawrence, an iconic figure of the 20th century, was a British archaeologist turned soldier, who created a unique name for himself due to his actions in leading the Arab Revolt against the invasion by Turkey in World War I. The invention of himself as Lawrence of Arabia could be considered his *sinthome*, a creative act that was both singular and unique. Florence Nightingale, the nurse and social reformer, became a crusader for the improvement of civilian and military healthcare, and whose ideas became foundational for modern nursing. Her *sinthome*, in the form of her singular and unique vocation could be considered in the same way. English physicist and mathematician Isaac Newton created his *sinthome* through his pioneering and unique work on the effects of gravity. It could also be argued that Hungarian mathematician Paul Erdős created a *sinthome* out of his unique gift for mathematics. He essentially created a name for solving mathematical problems that had remained unsolved for generations and for applying himself to any new problems that came to his attention (Hoffman, 1998, p. 49). Likewise, the pop singer Morrissey could be said to have created his *sinthome* through his musical creativity. Also, assuming his quote in the Introduction indicates an asexual orientation, the American writer Gore Vidal's *sinthome* can be seen in his political and creative writing (he was a co-writer on the 1959 movie *Ben-Hur*). Equally, if she is considered to have been asexual, Anna Freud's *sinthome* is to be seen in her perpetuation of her father's name through her unique work and writings about psychoanalysis and her dedication to child analysis.

Sinthome as Transformed Symptom

While the *sinthome* is the archaic way of describing the symptom, and is essentially a reparative transformation of the symptom, Lacan uses the term to describe something very different from a symptom. He introduces it late into his theory in *Seminar XXIII* where he explores the writing of James Joyce as the paradigmatic example of the concept. Essentially, the *sinthome* becomes the buckle that can repair the trefoil knot of Imaginary, Symbolic and Real which, in Joyce's case, was his desire to be an artist "who would keep the whole world busy" (2016, p. 72). Joyce's *sinthome* has its origins in his desire to be an artist, and it is what "compensates exactly for the fact that Joyce's father was never a father for him" (ibid.). According to Thurston (1996, p. 189), Joyce faced a radical non-function or absence of the Name-of-the-Father from childhood. However, he managed to avoid psychosis by "deploying his art as suppleance, as a supplementary cord in the subjective knot". Thurston says the Joycean canon from start to finish entails a "special relation to language", a refashioning of it as *sinthome* (ibid.). According to Lacan, "The name that is proper to him is what Joyce valorizes at the expense of the father", that is, Joyce's own name, elevated through an art that is aimed at "the whole world" and that acts as addition or suppletion for the failure of the signifier Name-of-the-Father (2016, pp. 72–73). The foreclosure of this signifier does not, in the case of Joyce, result in psychosis because his art, as *sinthome*, acts as the buckle that repairs the knot. In this final period of Lacan's work, his theorizing of the *sinthome* becomes an extension of his previous *Seminar, RSI*, in which he focussed on the Borromean knot. There, the three registers of Real, Symbolic and Imaginary that constitute the intertwined domains of the speaking subject are considered from a topological perspective and are conceived as linked together. In *Seminar XXIII*, however, Lacan concedes that they may not constitute a perfectly arranged knot, and so a fourth ring is necessary to bind them, and this ring is the *sinthome*.

Harari (1995, p. 246) says the invention of the *sinthome*, as that fourth element without which it is impossible to articulate RSI, is "one of the most powerful, uncompromising, and subversive propositions in all of Lacan's thought". The fourth ring is considered by Lacan to be beyond meaning to the extent that Joyce never questioned his relation to writing; it was something he had to do. According to Thurston (1996, p. 190), Joyce was able to invent a new way of using language to "organise enjoyment". He says the *sinthome* is a signifying formulation that is beyond the work of analysis and that represents what he calls a kernel of enjoyment which is immune to the efficacy of the symbolic register in which language operates. This is not to imply a redundant role for psychoanalysis because, on the contrary, if the *sinthome* is what "allows one to live" by providing a unique organization of *jouissance*, then the task of analysis becomes one of the analysand identifying it and, more specifically, identifying with it (ibid., p. 189).

Extending the Concept of the *Sinthome*

Some contemporary theorists are extending the application of Lacan's concept of the *sinthome* away from a purely literary association and into the domain of sexuality. In the area of sexual difference, Gherovici's (2010, p. 153) main contention is that the *sinthome* permits a new approach to the paradoxes of gender, in particular citing Lacan's idea a few years after his *Seminar* on the *sinthome* that there is a she-*sinthome* and a he-*sinthome* (Lacan, 1979b). In other words, the *sinthome* can become a supplement for grasping the impossible relation between the sexes or, as Gherovici puts it, "to tolerate the absence of the sexual relation" (2010, p. 154). In this theorizing, she takes the concept of the *sinthome* clearly into the domain of sexuality and, in this regard, gives a case study example of Victoria who remakes her male body and transforms it to female through what the author terms "transvestite artificiality" (ibid., p. 153).

Taking into account the complex relationship that transgender subjects have to the body, Gherovici says that an art similar to that of actual artists can be found in transgender artificiality. This is not an art on the level of Joyce's genius, but it is, she argues, tantamount to a creative *sinthome*, describing it as a "self created fiction" that allows a person to live their life (ibid., p. 216). But she points out, while James Joyce sets out to make a name for himself, he also aspired to create a universal language. Similarly, her thesis is that while transgender subjects demand singular recognition, a universal agency can be observed in them, nonetheless, and more precisely when they write (ibid., p. 217). For her, sex change memoirs are often symptoms, but they can also be *sinthomes* (ibid., p. 243). Equally, they may not be great literature, but they aspire to the most essential function of literature, a communication to the self or others that inscribes sexual difference. This leads to her proposition that, in some cases, transgender subjects writing about their transgender transformation is "of the order of the sinthome" (ibid.). The *sinthome* shapes the singularity of an "art", a *techne* that reknots a "workable consistency" which moves the subject from contingency to absolute necessity (ibid.). In short, transvestite artificiality, for Gherovici, is an example of a creative *sinthome* (ibid., p. 181), and in saying this, she is aware that her theorizing is a departure from Lacan's first formulations of the *sinthome* which insist on the Symbolic and on the father (ibid., pp. 185–186). She extends this line of thinking to the idea that, in the case of male-to-female transgender subject Hera, the *identification with* the surgical process whereby she would become a woman was itself a *sinthome* (ibid., p. 191). In another case, that of Linda, the subject's bulimia is transformed through analysis into a career making highly successful artisanal chocolates. In this case, the *sinthome* was creative confectionery (ibid., pp. 207–208).

I am proposing that asexuality is, in many instances, an identification with a non-sexually desiring position which, similar to Gherovici's point, may in some cases constitute a *sinthome*. However, my theoretical wager, if it can be called such, is that the *sinthome* can support asexual subjects who have *not* self-identified as asexual, not just in the era before self-identification was available but also for contemporary asexuals who are unable or unwilling to self-identify. My proposition is similar to the extent that the *sinthome* is being associated with supplementing a sexual positioning of the subject. It differs to the extent that asexuality, in and of itself, is not a *sinthome*, even though it remains possible to reinvent one's sexuality by identifying with one's *sinthome*. It also differs in that, as I have argued, the absence to be tolerated in asexuality is not the absence of the Name-of-the-Father or the sexual relation but the absence of the Imaginary phallus and the Symbolic phallus. For those asexuals for whom the stabilizing function of identification as asexual is not available either culturally or subjectively, the *sinthome* can offer the possibility of "creative unbalance" which "disrupts the symmetry" (ibid., p. 154) of heteronormative expectations and which helps the subject accommodate this absence. As I said, the consideration of asexuality as *sinthome* is not being proposed because it does not satisfy the twin criteria of singularity and creativity. Even though each asexual subject is a unique person, asexuality per se is not a singularly creative production which is unique to each subject, no more than heterosexuality or homosexuality. The *sinthome*, however, can effectively offer an alternative support and supplement for the foreclosure of the phallus to those asexuals who unconsciously choose it. In this way, it allows a non-phallic orientation to function within a dominant phallic discourse. The corollary of this proposition may be that non-sexual subjects who are unable to find support in either identifying as asexual or through the creation of a particular *sinthome* are potentially exposed to psychological distress and/or pathological effects.

The *Sinthome* as Sexual

Morel also broadens the concept of the *sinthome* beyond Lacan's particular frame, and like Gherovici, it could be said that she democratizes it by arguing that the *sinthome* is not only available to men of creative genius but that it is potentially available to everyone (Morel, 2019, p. 6). The logic she follows is that since every subject has a symptom, and since every *sinthome* is a unique transformation of, and solution to, the symptom, then every subject can potentially create a *sinthome*. She looks at how the child separates from the mother, and her focus is on how this is done without the Name-of-the-Father. In doing so, she extends Lacanian theory to a consideration that it is the *sinthome* which is capable of separating the child from the mother (2019, pp. 2–3). As well as its possible role in separation, she also hypothesizes that the *sinthome* will allow the subject to achieve sexual identity, and in Morel's reading of it, this may be in response to the experience of sexual ambiguity which is, presumably, why she refers to it as the "sexual" *sinthome* in the title of her book (ibid.). For her, the *sinthome* may result from successive symptomatic reductions obtained in analysis through the process of interpretation. But she also believes it may appear "out of the blue" without analysis (ibid., p. 306). The writing of James Joyce as *sinthome* is an example which appears without analysis, and she believes that Lacan's theory allows for an alternative to the Name-of-the-Father by generalizing the *sinthome*'s power of separation. "The sinthome is what enables the child to disengage itself from the law of the mother, by using a contingent element as a means of support", she says (ibid., p. 307). This contingent element *could* be the father, but of relevance to asexuality, she says it could also be an element "borrowed in a broader sense from the subject's social life" (ibid.). Morel also gives case history examples which include the case of Hector, mentioned earlier, whose *sinthome* is his craft of being a counterfeiter (ibid., p. 286), Claude whose *sinthome* is being a husband to his wife Ana (ibid., p. 274) and Bill whose *sinthome* is his writings as an Egyptologist (ibid., p. 297). The point of interest here is that the creative particularity of the *sinthome* is now being considered in a variety of new and different ways, which includes sexuality and which moves beyond the frame of Lacan's focus on a traditional understanding of what constitutes a creative act. In the traditional understanding, the *sinthome* is the intermediary signifier through which the absent signifier of the Name-of-the-Father is made operational (Harari, 1995, pp. 209–210). I am proposing that the *sinthome* for asexuality can be a signifying formulation that allows the subject to function in the absence of identification as a support and despite the foreclosure of the signifier Phallus. Harari's point is apposite when he says that while the hysteric is "clearly torn asunder", the "sinthomatic", although not tranquil, is "often without the surging anxiety that afflicts the former" (ibid., p. 233).

The *Sinthome* and No Sexual Desire

This allows for a consideration of the asexual subject as being capable of engaging in "an *intersinthomal* relation" (ibid., pp. 209–211) in which the *sinthome* operates as the signifier of a desire for no sexual desire. If this appears at first sight to be a strange form of sinthomatic *jouissance*, it is worth remembering that in *Joyce the Symptom II*, Lacan (1979a, p. 9) says that the *jouissance* proper to the *sinthome* is almost by definition "opaque", indicating something that is hard to understand, not clear or lucid, and which can even be obscure. He further refines what he means by opaque *jouissance* when he says that it "excludes meaning". This contrasts with phallic *jouissance* which, despite its prevalence, is the *jouissance* that fails, not only in terms of complete and full satisfaction but also in terms of providing meaning as to what it is to be a sexed subject. As such, the *sinthome* as it might be created by the asexual is not a metaphor, not a substitution, nor indeed a sublimation, but rather a making-up-for as suppletion. It is an additional signifier that compensates, not for the Name-of-the-Father as is found in psychosis but for the signifier Phallus whose foreclosure ensures that phallicized meaning effects remain void for asexual subjects. This addition that compensates with something new is an act of symbolic nomination (Harari, 1995, p. 240). But this act of nomination must be distinguished from a complementary form of creationism which is to be found in Lacan's early work. In the latter, according to Harari, it was enough to "name something" via the signifier in order to make "the Real emerge on the basis of the Symbolic" (ibid., p. 346). By contrast, the *sinthome* represents the *invention* of a name as either a proper name or as a noun (ibid., p. 347). He says this:

> Symbolic nomination is therefore alone capable of making a hole in the Real, determining it as not-all, as "fragmented". It is thus the concept that makes up for the sheer absence [*carence*] of the Name-of-the-Father.
>
> (ibid.)

I am proposing that the *sinthome*, for those asexuals who do not, or cannot, access identification as a signifying formulation, is also an act of symbolic nomination, the invention of a name, as a way of making up for the absence of the signifier Phallus. Lacan's phrase "to do without the Name-of-the-Father on condition of making use of it" means, for Harari, to choose a "good" form of heresy as an "unconditioned" Name-of-the-Father (ibid., p. 352). Indeed, in the context of the contemporary discourse of hegemonic sexuality, asexuality can be considered in some instances as a form of sexual heresy (Mosbergen, 2013). The creation of a *sinthome*, therefore, amounts to a working with the Real in a subjective identification with the thing created. The *sinthome*, and the agency of symbolic nomination which produces it, stops the *objet petit a* residing in the Other. In the case of asexuality, as I have proposed, the *sinthome* does allow for the *objet petit a* to reside in the Other but as the nothing which does not cause sexual desire and ensures that sexual *jouissance* is "no longer prescribed by the Other" (Verhaeghe and Declercq, 2002, p. 69). The subject of the symptom does and does not want his or her symptom, whereas the subject of the *sinthome* cannot live without the *sinthome* (Harari, 1995, pp. 358–359). I am proposing that asexuality can access a similar act of symbolic nomination, the invention of a name, which makes a Not-All of the Real of sexual desire. In this way, it makes up for the "sheer absence" (ibid., p. 347) of the phallic signifier and allows asexuality to represent a new way of organizing enjoyment, one that is immune to the efficacy of the Phallus and its production of sexualized meaning effects. In his new way of looking at the symptom, Lacan conceptualizes it as providing a *jouissance* that differs markedly from that of the traditional symptom. As Moncayo puts it, "Sinthome repairs and symptom damages or injures either in the form of pain or in the form of pleasure turned into pain" (2017, p. 85).

Verhaeghe and Declercq say that in analysis, a subject can choose either an *identification with* or *a belief in* their symptom (2002, p. 67). A *belief in* situates all *jouissance* on the side of the Other and involves the subject taking a stand against this in the fundamental phantasy. An *identification with*, however, sees the subject situate *jouissance* in the Real of their own body such as we find asexuals doing in validating their absence of sexual attraction for another person. This change in the subject's position vis-à-vis *jouissance* is resonant with the asexual experience of being able to sustain a sexual orientation which does not derive from, nor answer to, the demand of the Other and yet assimilating it as an authentic identity in the context of a sex-normative discourse.[12]

The *sinthome* is, therefore, an answer of the Real, and in *Seminar XXIII*, Lacan refers on more than one occasion to its emergence from and relation to the Real (2016, pp. 113–115, p. 120). In analysis, the subject is unaware that they are fashioning this "answer of the Real" which is consonant with Lacan's comment regarding James Joyce where he says, "Joyce didn't know that he was fashioning the *sinthome*, I mean, that he was simulating it. He was oblivious to it" (ibid., p. 99). Created without undergoing psychoanalysis, in the case of Joyce, he says it is achieved using savoir-faire, a know-how put to use in his role as artificer, inventor, creator and artist. A consequence of this is the new relation which the *sinthome* establishes between the subject and the Other. I am proposing that in asexuality, a *sinthome* can offer the necessary support in order to make up for the absence of sexual desire as both subjectively experienced and as the desire of the Other. In short, in the absence of the subjective support which self-identification as asexual undoubtedly offers those able to avail of it, the *sinthome* can make up for the foreclosure of the phallus. In terms of the *jouissance* which asexuality provides (i.e., one that is no longer prescribed by the Other) Moncayo (2008, p. 243) makes an interesting point when, adapting Freud's famous aphorism,[13] he says, "Where the jouissance of the Other and the symptom was, the Other jouissance of the *sinthome* shall be".

The *Sinthome* and Its Relation to the Other

Verhaeghe and Declercq's view is that if anything original or authentic is present in terms of a subject, it has to be looked for in the Real of the body and the drive (2002, p. 70). This, they argue, contrasts sharply with the subject constituted through the process of alienation who is dependent on the Other. The testimony of asexuals consistently points to a desire that ensures they are not dependent on, or responsive to, the sexual desire of another person. One asexual puts it this way:

> I am simply uninterested in having sex, not repulsed, and if my partner insisted on having sex I would oblige willingly. It's just not the emotional connection for me that it seems to be for most other people.
>
> (Carrigan, 2011, p. 467)

The emphasis in early Lacan was on the metaphor of the Name-of-the-Father to set the subject free from the desire of the (m)Other. In his later work, and in *Seminar XXIII* particularly, he moves away from metaphor to search for a new signifier that will do the same thing (Verhaeghe and Declercq, 2002, p. 71). The asexuals mentioned earlier, I would contend, are examples of those who have used the *sinthome*, Lacan's new signifier which offers a *jouissance* that is not prescribed by the Other, to support a desire for no sexual desire. The later Lacan focusses the goal of the subject on inventing something new, in particular on inventing a new signifier that can knot the three registers of the Real, the Symbolic and the Imaginary into a sinthomatic sexual rapport (ibid., p. 74).[14] This "self-created fiction" or *sinthome* is the new signifier that is built, as stated, "upon the lack of the Other" and, as such, is a creation "*ex nihilo*" (ibid.). Verhaeghe and Declercq refer to Lacan's invitation to all subjects to follow the example of Joyce and create their own *sinthome* at this place of the lack of the Other. They also point out that if this new signifier, like the Real, has no sense (*sens*), then it cannot be exchanged with other subjects, a reference to Lacan's point that the *sinthome* is particular to each subject. That is why the *sinthomes* of the examples earlier do not fit another subject because the act of sinthomatic creation is highly individual and particular to each (ibid., p. 75). Yet this aspect of the singularity of the *sinthome* has another dimension to it. Morel (2006, p. 68), similarly to Gherovici's point earlier regarding a universal aspect to the singularity of the *sinthome*, says the significance of the *sinthome* is that it combines the singularity of the individual with "the universality of a structure that belongs to all". She says the *sinthome* is a structure at the point of intersection between the universal and singular. In contrast, it is universal in that every speaking being responds to the trauma of the encounter with language by producing a symptom. However, it is singular because it depends on the contingency of that trauma in the context of each individual's personal history (ibid., p. 6).

Harari, for his part, believes that singularity is one of the "most radical features" of the *sinthome* and that this should be given its proper emphasis (1995, p. 30). When he comes to give an example of this, it is coincidental that he chooses an act of rejection of sexual advances by a woman who says no. He says, "Here we see a mode of singularity emerging: the 'but not that' is a way of putting down a mark – 'I don't do that sort of thing; I'm not that kind of woman (or: one of those women)'" (ibid., p. 32). Echoing a point made earlier regarding the asexual approach to the demand of the Other, Harari points out that in his example, the sexual demand invoked is manifestly related to the demand of the Other, to the extent that the "but not that" is essentially a "confrontation" with this demand. He says that in the face of the dominance of the demand of the Other, the "but not that" is a reaction which signals what he terms "the beginning of an escape from the subjection to the neurotic symptom". It is in this regard that the *sinthome* through its singularity entails a "break from these subjective positions" (ibid., pp. 32–33) and so becomes a route by which the asexual subject can effectively escape from the neurosis which responding to the sexual demand of the Other might impose. This, in turn, may offer greater perspective on the absence of subjective distress to be found in asexuality. Furthermore, Harari's example is not linked to any typical symptom of obsessional neurosis, hysteria or phobia, but bears ultimately on an "ethical dimension" (ibid.). Morel also includes this aspect when she says that the *sinthome* has the advantage, as far as theory is concerned, of considering neurosis, psychosis and perversion from one common perspective (2019, pp. 42–43). In fact, underlining Lacan's successful avoidance of a pronouncement of psychosis in the case of Joyce, Harari believes it would be wrong to consider Joyce's writing to be a symptom of any kind. "The only person to suffer from a symptom for us, as analysts, is the one who says that he or she does", he says (1995, p. 45). Savoir-faire, then, becomes the means by which an anchored, subjective position can be achieved (ibid., p. 116); in Borromean terms, the self-created invention or creation of a fourth ring to tie the other three rings together. If sexually desiring subjects remain unconscious of it (ibid., p. 222), then asexuals who are supported by it are equally so. In a similar way to James Joyce whose art is his self-created *sinthome* which acts as the buckle that repairs the Borromean knot, the *sinthome* can do the same for the asexual subject. Joyce creates a special relation to language and refashions it as *sinthome*, while asexuals, through a variety of sinthomatic creations, refashion a special relation to their sexuality.

Notes

1 See Lacan, 1993, p. 321; Lacan, 2006, p. 465, 470.
2 See Lacan, 2006, p. 811, translator's endnotes, no. 535 (3).
3 For *Verwerfung's* history in psychoanalysis, see Roudinesco, 1997, pp. 281–283. She points out that one of Lacan's translations of *Verwerfung* before he settled on foreclosure was *"retranchement"* or "cutting off".
4 Harari (1995, p. 240) emphasises this point of fundamental signification which underpins all further metaphorizations thus: "For any metaphor only functions on the basis of an effectively working paternal metaphor".
5 Fink (1995, p. 110) indicates that foreclosure can be found on both the woman's and the man's side of Lacan's *Formulae of Sexuation*. On the man's side, he says the primal father in the position of exception, $\exists x \overline{\phi x}$, does not *exist* but rather ex-sists which means the entire phallic function (i.e., the no of the Father plus the phallic signifier it is required to bestow on the castrated subject) is not simply negated but is foreclosed. As a result, he says the primal father, as unbridled sexual enjoyer of all the women is psychotic. He makes a related argument regarding "ex-sistence" in terms of the woman's side. Lacan's feminine *jouissance* or other *jouissance* in the place of the Not-All ($\overline{\forall x} \phi x$), similarly, does not "exist" but rather "ex-sists" as a "radical alterity" in relation to the symbolic order and is "akin to that of a logical exception" similar to that found on the man's side (ibid., p. 113, and see note 32, p. 194).
6 Lacan says, "all human desire is based on castration" (1977, p. 118).
7 According to Leader (2012, p. 62), this is the paternal metaphor whereby the father is substituted in for the child's desire to "complete" the mother. In his later writings, Lacan argued that this symbolic function was not necessarily linked to paternity. Leader says, "Anything could count as a Name-of-the-Father as long as it worked to introduce limits and bind together the registers of the symbolic, the imaginary and the real".
8 A philosophical version of this can be found in Kojève's (1969, p. 5) reading of Hegel whereby the individual uses negation to create the "I" by forming a futurity from a present based on its past. Kojève says, "Thus, this I will be its own product: it will be (in the future) what it has become by negation (in the present) of what it was (in the past),

this negation being accomplished with a view to what it will become". In psychoanalytic terms, this process begins with the earliest "choices" of infancy.

9 Freud says that sexuality is composed of a number of partial drives, such as the oral drive and the anal drive, each with a different source (erotogenic zone) and which function independently until, at puberty, they become organised together under the genital zone. Lacan, in contrast, says the partial drives never come to a complete harmonization in the genital phase which posits that there is no single sexual drive. Instead, the drives remain partial, not in the sense that they are parts of a whole genital drive but that each only represents sexuality partially.

10 Writing about the death drive and drawing on the concepts of physics, Žižek (2012, p. 21) believes "living systems" are best characterized as systems "that dynamically avoid attractors", thus, maintaining a "state of tension". This dynamism offers an opposing interpretation of the Freudian death drive as a tendency of life towards Nirvana or zero tension, suggesting in contrast an insistence on maintaining tension. This interpretation lends support to the concept of a desiring subject desiring no sexual desire.

11 This is what Lacan might term "signifierization" (2014, p. 174).

12 Asexuality researcher Ela Przybylo (2019) calls into question the naturality of sexuality with the term "compulsory sexuality" which she draws from American poet, essayist and feminist Adrienne Rich's term "compulsory heterosexuality" (1980).

13 "Where *id* was, there ego shall be" (Freud, 1933, p. 80).

14 "Why would we not invent a new signifier? Our signifiers are always received. A signifier for example which would not have, like the Real, any kind of sense" (Lacan, *Seminar XXIV*, 1976–1977, session of 17 May 1977, p. 124).

References

Carrigan, M. (2011) 'There's more to life than sex? Difference and commonality within the asexual community', *Sexualities*, 14(4), pp. 462–478.

Evans, D. (1996) *An introductory dictionary of Lacanian psychoanalysis*. London: Routledge.

Fink, B. (1995) *The Lacanian subject – Between language and jouissance*. Princeton, NJ: Princeton University Press.

Fink, B. (1999) *A clinical introduction to Lacanian psychoanalysis*. Cambridge: Harvard University Press.

Foster, A. B. and Scherrer, K. S. (2014) 'Asexual-identified clients in clinical settings: Implications for culturally competent practice', *Psychology of Sexual Orientation and Gender Diversity, American Psychological Association*, 1(4), pp. 422–430.

Freud, S. (1916–1917) *Introductory lectures on psycho-analyses*, Standard Editions XV–XVI. London: Vintage/Hogarth.

Freud, S. (1933) 'The dissection of the psychical personality', in *New introductory lectures on psycho-analysis and other works*, Standard Edition XXII. London: Vintage/Hogarth.

Gherovici, P. (2010) *Please select your gender: From the invention of hysteria to the democratizing of transgenderism*. New York: Routledge.

Grigg, R. (2017 [1998]) 'From the mechanism of psychosis to the universal condition of the symptom: On foreclosure', in Nobus, D. (ed.), *Key concepts of Lacanian psychoanalysis*. Oxfordshire: Routledge, pp. 48–74.

Harari, R. (1995) *How Joyce made his name – A reading of the final Lacan* (Thurston, L., trans). New York: Other Press.

Hoffman, P. (1998) *The man who loved only numbers*. London: Fourth Estate.

Kojève, A. (1969) *Introduction to the reading of Hegel – Lectures on the phenomenology of spirit* (Bloom, A., ed.) (Nichols, H. J. Jnr., trans). Ithaca, NY: Cornell University Press.

Lacan, J. (1966–1967) *The logic of phantasy*, Seminar XIV, unpublished (Gallagher, C., trans). Available at: www.lacaninireland.com [Accessed 21 November 2021].

Lacan, J. (1976–1977) *L'insu que sait de l'une-bévue s'aile à mourre*, Seminar XXIV, unpublished (Gallagher, C., trans). Available at: www.lacaninireland.com [Accessed 29 November 2021].

Lacan, J. (1977 [1964]) *The four fundamental concepts of psycho-analysis*, Seminar XI (Miller, J-A., ed.) (Sheridan, A., trans). London: Penguin.

Lacan, J. (1979a) *Joyce the symptom II* (Collins, D., trans), unpublished. Available at: www.apwonline.org/download/joyce-the-symptom-ii.pdf [Accessed 3 December 2021].

Lacan, J. (1979b) 'On transmission', *Lettres de l'Ecole, Bulletin intérieur de l'Ecole freudienne de Paris*, 2(25), June, pp. 219–220, cited in Gherovici, P. (2010) *Please select your gender: From the invention of hysteria to the democratizing of transgenderism*. New York: Routledge.

Lacan, J. (1992 [1959–1960]) *The ethics of psychoanalysis*, Seminar VII (Miller, J.-A., ed.) (Porter, D., trans). London: Routledge.

Lacan, J. (1993 [1955–1956]) *The psychoses*, Seminar III (Miller, J.-A., ed.) (Grigg, R., trans). New York: Norton.

Lacan, J. (2006 [1966]) *Écrits – The first complete English edition* (Fink, B., trans). New York: W. W. Norton.

Lacan, J. (2007 [1969–1970]) *The other side of psychoanalysis*, Seminar XVII (Miller, J.-A. ed.) (Grigg, R., trans). New York: Norton.

Lacan, J. (2014 [1962–1963]) *Anxiety*, Seminar X (Miller, J.-A. ed.) (Price, A. R., trans). Cambridge: Polity Press.

Lacan, J. (2016 [1975–76]) *The sinthome*, Seminar XXIII (Miller, J.-A., ed.) (Price, A. R., trans). Cambridge: Polity.

Lacan, J. (2017 [1957–1958]) *Formations of the unconscious*, Seminar V (Miller, J.-A., ed.) (Grigg, R., trans). Cambridge: Polity Press.

Lacan, J. (2019 [1958–1959]) *Desire and its interpretation*, Seminar VI (Miller, J.-A., ed.) (Fink, B., trans). Cambridge: Polity Press.

Lacan, J. (2020 [1956–1957]) *The object relation*, Seminar IV (Miller, J.-A. ed.) (Price, A. R., trans). Cambridge: Polity Press.

Leader, D. (2012) *What is madness*. London: Penguin.

Moncayo, R. (2008) *Evolving Lacanian perspectives for clinical psychoanalysis – On narcissism, sexuation, and the phases of analysis in contemporary culture*. London: Karnac.

Moncayo, R. (2017) *Lalangue, sinthome, jouissance and nomination*. London: Karnac.

Morel, G. (2006) 'The sexual sinthome' (Végső, R. K., trans), in *Umbr(a)*, Incurable, No. 1., pp. 65–83. University of Nebraska – Lincoln, Faculty Publications, Department of English, 94. Available at: https://digitalcommons.unl.edu/cgi/viewcontent.cgi?referer=www.google.com/&httpsredir=1&article=1093&context=englishfacpubs [Accessed 4 December 2021].

Morel, G. (2019) *The law of the mother: An essay on the sexual sinthome*. New York: Routledge.

Mosbergen, D. (2013) 'LGBT+, asexual communities clash over ace inclusion', *Huffington Post*, 21 June (updated 6 December 2017). Available at: www.huffpost.com/entry/lgbt-asexual_n_3385530 [Accessed 3 December 2021].

Przybylo, E. (2019) *Asexual erotics: Intimate readings of compulsory sexuality*. Columbus, OH: Ohio State University Press.

Rich, A. (1980) 'Compulsory heterosexuality and lesbian existence', *Women: Sex and sexuality*, Summer, University of Chicago Press, pp. 631–660.

Roudinesco, É. (1997 [1993]) *Jacques Lacan – Outline of a life, history of a system of thought* (Bray, B., trans). New York: Columbia University Press.

Scherrer, K. S. (2008) 'Coming to an asexual identity: Negotiating identity, negotiating desire', *Sexualities*, 11(5), 1 October, pp. 621–641.

Swales, S. (2012) *Perversion – A Lacanian psychoanalytic approach to the subject*. New York: Routledge.

Thurston, L. (1996) 'Sinthome', in Evans, D. (ed.), *An introductory dictionary of Lacanian psychoanalysis*. London: Routledge, pp. 188–190.

Vanheule, S. (2011) *The subject of psychosis: A Lacanian perspective*. New York: Palgrave Macmillan.

Verhaeghe, P. and Declercq, F. (2002) 'Lacan's analytical goal: "Le Sinthome" or the feminine way', in Thurston, L. (ed.), *Essays on the final Lacan. Re-inventing the symptom*. New York: Other Press, pp. 59–83.

Verhaeghe, P. (2005) 'Sexuality in the formation of the subject', *Psychoanalyse. Aesthetik. Kulturkritik.*, 25, Heft 3/05, Passagen Verlag, Wien, pp. 33–53.

Žižek, S. (2012 [2004]) *Organs without bodies*. Abingdon, Oxfordshire: Routledge.

Chapter 7

Conclusion

The challenge of seeking an understanding of asexuality using Freudian theory is that the latter posits that there may well be "nothing of considerable importance that can occur in the organism without contributing some component to the excitation of the sexual instinct (drive)" (1905, p. 205). From this perspective, there appears to be no place given to the absence of libido as the ubiquitous energy of the sexual instinct (drive). It, therefore, becomes necessary to theorize not an absence but a presence of libido for the asexual subject and to hypothesize that the satisfaction of this libido must be achieved in a hitherto unrecognized manner.[1]

Freudian theory, as shown in Chapter 2 and Chapter 3, sees the sexual instinct (drive) as problematic and points to the unsettling quality of libido as a central aspect of human sexuality. So much so, human civilization, in several of Freud's formulations, is depicted as being built on the suppression of the sexual drive. The relevance of this thematic is that it emphasizes the contrariety which the human sexual drive represents – that is, as well as a potential source of pleasure it can also represent a potentially disruptive and confusing experience for the subject, even before the effects of morality or societal constraints are felt.[2] As Copjec (2016, p. 109) puts it, for Freud, sex manifested itself in *negative* phenomena, such as lapses, slips of the tongue and so on, and that this signalled a "discontinuity in the causal chain" and represented "unexpected dislocations in linearity". This leitmotif of disruption challenges the implicit assumption of sexuality as solely concerned with the pleasurable expression of sexual impulses or the seamless acquisition of a consistent sexual identity. For Freud, in contrast, the sexual drives might actually need to be defended against, and to this end, there are "motive forces" within each subject that work against the drives being carried through to satisfaction in an unmodified form. He says that these "vicissitudes" of the drives can be considered methods of *defence* [emphasis in original] (1915a, pp. 126–127).

Another important concept within Freudian theory is that there is no natural link between the sexual drive and its satisfying object – that is, the sexual drive is independent of its object. Nor is the sexual drive's origin likely to be due to the object's "attractions", as he puts it in *Three Essays on Sexuality* (p. 148). The object of the drive, in other words, is not important, other than the fact that *some*

DOI: 10.4324/9781003214946-8

object is necessary. In non-psychoanalytic theorizing of asexuality, the absence of an object is considered as a concrete absence, one which is written in to asexuality's definition of "no sexual attraction" for another person. In psychoanalysis, however, this absence can be just as much a presence which drives the subject, sexual or asexual. The Freudian view that there *must* be an object, in contrast, is of distinct importance when considering asexuality. Intuitively, the object of asexuality is quite obviously not only a desexualized object but also a non-specular one. This allows for a theory of asexuality that has two central tenets: first, that, contrary to other approaches, asexuality is *not* without an object, and second, that it is free from the edict of a manifestly *sexual* object in the form of an Other and against which the presence or absence of a sexual drive is usually evaluated. A further and often overlooked implication of Freud's view that the sexual drive is independent of its object is that if the object is not of primary importance, then the priority would appear to be the drive itself. In other words, it would suggest that, for sexual and asexual alike, the desire for a desire is the key factor here.

Asexuality and Infantile Sexuality

Freudian theory provides a valuable context whereby the child's relation to their primary caregivers is privileged as the most important infantile experience (ibid., p. 228). Freud explains that the "innumerable peculiarities of the erotic life of human beings" and even the "compulsive character" of falling in love are unintelligible unless seen as the "residual effects of childhood" (ibid., p. 229, fn. 1). He is also consistently pointing to the overwhelming nature of the sexual drives for the infant; they are the most abundant sources of this internal excitation, and they can have traumatic effects due to the unpreparedness of the infant for them (1920, p. 34). Although Freud was theorizing in the context of sexually desiring subjects, these aspects of his theory, I would argue, are not only applicable to asexuality but are also key to an understanding of it.

In one of the few instances where Freud does use the word "asexual", he gives the example whereby "almost all infantile sexual activities" are forbidden so that an ideal is set up making the life of the child asexual (1916–1917, p. 312). He says that over time, people really believed the life of children was asexual, and following this, science pronounced it as a doctrine (ibid.). But for Freud, there is no such thing as an asexual childhood. The period up to the age of 5 or 6 is the first phase of infantile sexuality which is forgotten as a result of "the veil of amnesia" (ibid.). This latter concept allows for a different perspective on the subjective experience of asexuality as one of "being born with it".[3] For Freud, the reason for forgetting these infantile experiences is that they relate, in particular, to the Oedipal relationship of the child with its parents which needs to be repressed. His theory is that infantile amnesia erases any memory of early sexuality, and so, as with heterosexuality and LGBTQIA+ orientations, it might appear as if the subject *is* born with it. Nevertheless, as I have discussed in previous chapters, the early infantile experience of asexuals is qualitatively different to that of sexual subjects.

Within Freud's work, one apparent point of commonality between sexual and asexual subjects emerges when he includes an asexual phase in all human sexual development. This period occurs from about 5 years of age when the Oedipus complex comes to an end and there is a diversion of libido away from sexual aims to new non-sexual aims through a process of sublimation. Freud calls this the period of sexual latency of childhood (1905, p. 178) where libidinal trends associated with the Oedipus complex are in part "desexualized and sublimated . . . and in part inhibited in their aim and changed into impulses of affection" (1924, p. 177). During latency, sexual impulses still exist even though they cannot be used because the reproductive functions of the sexual drive have yet to develop. The latency period, therefore, is a time when the sex drive is still active, and this, I have argued, offers a Freudian template on which asexuality can be modelled: an apparent absence of sexual desire behind which lies concealed an active libido.

However, the main point of difference between asexuality and an extended, or permanent, latency period is that for sexually desiring subjects, latency is inaugurated by a repression which brings the Oedipus complex to an end. For asexuals, I have proposed that repression at the phallic stage is not the mechanism which ensures the desexualization of the libidinal trends but an earlier foreclosure of the Imaginary phallus. Similarly, I have proposed that, in contrast, the libidinal trends directed towards the Other within asexuality are desexualized, not at the end of Oedipal phase when latency begins but during the earlier pre-Oedipal phase. This implies that the passage of the asexual subject through not only the latency period but also the preceding stages of infantile sexuality is qualitatively different to that of the sexually desiring subject. For the asexual, sexual desire for the desire of the Other is not sublimated away from achieving sexual aims but is, instead, foreclosed.

In sum, in Freudian theory, there are two aspects which are of particular relevance to asexuality: first, libido can find a way towards satisfaction which differs from normative expectations, and second, it can be difficult to see that libidinal satisfaction is being derived by the subject because of this (1916–1917, pp. 365–367). I have proposed that this supports my theory of the possibility that the asexual subject is deriving a libidinal satisfaction which has not been considered to date.

The Limits of Freudian Theory

There are, however, points at which Freudian theory reaches a limit in terms of providing the fullest possible understanding of asexuality. In the most general sense, there is no theoretical consideration given to a subject who does not experience sexual attraction or, indeed, one who experiences the absence of the sexual drive in a distress-free manner. In terms of specific Freudian mechanisms, the concept of repression does not adequately explain the phenomenon of asexuality. In repression, there is a psychical action which consigns repressed ideas to the unconscious, but equally, there is an attraction emanating from the repressed idea that extends to "everything with which it can establish a connection" (1915b, p. 148). In other words, the repressed idea continues to make its presence felt. Also, repression does not merely happen once and, therefore, brings about a permanent result (ibid., p. 151). Instead, it demands a persistent expenditure of energy. This is because a key feature of repression is that the repressed continues to return in the form of "substitute formations and symptoms" (ibid., p. 154).

In asexuality, there is quite obviously a withdrawal of the cathexis of libido (ibid., p. 155) which is characteristic of repression, but the repressed does not return in the form of symptoms that might cause subjective distress. Freud also argues that frustration must affect the mode of satisfaction which "alone the subject desires, of which alone he [*sic*] is capable" (1916–1917, p. 345). This means that frustration only emerges when it blocks a path to satisfaction which is desired in the first place. The experience of asexuality is that, since there is no sexual satisfaction being desired in the first place, there is no path to sexual satisfaction being blocked. This has led me to conclude that repression is not a satisfactory explanation of the operative cause of asexuality.

In terms of regression, both of the types that Freud distinguishes also fail to adequately explain asexuality. The classical understanding is that, firstly, if the libido is pushed back to an earlier stage or, secondly, if the genital organization is repressed, neurosis ensues, and its symptoms are a substitute for frustrated satisfaction (ibid., p. 342). On this basis, regression does not apply to asexuality because with the first type, there would be signs of regressed infantile sexuality, and there are none. The second type would see a return of the repressed genital organization in the form of symptoms of which, again, there are none. I have proposed that, rather than a regression, asexuality represents an *egression* whereby an early pre-Oedipal experience of unpleasure is carried forward by the subject rather than one which, post-Oedipally, regresses the subject back.

Sublimation, too, would appear to offer prima facie material for an explanation of asexuality. It is the ability to displace or find a substitute for the sexual drive in order to avoid or reduce frustration. Sexual trends are attached to non-sexual pursuits, and so sublimation offers an explanation as to how sexual drives can change their object and, most importantly from an asexual perspective, can be transformed into non-sexual satisfactions. However, as outlined in Chapter 2, Freud says that with sublimation, "there is a limit to the amount of unsatisfied libido that human beings on the average can put up with" (ibid., p. 346). Also, libido itself "makes a person's satisfaction depend on the attainment of only a very small number of aims and objects" (ibid.). As well as that, any imperfect development of the libido leaves behind numerous fixations to early phases and to objects which are mostly incapable of real satisfaction. Asexuals appear to be unperturbed by their non-sexual orientation, highlighting how the motive force necessary for sublimation – that is, finding a substitute satisfaction for a sexual drive aimed at an object – is missing. Sublimation also presumes the existence of a sexual trend which must attach to a non-sexual one, and as I have argued, asexuality does not appear to have a pre-existing sexual trend with either a manifest sexual object or a sexual

aim. Nevertheless, as stated, the Freudian view is that behind what we are considering as asexual (i.e., non-sensual or affectionate trends) lie originally sexual
aims. An "affectionate feeling" is, for Freud, the "successor to a completely 'sensual' object-tie" (1920, p. 34). It is for this reason that I have proposed that asexual
affection in romantic asexual relationships, while not having an underlying sexual
aim, is underpinned by an active libido aimed at a particular desexualized object.
However, the Freudian concept of sublimation does not offer a complete understanding of asexuality, and so it becomes necessary to revisit this concept in terms
of Lacan's theorizing.

I have also contended that an understanding of asexuality is not to be found in
the Freudian concept of hysteria. Hysterics show a number of sex-averse characteristics, such as a degree of sexual repression in excess of what Freud calls the
"normal quantity", an intensification of the resistance against the sexual instinct
(drive) and an instinctive aversion "to any intellectual consideration of sexual
problems" (1905, p. 164). This is a set of characteristics that asexuality shares,
but the point at which asexuality differs from Freudian hysteria is the paradoxical
one of the *predominance* of the sexual instinct (drive). As stated earlier, hysteria is
characterized by a simultaneous "exaggerated sexual craving and excessive aversion to sexuality" (ibid., p. 165). Asexuality does not match these simultaneous
criteria, and on this basis, it represents something distinct from a symptomatology
of hysteria.

Asexuality and Lacanian Theory

Lacan has pointed to an important concept, not found in Freudian theory, which
is a mechanism whereby the breast as object is annulled as symbolic by the infant
in order to reverse its relation of dependence (2020, p. 179). This is a theoretical
account of how the infant can experience dependence on and libidinal excitation with the Other as a negative and seek to reverse its position in relation to
it. As outlined in Chapter 4, this theory offers a point of difference to concepts
such as repression, regression and sublimation where the cause of lack of sexual
desire is usually to be found in an Oedipally activated refusal of, or aversion
to, sexual interaction. Instead, Lacan's concept of a reversal of dependence posits an originary pre-Oedipal experience of the omnipotent desire of the Other as
unpleasurable, manifesting in the first oral activity of feeding. This activity takes
on an eroticized function on the plane of desire which is organized in the symbolic
order (ibid., p. 177) and where a sexual relation becomes substituted for a feeding
relation (1966–1967, session of 18 January 1967, p. 4). This is the primary and
contingent infantile sexual experience from which I have proposed that the choice
of asexual orientation originates.

The reversal of the relation of dependence on the mother is, for Lacan, an eating
of nothing which is a something that exists on the symbolic plane (2020, p. 177).
In this way, the child uses "a savoured absence" to make the mother depend
on him rather than him depend on the mother, thereby reversing the relation of

dependence (ibid.). He says the drive to reverse the relation of dependence is due to a realization for the child that this real being as mother is omnipotent – that is, the being on whom "the gift or the non-gift depend, absolutely and with no recourse" (ibid.). Lacan broadens its applicability beyond orality to subsequent psychosexual stages with infantile sexuality, and in Chapter 6, I have proposed how this concept of a reversal of dependence can be applicable to the formation of the asexual subject. In doing so, I have argued that this reversal does not establish a fixation point at the oral drive but egresses or moves forward as an established tendency through subsequent stages. I have also proposed that this infantile experience at the oral stage lays the foundation upon which, post-Oedipally, the Symbolic phallus as the sexualized signifier par excellence is foreclosed by the asexual.

As examined in Chapter 5, psychoanalytic theory emphasizes that libido is present irrespective of the conscious experience of the subject and that the sexual drive is a permanence within the subject's unconscious. I have proposed that, due to this theorized reversal of dependence, asexuality is *libidinally* directed to experience a void in terms of sexual excitation because this is the very satisfaction which asexuality seeks and derives. Lacan moves the concept of reversal beyond the oral phase when he speaks about a desire for nothing in the "fresh brains" case of the would-be plagiarist (2006, pp. 500–502). It is not that the patient does not steal anything, it is that he steals *nothing*. For Lacan, the absence *is* the desire, the actual desire on which the idea lives (ibid., p. 502). This has provided a foundation on which I have theorized an aetiology of asexuality which, fundamentally, emerges from a psychical reversal of the relation of dependence on the first Other by the infant. A central proposal of this book is that this reversal, in turn, brings about a pivotal reversal in the child *not* taking up the position of the Imaginary phallus. Since this is an important concept for this book, I will elaborate on it more fully.

Asexuality and the Imaginary Phallus

For Lacan, the child must become the Imaginary phallus in order to become what it is the mother desires. This is how the first identification begins, and so if the mother's desire *is* for the phallus, then the child wants to be that for her (ibid., p. 582). The generally understood implication of this statement is that this is the case for all subjects. Yet as I have pointed out, Lacan's teaching in *Seminar IV* suggests that becoming the Imaginary phallus for the mother is *not* inevitable and can even be rejected. Indeed, in *Seminar VI*, he identifies a moment when this reversal might conceivably take place, and it is when the child reaches an awareness that the breast is the possession of the mother, not of the child (2019, p. 219). This is the moment of the child understanding the possibility of being deprived of the desired object. Lacan equates this time with the onset of the Kleinian depressive position, "when the mother as a totality" is realized (ibid.).

The traumatic inflection associated with the infantile sexual Real as represented by the first Other transfigures the dyadic foundations of the dialectic of need, demand and desire. I have proposed that for the asexual, it represents an unconscious intention, starting in the oral phase and repeating through subsequent psychosexual phases, which will ultimately orient the asexual position towards an annulment of the phallic signifier at the phallic stage of the Oedipus complex. If this proposition holds, then asexual libidinal desire is potentially delimited from its very beginning by the elision of the libidinal element of the symbolic part-objects that come to represent the relation between the subject and the first Other. For Lacan, the refusal of the breast as the symbolic object of the subject-Other dialectic appears, as he says clearly, under the sign of the nothing (2020, p. 179). He identifies the mechanism which brings this refusal about when he says that it is with regard to the "annulled object qua symbolic object" that the child puts his dependency on the mother in check "precisely by feeding on *nothing*" [emphasis in original] (ibid.). He speaks in *Seminar IV* about the Freudian concept of *Versagung* in terms of the child quashing what is disappointing in the Symbolic. By disappointing, I interpret him to mean not only that the demand for love (ibid., p. 210),[4] implicit in the demand for the satisfaction of need, can never be completely satisfied but also that the disappointment might include the child's experience of helplessness in the face of mother's omnipotence.

This theorization posits the conditions whereby an unconscious, prototypical annulment of the eroticization of the first part-object determines asexuality and distinguishes it from sexually desiring orientations. It is *Versagung*, as Lacan has referred to it, as "the notion of reneging, in the sense one says *to renege a treaty* [emphasis in original], to withdraw from an engagement" (ibid., p. 172). As stated, Laplanche and Pontalis point out that *Versagung* includes an active sense, and they define the word as a "condition of the subject who is denied, *or who denies himself* [emphasis added], the satisfaction of an instinctual demand" (1973, p. 175). I have proposed that it is annulment by the child which brings about the reversal of the relation of sexualized dependence on the Other, a characteristic which is central to asexuality. Although the choice of annulment begins with the breast as oral object, it does not fixate on the oral object and, instead, carries on as the preferred choice through anal and phallic phases.

In *Seminar VI*, Lacan elaborates on how *Versagung* as annulment might transmit through oral, anal and phallic phases. What he terms a "code of demand" or "vocabulary" (2019, p. 120), passes through relationships to the part-objects via food, excrement and so on. I have proposed that the stamp of a renunciation or annulment of the object as symbolic carries through from the first relation to the breast as object in the dialectic of substitution. Rather than repression or regression, the aetiology of asexuality might, rather, begin with the choice of annulment which, through egression and forward movement, becomes an unconscious choice and intention to annul the libidinal aspects of the subject-Other relation. When it comes to the phallic phase, Lacan says that it is by a type of "continuation of the subject's signifying fragmentation in relations involving demand", established in the oral and anal relationships, that the signifier phallus of the genital stage comes to appear, albeit in what he calls a "morbid way, including all its symptomatic forms of impact" (ibid.). Therefore, my proposal is that *Versagung* as annulment is capable of bringing about an unconscious and prototypical nullification of Other-directed eroticization. As a result of the "continuation" of this "code of demand" passing through oral, anal and into the phallic phase, the Symbolic phallus can emerge annulled in order to ensure the relation to subsequent others is similarly desexualized. In the process, the phallus as an annulled signifier becomes variously stripped of some or all its phallicized signifying effects but continues to operate as an essential space holder and cause of movement, in terms of both desire and the signifying chain, analogously to how I have described the zero operating in mathematics.

Asexuality as Non-Psychotic Foreclosure

In proposing that asexuality's inaugural moment is the choice not to take up the position of Imaginary phallus, I have made use of Lacan's term "annulment" to explain the mechanism that brings this about. But as I have also pointed out, the unconditional nature of the unconscious elision of sexual desire in asexuality, even among asexuals who engage sexually with a partner, suggests that something irrevocable is taking place. On this basis, I believe it is necessary to consider that the term "foreclosure" rather than "annulment" may be more appropriate to describe the mechanism for this. As noted in Chapter 6, when the term "foreclosure" is introduced into a Lacanian consideration of the aetiology of asexuality, it raises the question of psychosis. I have argued that the term "foreclosure" as applied to asexuality does not require that the latter should be assigned a psychotic structure. In psychotic foreclosure, "whatever is refused in the symbolic order", as the Name-of-the-Father is, then "reappears in the real", in the form of paranoia or psychotic hallucination because the Name-of-the-Father's metaphoric role in anchoring meaning has been lost to the subject (Lacan, 1993, p. 13). In asexuality, there is no return in the Real of psychotic symptoms which, I have proposed, supports the concept of a non-psychotic foreclosure. Equally, asexuality is not associated with any forms of language disturbance which foreclosure of the Name-of-the-Father opens up in terms of the subject's initial introduction to fundamental signifiers (ibid., p. 252, 323).

In contrast, for the asexual subject, the Name-of-the-Father, as agent of castration and separation, is experienced and acknowledged no matter how "slight" it happens to be (Lacan, 2016, p. 102). This theorizing requires that while the Imaginary phallus and, by extension the Symbolic phallus, is foreclosed, the Name-of-the-Father is not, so that a separation exists between the two. In Lacan's theorizing, particularly in *On a question prior to any possible treatment of psychosis*, he clearly places the two foreclosures as linked and taking place at the same time. However, I have proposed that in asexuality, the Name-of-the-Father is *not* foreclosed because the subject has already brought about a foreclosure of the Imaginary phallus, effectively a pre-Oedipal form of psychical separation from the mother. Therefore, the motive force necessary to foreclose the Name-of-the-Father as "primordial signifier" and cast it "into the outer shadows" (Lacan, 1993, p. 150) is absent in asexuality. The Name-of-the-Father is *not* foreclosed while the Phallus *is* foreclosed, and I have included an example from a case study by Morel in support of the possibility of this.

The foreclosure of the Imaginary phallus, as I have been proposing it, is the psychical mechanism which inaugurates separation in the form of a reversal in the relation of dependence on the mother and which does not produce psychosis. If, as Lacan suggests, the Name-of-the-Father is something slight and if, as Harari suggests (1995, p. 341), it is a precarious signifier which is structurally deficient and "cannot account with sufficient rigor for the status of foreclosure", then this allows for the possibility of other, non-psychotic forms of foreclosure (ibid., p. 344). This permits asexuality to potentially represent an alternative foreclosure (i.e., of the Imaginary phallus), which has not, so far, been considered within existing Lacanian theory. It also permits the Name-of-the-Father, as structuring agent of the child's desire, to function. This theorized relation to the Imaginary phallus in asexuality is different to the position of perversion which, Lacan says, sees the child's relationship to the mother "constituted" by its "dependence on her love" (2006, pp. 462–463). In identifying with the Imaginary phallus in perversion, or indeed becoming the Imaginary phallus in neurosis, Lacan is saying that there is a "phallocentrism produced by this dialectic" between mother and child which is due to an "intrusion" of the phallic signifier into the child's psyche (ibid.). I have proposed that the asexual neither *identifies* with nor *becomes* the Imaginary phallus. Instead, the latter is foreclosed as the child seeks to defend itself from, and reverse its dependence on, the omnipotent desire of the first Other. It follows from this line of reasoning that, if the Imaginary phallus is foreclosed, there is little, if indeed any, intrusion of the phallic signifier into the child's psyche. In Lacan's view, the Imaginary phallus is the "pivotal point in the symbolic process" for both sexes (ibid.). On this basis, I have proposed that a foreclosed Imaginary phallus is, by extension, going to bring about a foreclosure of the Symbolic phallus so that desire as the desire of the Other is voided of phallic signification.

Asexuality and the *Sinthome*

I then proposed that asexuals who do not access or avail of self-identification for psychical support can have access to the *sinthome*. The *sinthome* is a conceptual device elaborated in Lacan's later teaching whereby a subject-specific act of artifice creates a fourth ring that ties the Borromean knot of Real, Symbolic and Imaginary together (2016, p. 131). This, I have maintained, allows asexuality to participate in a productive and creative engagement with desire. The emphasis in early Lacan was on the metaphor of the Name-of-the-Father whose function, inter alia, was to set the subject free from the desire of the mother (i.e., bring about a separation from her). In his later work, and in *Seminar XXIII* particularly, he moves away from metaphor to search for a new signifier that will provide the same function (i.e., to knot the three rings together). This self-created fiction which is the *sinthome* is the new signifier built upon the lack of the Other. I have proposed that in asexuality, the *sinthome* is also built upon the lack/omnipotent desire of the first Other as the desire of the mother, and the lack which it seeks to fill is experienced as an omnipotence which engenders psychical helplessness and is, therefore, traumatic. In this sense, while the desire of the first Other is experienced as overwhelming, so, too, is its correlative lack which is experienced by the child as unfillable and, indeed, unfathomable. Lacan's invitation is for all subjects to follow the example of James Joyce and create their own *sinthome* at this place of the lack of the Other. In the traditional psychoanalytic understanding, the aim of this creative act is to be able to function without dependence on the signifier of the Name-of-the-Father (i.e., the Other) (Verhaeghe and Declercq, 2002, p. 75).

However, in creating the *sinthome*, the asexual subject is not making up for the absence of the Name-of-the-Father but for the absence of the phallic signifier. Morel believes Lacan's concept of the *sinthome* frees the subject from any obligation to "become inscribed in the phallic function in order to subsume a relation to sex and sexuation" (2019, p. 308). What this effectively says is that via the *sinthome*, the subject can do without the phallus and still be a sexual and sexuated or gendered being. This is essentially what Lacan is saying in *Seminar XXIII* when he says of James Joyce's *sinthome* that his art is "the guarantor of his phallus" (2016, p. 7). In asexuality, the effects of the phallic signifier are absent because the Imaginary phallus, which is the foundation for the Symbolic phallus, has been foreclosed by the child. The lack of the mother, manifest through her desire, has been experienced as overwhelming, and the child has unconsciously chosen not to become the Imaginary phallus which might fill that lack. In this regard, Harari makes the point that the *sinthome* becomes the means by which the subject effectively escapes from the neurosis which is in response to the sexual demand the Other might impose (1995, pp. 32–33). As stated, the *sinthome* is an act of artifice, a personal, subjective creation and, as such, savoir-faire becomes the means by which it can be achieved (ibid., p. 116). Lacan is clear that in the case of James Joyce, the latter is unconscious of the fact that he is creating a *sinthome* (2016, p. 99). In a similar way, I have proposed that the non-self-identified asexual who might need the support of, or indeed the self-identified asexual who might need the *additional* support of, the creation of a *sinthome* can do so and remain unconscious of it.

The Absence of Subjective Distress

I have also proposed that the *objet petit a* as the nothing, as the cause of a desire for no sexual desire, is central to the phantasy which supports the asexual subject. The absence of subjective distress for self-identified asexuals is due to the relative tranquillity of the sexual drive in relation to phallic *jouissance*. If the *sinthome* compensates for the foreclosed signifier Phallus and allows the subject to func-tion, then the absence of subjective distress in sinthomatic asexuality is due to the comparatively "tranquil" (Harari, 1995, p. 233) effect of its function in knotting the three registers of Real, Symbolic and Imaginary together. As stated, the *sin-thome* is not a metaphor, not a substitution, nor indeed a sublimation, but rather a "making up for" as suppletion. It is an additional signifier that compensates in asexuality for the foreclosed signifier Phallus which does not now create phal-licized or sexualized meaning effects.

The *objet petit a* as the nothing in asexuality maintains a void whereby no substitute object, or *semblant*, takes up this position other than the object as void or zero, as I have proposed earlier. In this sense, the asexual fundamental phan-tasy could be said to represent a similar position to someone who has "traversed the radical phantasy", the term Lacan uses just once to describe the end of psy-choanalysis as a treatment (1977, pp. 273–274). As Neill (2014, p. 69) puts it, traversing the fundamental phantasy involves the subject assuming a position of responsibility for their phantasy. He says it is an acceptance of one's desire for what that desire is and "not attaching oneself to the illusory dream of attaining lost jouissance 'elsewhere'" through the "perpetual sliding of *objet petit a*". In keeping with the theory as it applies to sexually desiring subjects, he goes on to say that, insofar as *objet petit a* has no content and is a "no-thing", it must be marked by "some" content, even if whatever is chosen is never "it" (ibid.). I am proposing that the asexual puts the nothing in the place of *objet petit a*, not as something without content but as something similar to Miller's conception of zero as a "first object" (*Seminar XII*, session of 24 February 1965, p. 119). In this way, the asexual is, thus, assuming responsibility for their desire and not attaching to the illusory dream of attaining *jouissance* through metonymically shifting *objets petit a*. According to Harari, the *sinthome*, and the agency of symbolic nomination which produces it, alters the manner in which the *objet petit a* resides in the Other. As an act of symbolic nomination, or the invention of a name, it makes a Not-All of the Real of sexual desire, and when applied to asexuality, I have proposed that it makes up for the "sheer absence" of the phallic signifier. In short, the *sinthome* allows for the *objet petit a* to reside in the Other as the nothing as cause of desire in a manner that does not include sexual desire and without the experience of subjective distress.

Asexuality and "Delusional Normalism"

So far, I have highlighted how asexuality, in a similar way to Lacan's view of sex-uality, does not "satisfy the delusional normalism of the genital relation" (2006, p. 507). The asexual subject, through a hypothesized reversal of the relation of dependence at the oral and subsequent stages, and a consequent foreclosure of the Imaginary phallus, has subjectified lack.[5] From this perspective, the lack of sexual attraction is not a lack of libido but, instead, an active libidinal desire for no sexual desire. This is because the experience of the desire/lack of the Other begins with a traumatic inflection that is unpleasurable. This, I am proposing, is what shapes the asexual orientation and becomes concretized when the choice to become the Imaginary phallus for the mother is foreclosed. Gherovici (2017, p.375) says that the way subjects relate to lack determines the way they relate to their "sexual bodies", which is what psychoanalysis calls castration. She says the relation to lack will provide the foundation for "diverse structures of desire" whether those structures are "neurotic, perverse, fetishistic or homosexual" (ibid.). In this context, my proposition has been that asexuality is one further possibility that can manifest within these diverse structures of desire. Regarding such a diversity, Chen (2020, p. 181) points out that asexuality is often narrowly conceptualized as a negative space because of its lack of sexual desire, and she, too, argues that it is more than that. Her view, which supports an active libido operating within asexuality, is that the lived experiences of asexuals open onto other forms of eroticism and ways of living that can be just as fulfilling. While she says that it was through Freud's body of work that the erotic became bound to the sexual, she can equally point out that Freud also said it was not easy to decide what is covered by the concept of "sexual" (1916–1917, p. 303). He grapples with this question in his 1917 lecture *The Sexual Life of Human Beings*, concluding, inter alia, that the human sexual drive has always been independent of the twin binaries of having a reproductive aim and having a solely heterosexual object. He further adds that it has been this way, in his view, "from time immemorial" and "among all peoples" (ibid., p. 307). If the libido as the energy of the sexual drive is, and always has been, free to pursue its satisfactions in a wide variety of ways, then I would argue that it is feasible to include asexuality as another viable form of its expression.

Przybylo is working in similar terrain when she embraces the concept of an asexual "erotics" in order to think through a form of sexuality which is beyond sexual and bodily regimentation (2019, p. 26). In her argument, there are many ways to be desired and to desire, even to be aroused and to arouse, which are not "reducible to sex or encompassable by sexuality". She builds on the concept of a non-sexual "erotics", the term taken from a 1978 essay by American writer, feminist and activist Audre Lorde (2019, pp. 43–50),[6] and her aim is to establish such an erotics while distancing it from a Freudian understanding in which sexuality is at the base of all erotics. Her "erotics" is one in which it is possible to desire/be desired, arouse/be aroused, touch/be touched, love/be loved and attract/be attracted. But all this in a way that is not sexual or have a sexual base and without Freudian libido which, in her reading of it, conflates the erotic with sexuality. In contrast, I am theorizing that asexuality is a form of libidinal expression driven towards satisfactions which are non-sexual. In other words, the asexual derives a Freudian libidinal satisfaction from *not* having a sexual attraction towards the Other,[7] and I have included Lacan's theorizing of sublimation-as-equivalence in support of this. Przybylo (2019, p. 22) points out, in this instance similar to a Freudian view, that the "erotic" is an inner source of power that fuels "action and intimacy in the world". This, however, is not a sexually motivated energy but rather what she calls a reverse sublimation whereby the erotic, as a non-sexual life energy, is transferred into various activities which can include sex (ibid.). It is not possible to adequately summarize Przybylo's extensive theorizing, but suffice to say, it has elements which run parallel to the thesis proposed in this book while at the same time privileging a position which opposes a Freudian emphasis on the ubiquity of a sexual libido. However, the task which she sets herself – that is, how to rethink relationality when it is read as asexual and is without an investment in the "promises of sex and the sexual universal" (ibid., p. 26) – is in some ways similar to the objectives of this book.

Returning to a Lacanian perspective, and given that I have already proposed that the Phallus does not have the same use-function for asexual subjects as it does for sexual subjects, it is interesting to note how Gherovici posits the *sinthome* as that which allows Lacanian theorizing to move *beyond* the Phallus.[8] She describes the latter, variously, as that which is an "obstacle" and what she believes to be a "failed answer to the conundrum of sexual difference" (2017, p. 378), as well as a "defective tool to navigate the Real" (ibid., p. 374), that is, of sexualized bodily *jouissance*. Although her focus is on transgender issues, some of her comments are equally applicable to asexuality. Asexuals, too, could be said to have a "complex relationship" to their bodies, evidenced in their very different relation to sexual desire and in the particular way they derive *jouissance*. Extending the concept of a creative *sinthome*, she says a "push-towards-writing" is evident in transgender experience as a way in which "the body finds its anchor in the sea of language" (ibid., p. 379). While not intended to be comparable to the singular and creative writings of James Joyce, a similar "push-towards-writing" can be seen in the work of numerous published asexual writers as well as asexual bloggers writing about their experiences on the internet. In other words, writing has become the register in which the asexual subject has sought to creatively establish a support in a Symbolic order which has hitherto not had signifiers or discursive space for their subjectivity or lived experience.

The *sinthome* allows for a creation in the Symbolic, out of language, ex nihilo, which in turn allows the subject to deal with the "unbalance" of the "impossible relation between the sexes" (ibid., p. 374). The asexual experience can be free of subjective distress once identification as asexual has been accessed to support it. Without the support of self-identification, a *sinthome* can be created which allows for a relation to the Other which does not rely on a phallicization or sexualization of the relation within and between the sexes. This sex-free domain, or beyond of sexuality, is strikingly similar to the one on which some contemporary writers on homosexuality have been focussing. Tim Dean, for example, says that homosexuality should try to situate itself in a place that is "outside – or apart from – genitality". Arguing for the addition of an aesthetic practice to situate alongside an erotic practice, he says that far from a "poor substitute for sex, art may represent a more inventive mode of approaching jouissance". He says, "Beyond sexuality lie the myriad possibilities of aesthetics" (2000, p. 279). Needless to say, the co-option of art as a support for the impossibility of sex and sexual difference evokes

Lacan's concept of the *sinthome*. Leo Bersani goes further in terms of considering an alternative view of sex. In the opening lines of his essay, again with a focus on the homosexual experience, he says, "There is a big secret about sex: most people don't like it" (2010, p. 3). He goes on to reference the "immense body of contemporary discourse" that argues for a radical revision of thinking around "the body's capacity for pleasure" (ibid., pp. 20–23). In an earlier work, *The Culture of Redemption*, he is writing on Freud's theories of narcissism and sublimation and refers to what he calls "the peculiar idea of a sexuality independent of sex" (1990, pp. 32–33), a topic which has also been a focus of this book.

Some Questions to Be Addressed

The theoretical positions proposed in this book are not intended to be a closed or final representation with regard to a psychoanalytic understanding of asexuality and will require further discussion and will, hopefully, encourage further research. One area for consideration might be asexuality's position with regard to sexual difference, or "sexuation", to use the Lacanian term. I have proposed that the asexual position begins for both men and women with a pre-Oedipal foreclosure of the Imaginary phallus which, in turn, has forclusive consequences for the Symbolic phallus. In this way, a subject emerges who is not without having a sexual orientation but a sexual orientation that is not a phallically enjoying one. Proposing that such a subject might fit within the centre of Lacanian sexual theory (i.e., on both sides of the *Formulae of Sexuation*) was not intended to suggest that asexuality could only be thought as an offshoot, if you like, of dominant sexual discourses. Rather, the intention behind this proposal was twofold: firstly, that asexuality could be considered a part of sexuality and so exist as a radical alterity alongside and, indeed, within a theory of sexuality. Secondly, that it could do so in a way which has gone unnoticed in Lacan's overall theory, similar to what we find in Freud's theory with regard to his daughter Anna's hypothesized asexual orientation.

While Lacan has theorized an asexual *jouissance* on the woman side, one that is achieved through sublimation, I have been proposing an asexual on the woman side who has taken up that position due to a foreclosure of the phallic signifier. On the face of it, the two approaches are very different, but some ground for commonality can be found if Lacan's later theorizing with regard to sublimation-as-equivalence is taken into account. In contrast to Freudian sublimation which finds a substitute for sexual satisfactions in non-sexual activities, Lacan's version, which we find making its way into the thinking of current theorists, is that sublimation might instead offer an equivalent enjoyment which is sexual. This, then, raises the question as to whether sublimation might be the correct term given that there is no substitution being made in the classic sense of the non-sexual for the sexual. Rather this later theorizing appears to suggest that *jouissance* is being derived via sublimated activities which are in themselves sexual (i.e., carriers of libido). In this sense, we find that our understanding of what constitutes the sexual is being broadened to include activities which had traditionally been considered non-sexual. The question which then arises is whether the term "sublimation" which appears to have taken on a catch-all function should be opened up to further examination in the same way that we find Braunstein (2003) and Leader (2021) revisiting the term *jouissance* and refining what it might and might not mean.

My proposal that an asexual position could be included on the man side of the *Formulae* holds out the possibility that asexuality can be viewed not as a theoretical add-on to existing and dominant sexual discourses but rather as the opposite. If asexuality is viewed as a viable, but hitherto unconsidered, form of expression of the sexual drive, then two points emerge: first and the most obvious one, perhaps, is that it has a place within sexual discourse and is a sexual orientation. Second, this reading of a male asexuality at the heart of a phallically structured theory of maleness represents not a support for but a critique of the psychosocial centrality of masculine sex and sexuality in Western cultures. In other words, this book has been an attempt to use psychoanalytic theory and its assumption of the primacy of phallic sexuality in order to propose that a different form of sexuality is possible on the side of men also which offers equally viable forms of libidinal satisfaction and desire.

I have argued that on the man side, an asexual exception which arrives there as the result of foreclosure of the phallic signifier still supports the exceptional quality of this position in relation to all men who phallically enjoy. I have also argued that this provides a possible answer to the question posed in Freud's myth as to why the sons after his murder implement the very rule which the Father had imposed on them. However, these are aspects which are beyond the scope of this book and which will undoubtedly benefit from further attention. One further point might be whether the theorizing of the asexual position supports the distinct sexuated positions between man and woman. Positing a common origin for male and female asexuality (i.e., foreclosure) might at first sight appear to threaten this dissymmetry, but while again it is a topic for further discussion, I would offer that dissymmetry between the sexes still remains intact in that the exception is still valid on the man side just as the Not-All is on the woman side.

That an asexual subject functions without the phallic signifier has implications for the Lacanian theoretical position of the phallus as the universal signifier of sexual desire and the signifier which distinguishes between the sexes in terms of "being" the phallus (woman) or "having" the phallus (men). As Buhle (1998, p. 327) puts it, by translating the Oedipus complex into a linguistic event, Lacan offers a theory of sexual difference which "fully evades the lure of biologism", and the signifier phallus as symbolic, "is, simply, that which functions to produce a subjectivity that is sexed". But some psychoanalytic theorists, as mentioned earlier, are questioning whether the phallus is an adequate signifier of sexual difference,[9] or the sole possibility for distinguishing male and female positions, particularly in the light of Lacan's later theorizing. If, as I have proposed, the asexual can function without the signifier phallus, what does this imply for the latter's all-encompassing role? As stated, Morel (2019, p. 308) says that Lacan's invention of the *sinthome*, which is a concept that "crowns" the Name-of-the-Father,[10] means that there is no longer any obligation for the subject to "become inscribed in the phallic function" in order to take up a position in relation to sex or sexuation (ibid.). She says, "Sexual difference, which since Freud's time has been measured using the yardstick of the phallus, now also needs to be considered in quite another way" (ibid., p. 309). Similarly, Gherovici says the phallus only refers to phallic *jouissance* (i.e., sexual *jouissance*) and that "other forms" of non-phallic *jouissance* exist and can be experienced. She says, "Sexual positioning is predicated on an 'error' that consists of taking the real organ for a signifier of sexual difference. The error is to take the phallus as a signifier of sexual difference" (2011, p. 13). Dean argues that sexual difference is secondary in determining sexual desire because desire originates in the unconscious which knows nothing of sexual difference (2000, pp. 87–88). From his perspective, it is the *objet petit a* which "demotes or relativizes" the concept of the phallus because, while the latter implies a univocal model of desire, the former offers multiple possibilities (ibid., p. 250). Minsky (1996) is of the view that Lacan himself "pulls the theoretical rug" from under the phallus with his idea that it only *seems* to have power because of its value as a signifier.[11] As a signifier, it has an arbitrary value, lacks status in itself and is, therefore, a "bogus" signifier. "If the status of the phallus is false and arbitrary, then so are all these other oppositions modelled on the binary meanings of the phallus and the lack, 'masculinity' and 'femininity', by which we structure our world", she says (1996, p. 159). Cox Cameron says that Lacan was operating from within an ineluctably androcentric symbolic order which had begun the reinstallation of the patriarchy after World War II. His concept of the phallus, therefore, enters the vocabulary of psychoanalysis, "freighted with centuries of semantic ballast which cannot but render questionable its all-encompassing range of reference" (2021, p. 202).[12] While these approaches might appear critical of this aspect of Lacanian theory, they also throw light on fertile possibilities within it to consider new pathways for conceiving gender difference as well as sexuality and, for the purposes of this book, asexuality. Each in their way are inviting a reconsideration of an accepted tenet of Lacanian theory by questioning the efficacy of the phallus in its role as the universal determinant of sexual difference and signifier of sexual desire. As stated, such a reconsideration has not been the direct focus of this book, but it has been raised by implication as a result of the theorized aetiology of asexuality.

Other questions which would benefit from further consideration include: the proposed foreclosure of the Imaginary phallus; the theorized concomitant foreclosure of the Symbolic phallus; the functioning of the Name-of-the-Father as agent of metaphoric substitution despite these foreclosures; the operative unconscious presence of a fundamental phantasy which includes the *objet petit a* as the nothing; the functionality of a *jouissance* that is non-phallic for both male and female asexuals on both sides of the *Formulae of Sexuation*; and the *sinthome* as it might operate in the lived experience of both self-identified and non-self-identified asexual subjects. An area that would also benefit from further examination is asexuality's relation to the Freudian concepts of female frigidity and male impotence. Are clinically significant forms of female frigidity and male sexual impotence distressing because of the *absence* of either identification or the *sinthome* as support? Has there been a similar foreclosure of the Imaginary phallus in lifelong frigidity and impotence as I have been proposing for asexuality? If so, what are the factors that allow for identification or a *sinthome* to be created in asexuality while frigidity and impotence can produce distress for the subject?

Within Lacanian theory, there is a sense of conflicting importance given to the pre-Oedipal phase. On the one hand, Lacan places great emphasis on this area in his theorizing in *Seminar IV* and in his regard for Melanie Klein's work (2020, pp. 177–178). It can also be found elsewhere in his writings on the oral stage.[13] On the other hand, he is also capable of describing pre-Oedipal stages as "analytically unthinkable" (2006, p. 462). He suggests considering the term "pregenital stages" which are amenable to psychoanalysis via the retroactive effect of the Oedipus complex (ibid.). Further theoretical research might allow for a synthesis between Lacan's concept of the analytically unthinkable aspect of pre-Oedipal stages with what I have proposed in terms of the theoretically thinkable aspects of them.[14] Further work is also necessary to elaborate on my proposed egressive effects of the pre-Oedipal on the Oedipus complex, compared to Lacan's and Freud's emphasis on the retroactive signifying effects of the Oedipus complex.

Finally, it is clear that the work of Lacanian theorists, as well as theorists from other approaches, is broadening out the concept of sexuality itself. In particular, the idea that the sexual at the heart of human experience might escape any meaning we might apply to it is shaping theoretical endeavour more than at any other time. As such, this is the terrain in which we find asexuality as a sexual orientation which experiences no sexual attraction to another person. Its proponents argue that, on account of this characteristic, asexuality asks some fundamental questions about sexuality, and so, in this context, further research might allow for a fuller examination of areas of commonality or disparity between asexuality and, inter alia, the "redemptive reinvention" of sexuality proposed by Bersani (2010, p. 22) and the "eroticism beyond genitalia" proposed by Dean (2000, p. 279)

Notes

1 Chen (2020, pp. 20–21) also makes this point about the presence of libido as a sexual drive in asexuality. She says, "aces" (asexuals) have a libido but without sexual *attraction* – that is, libido that is not aimed at the Other.

2 This is in contrast to Foucault's view (1990, p. 105, 155, 157) that sexuality is a "historical construct", the product of a societally based "surface network" of power agencies.

3 See, in Engelman, 2008, online pagination, p. 8, the comment submitted by "Guest". See also, Bogaert, 2004, p. 284; Brotto et al., 2010, p. 615.

4 See also, Lacan, 2006, p. 580.

5 Fink (1999, pp. 215–216) describes subjectification, in analytic treatment, as a coming into being of the subject where *it* was (i.e., where the drives were). He says, "To subjectify them (drives) is to give them a place, and perhaps an importance, otherwise refused them. To see them as one's own is already a step toward allowing them expression".

6 In Lorde's writing of it, "erotics" is conceived as a resource/source of power which is purely available to women, a potentially limiting gender binary which Przybylo acknowledges. This puts it in close accord with Lacan's concept of feminine *jouissance*, except that Lacan's feminine *jouissance* can also be accessed by men. Lorde's version is female, has a "spiritual" element and has an arcane quality of being "unrecognised" by women, elements also found in Lacan's concept. See Lacan, 1999, pp. 74–76, and see Lorde, 2019, pp. 43–46.

7 Minsky (1996, p. 162) similarly refers to "sources of pleasure" in Lacan's concept of Feminine *jouissance* which "lie beyond the reach and meaning of heterosexual physical satisfaction based on the phallus". She cites Lacan's reference to Bernini's statue of Saint Theresa as depicting a form of bliss "entirely separate from the phallic function".

8 For a similar approach, see also Morel, 2019, p. 304, 309.

9 We can also note gender theorist Judith Butler's (1990, p. 67) criticism that the phallus supports a binary and masculine heteronormativity.

10 See Lacan, 2016, p. 147.

11 Lacan, it could be argued, does something similar with his idea of feminine *jouissance* which he associates quite clearly with a *jouissance* that is "beyond the phallus" (2016, p. 74).

12 Cox Cameron (2021, p. 203) describes Lacan's "ever-widening" role of the phallus as the signifier "upholding the whole world of meaning" as "a leap into the ludicrous".

13 See Lacan's comment on the child who is most lovingly fed being the one who refuses food and employs this refusal as if it were a desire (2006, p. 524).

14 Leader (2021, p. 45) says, "To simply call the infant's state prior to the mirror phase a 'chaos', as Lacan does several times, shuts down a rich field of research on early symbolic, corporeal and affective processes".

References

Bersani, L. (1990) *The culture of redemption*. Cambridge, MA: Harvard University Press.

Bersani, L. (2010) *Is the rectum a grave? And other essays*. Chicago: University of Chicago Press.

Bogaert, A. F. (2004) 'Asexuality: Its prevalence and associated factors in a national probability sample', *Journal of Sex Research*, 41(3), pp. 279–287.

Braunstein, N. A. (2003) 'Desire and jouissance in the teachings of Lacan', in Rabaté, J.-M. (ed.), *The Cambridge Companion to Lacan*. Cambridge: Cambridge University Press, pp. 102–115.

Brotto, L. A., Knudson, G., Inskip, J., Rhodes, K. and Erskine, Y. (2010) 'Asexuality: A mixed-methods approach', *Archives of Sexual Behavior*, 39(3), pp. 599–618.

Buhle, M. J. (1998) *Feminism and its discontents – A century of struggle with psychoanalysis*. Cambridge, MA: Harvard University Press.

Butler, J. (1990) *Gender trouble – Feminism and the subversion of identity*. New York: Routledge.

Chen, A. (2020) *ACE – What asexuality reveals about desire, society and the meaning of sex*. Boston: Beacon Press.

Copjec, J. (2016) 'The sexual compact', in Cerda-Rueda, A. (ed.), *Sex and nothing – Bridges from psychoanalysis to philosophy*. London: Karnac, pp. 107–137.

Cox Cameron, O. (2021) (with Owens. C.), *Studying Lacan's seminar VI: Dream, symptom, and the collapse of subjectivity*. Oxford: Routledge.

Dean, T. (2000) *Beyond sexuality*. Chicago: University of Chicago Press.

Engelman, J. (2008) *Asexuality as a human sexual orientation*. Available at: https://serendipstudio.org/exchange/serendipupdate/asexuality-human-sexual-orientation [Accessed 1 November 2021].

Fink, B. (1999) *A clinical introduction to Lacanian psychoanalysis*. Cambridge: Harvard University Press.

Foucault, M. (1990 [1978]) *The history of sexuality*, Vol. 1, An introduction (Hurley, R., trans). New York: Vintage.

Freud, S. (1905) 'Three essays on sexuality', in *A case of hysteria, three essays on sexuality and other works*, Standard Edition VII. London: Vintage/Hogarth.

Freud, S. (1915a) 'Instincts and their vicissitudes', in *On the history of the psycho-analytic movement, papers on metapsychology and other works*, Standard Edition XIV. London: Vintage/Hogarth.

Freud, S. (1915b) 'Repression', in *On the history of the psycho-analytic movement, papers on metapsychology and other works*, Standard Edition XIV. London: Vintage/Hogarth.

Freud, S. (1916–1917) *Introductory lectures on psycho-analyses*, Standard Editions XV–XVI. London: Vintage/Hogarth.

Freud, S. (1920) 'Beyond the pleasure principle', in *Beyond the pleasure principle, group psychology and other works*, Standard Edition XVIII. London: Vintage/Hogarth.

Freud, S. (1924) 'The dissolution of the Oedipus complex', in *The ego and the id and other works*, Standard Edition XIX. London: Vintage/Hogarth.

Gherovici, P. (2011) 'Psychoanalysis needs a sex change', *Gay & Lesbian Issues and Psychology Review*, 7(1), pp. 3–18.

Gherovici, P. (2017) 'Sexual difference: From symptom to sinthome', in Giffney, N. and Watson, E. (eds.), *Clinical encounters in sexuality: Psychoanalytic practice & queer theory*. California: Punctum Books.

Harari, R. (1995) *How Joyce made his name – A reading of the final Lacan* (Thurston, L., trans). New York: Other Press.

Lacan, J. (1966–1967) *The logic of phantasy*, Seminar XIV, unpublished (Gallagher, C., trans). Available at: www.lacaninireland.com [Accessed 21 November 2021].

Lacan, J. (1977 [1964]) *The four fundamental concepts of psycho-analysis*, Seminar XI (Miller, J-A., ed.) (Sheridan, A., trans). London: Penguin.

Lacan, J. (1993 [1955–1956]) *The psychoses*, Seminar III (Miller, J.-A., ed.) (Grigg, R., trans). New York: Norton.

Lacan, J. (1999 [1972–1973]) *Encore*, Seminar XX (Miller, J.-A., ed.) (Fink, B., trans). New York: Norton.

Lacan, J. (2006 [1966]) *Écrits – The first complete English edition* (Fink, B., trans). New York: W. W. Norton.

Lacan, J. (2016 [1975–1976]) *The sinthome*, Seminar XXIII (Miller, J.-A., ed.) (Price, A. R., trans). Cambridge: Polity.

Lacan, J. (2019 [1958–1959]) *Desire and its interpretation*, Seminar VI (Miller, J.-A., ed.) (Fink, B., trans). Cambridge: Polity Press.

Lacan, J. (2020 [1956–1957]) *The object relation*, Seminar IV (Miller, J.-A. ed.) (Price, A. R., trans). Cambridge: Polity Press.

Laplanche, J. and Pontalis, J. B. (1973) *The language of psycho-analysis* (Nicholson-Smith, D., trans). London: Hogarth Press/Institute of Psycho-Analysis.

Leader, D. (2021) *Jouissance – Sexuality, suffering and satisfaction*. Cambridge: Polity.

Lorde, A. (2019 [1978]) 'Uses of the erotic: The erotic as power', in *Sister Outsider*. London: Penguin.

Minsky, R. (1996) *Psychoanalysis and gender, An introductory reader*. Routledge: New York.

Morel, G. (2019) *The law of the mother: An essay on the sexual sinthome*. New York: Routledge.

Neill, C. (2014 [2011]) *Without ground – Lacanian ethics and the assumption of subjectivity*. London: Palgrave Macmillan.

Przybylo, E. (2019) *Asexual erotics: Intimate readings of compulsory sexuality*. Columbus, OH: Ohio State University Press.

Verhaeghe, P. and Declercq, F. (2002) 'Lacan's analytical goal: "Le Sinthome" or the feminine way', in Thurston, L. (ed.), *Essays on the final Lacan. Re-inventing the symptom*. New York: Other Press, pp. 59–83. Available at: https://biblio.ugent.be/publication/8513109/file/8513112.pdf [Accessed 4 November 2021].

Index

absence 5–10, 13–14, 20, 22, 28, 39,
42, 52–53, 67–68, 74–75, 78, 82,
89–93, 95–96, 107–109, 112, 135, 138,
143, 145–150, 155–157, 159–160,
164–165, 171; savoured 85, 89, 93, 95,
123, 140, 159; sexual attraction 2, 6, 14,
25, 70, 72, 83, 90, 122, 142, 149;
see also lack, of sexual attraction
abstinence 33, 38, 76, 121
Aicken, C. R. H. 3
ambivalence 73, 121
annulment 13–14, 88, 91, 101, 107–108,
117, 125–127, 133, 139, 161–162
anxiety 30, 64, 67, 73–74, 83, 95, 137, 147
aromantic 26
asexual erotics 5, 166
asexuality: definition 1–3, 11, 14, 20–23,
25–26, 50, 92, 107, 156; history 3–5;
pathology 2, 13, 21, 23–24, 142;
subjective distress 2, 8, 12, 21–22, 28,
42, 67, 72, 74, 78, 90, 95, 138, 150, 158,
164–165, 167
AVEN 1–4, 23–26

Baumle, A. K. 3
Bernini, G. L. 117
Brajterman Lerner, R. C. 29
breast 11, 41, 43, 47–49, 83–86, 93, 112,
114, 126–127, 138–139, 159
Bogaert, A. 2–3, 20–22, 24–25,
28, 39
Boston Marriage 5
Bostridge, M. 4
Braunstein, N. 169
Brehony, K. A. 5
Brotto, L. A. 1–2, 23, 25, 27, 39, 45, 50,
66, 71–72, 74, 108
Buhle, M. J. 90, 169
Burlingham, D. 32

Carrigan, M. 12, 26–27, 44, 51, 68,
70–71, 96, 122, 142, 149
castration 29–30, 95, 107, 110–115,
119–120, 123–124, 133, 137, 139,
162, 166
celibacy 1, 4, 23, 43
Chassaing, J-L. 29–30
Chen, A. 1, 8, 87, 166
choice 1, 6–7, 10, 23, 30, 40, 42–43,
47–55, 63–65, 69, 79n10, 84, 89,
99–101, 127, 134, 139, 159,
161–162, 166
code of demand 139, 161–162
Cole, E. 22
compulsory sexuality x, 152n12
Copjec, J. 4, 155
courtly love 124
Cox Cameron, O. 170

das Ding 82–83, 109
death drive 141
debasement, psychical 76–77
Decker, J. S. 122
delusional normalism 165
demand: ego 63; libidinal 2, 13, 46, 65, 67,
87, 89, 91, 95, 109–110, 138–139, 150,
161, 164; Other's 85, 89, 95, 112, 116,
122–127, 149, 150
De Paulo, B. 121
dependence 84–85, 93–95, 98, 112–113,
134, 159–160, 163, 165; *see also*
reversal of dependence
desexualization 43–44, 47, 54, 60, 62,
69–70, 86–88, 108, 127, 141, 157
desire 1–6, 9–14, 20–27, 29–32, 37–43,
46, 50–51, 53–54, 62–65, 67–71, 75,
78, 82–93, 95–96, 98, 101, 107–119,
121–125, 133–134, 136–144,
147–150, 156–167, 169–170

Diagnostic and Statistical Manual
(DSM-5) 2
dialectic of frustration 93, 96
dialectic of substitution 89, 93, 96,
139, 161
Diana, Roman goddess 4
Dora case study 60, 96, 121, 124
drive, the 10, 14, 40–41, 61, 69, 71, 87,
94, 96, 99–100, 118, 124, 149, 154,
156, 160
dustuchia 98

ego 9, 13, 32, 42–45, 47, 52, 60–66,
68–70, 74–75, 88, 97, 99, 107
ego ideal 13, 62–64, 70
ego instincts 44, 61
ego syntonic 63, 75, 78n5
egression 158, 161
Engelman, J. 4–5
Erdős, P. 4, 143
Eros 43, 141
erotic, the 5, 166–167
erotic fantasy 20
eroticism 48
erotogenic zones 43, 52
Evans, D. 134
exception, the 119–121, 129n17, 129n28,
151n5, 169
ex-sistence 117, 151n5

fantasy 7, 16n30, 20, 29, 31, 34n3, 39, 42,
50, 85, 88–89, 98, 108–109, 111, 120;
see also fundamental phantasy; phantasy
Feminine *jouissance* 117, 119, 128n4,
128n19, 151n5, 172n6, 172n7, 172n11;
see also jouissance
Fink, B. 83, 102n20, 119, 125, 128n15,
129n23, 133, 151n5, 172n5
foreclosure 13–14, 78, 133–139, 141,
143–144, 146–147, 149, 151n5, 157,
162–163, 165, 168–171
Formulae of Sexuation 121, 117–119,
151n5, 168–170
Fort-Da game 98
Foster, A. B. 143
Frege, G. 91–92, 102n19
Freud, A. 32–33, 34n11, 78n1, 144, 168
Freud, S. 2, 6–13, 32–33, 37–55, 60–78,
82, 84, 87–90, 94, 96, 98–99, 107,
117–121, 124–126, 138, 149, 155–159,
166, 168–171
frigidity 9, 13, 33, 34n17, 72, 75–78,
79n16, 79n21, 129n20, 171

frustration 43, 49, 50, 93, 96, 126–127,
138, 158
fundamental phantasy 10, 30, 82–83,
85–87, 89–90, 109, 140–141, 148, 165,
170; *see also* fantasy; phantasy

genital primacy 49
Gherovici, P. 2, 83, 123, 143, 145–146,
150, 166–167, 170
gift, the 84, 94, 127, 160
Graham, C. A. 21, 23
Green, A. 102n17
Grigg, R. 120–121, 133–134, 136
groups 21, 26–27, 61–62, 78n2, 142
GuéGuen, P-G. 122

hainamoration 121
hallucinatory satisfaction 87
Hansen de Almeida, R. 29
Harari, R. 135–136, 144, 147–148,
150–151, 163–165
Haven for the Human Amoeba 3, 79n9
Heisenberg uncertainty principle 125
helplessness (*hilflosligkeit*) 11, 84, 89, 95,
101n1, 102n11, 140–141, 161, 164
heterosexuality 2, 12, 21, 71, 94,
146, 156
Hinderliter, A. C. 3
homosexuality 2, 14n6, 21, 39, 129n31,
146, 167
Hook, D. 112, 116, 128n6
hypoactive sexual desire disorder 3,
20–21, 24–25
hysteria 7, 49, 72, 74, 90, 98, 102n14,
121–125, 129n29, 150, 159

id 44–45, 57n22, 60, 63–64, 74–75, 88,
152n13
idealization 9, 76, 129n22
identification 142
imaginary phallus *see* phallus
impotence 9, 13, 72, 75–78, 171
incest 48, 54, 57n28, 75–76, 78, 87,
119–120
infantile amnesia 39, 156
infantile masturbation 48; *see also*
masturbation
infantile psychosexual stages 12, 14, 55,
89, 94, 139, 160
infantile sexuality 7–8, 11, 13, 37,
39–41, 47–55, 65, 67, 71, 78, 89, 126,
156–158, 160
inhibition 13, 33, 73–77, 93

instinct 9, 33, 41–43, 46–54, 56n11, 56n14, 61, 67, 69, 72–73, 155, 159; *see also* ego instincts; sexual instinct
introjection 60, 62, 78n4

Jay, D. 3
Joan of Arc. 4
jouissance 5, 10, 12, 15n21, 30–31, 69, 89, 90, 92, 100, 108, 117, 123–124, 129nn16–19, 129n21, 129n26, 129n31, 135, 143, 145, 147–149, 165, 167–169; asexual 11, 118, 128n4, 128n15, 133, 138, 168; non-phallic 117, 119, 170; not prescribed by the Other 12, 148–150; phallic 10, 90, 108–109, 117, 121, 129n26, 147, 165, 170; *see also* Feminine *jouissance*
Joyce, J. 135–136, 144–145, 147, 149–151, 164, 167

Kahn, K. 31
Kaplan, R. 102n15
Kierkegaard, S. 128n4
Klein, M. 84, 94, 111–112, 160, 171
Kojève, A. 151n8
Kris, E. 140

Lacan, J. 5, 7, 10–14, 31, 38, 41, 43, 45, 69, 82–101, 107–127, 133–141, 143–151, 159–166, 169–171
lack 13, 29–30, 33, 83, 86, 88–89, 91–92, 101n1, 107–108, 110–112, 115, 121–123, 129n18, 129n31, 135, 140, 150, 164–166; of sexual attraction 2, 9, 11, 13–14, 20–25, 33, 41, 51, 53, 70, 75, 93, 96, 126, 133, 141, 159, 165; *see also* absence
Laplanche, J. 90, 126, 129n22, 161
latency period 8, 13, 39, 48, 51–54, 73, 157
Lawrence, T.E. 4, 143
Leader, D. 15n21, 29, 40, 102n22, 127, 128n8, 151n7, 169, 172n14
Le Gaufey, G. 102n8, 119
LGBTQIA+ 2–3, 19, 39, 52, 123, 156
libido 2, 6–10, 12–14, 33, 37, 41–47, 49, 52, 55, 60–65, 68–70, 72–74, 76–78, 85, 87, 89, 92–93, 96, 101, 108–109, 117–118, 128n15, 138, 155, 157–160, 165–168, 171n1
Lorde, A. 166, 172n6

Masters and Johnson 27–28
masturbation 1, 9, 21, 23, 25, 29, 48, 50–51, 66, 68, 85, 108
Miller, J-A. 92, 165
Miller, N. E. 4–5
Minsky, R. 170, 172n7
Mirror Stage 31, 94, 97
Moncayo, R. 95, 135, 148–149
Morel, G. 10, 79n10, 100, 136–137, 143, 146–147, 150–151, 163–164, 169
Morrissey. 4, 143
mother 37, 43, 63, 126–127, 128n5, 128n6, 140; breast 43, 48; desire 11, 94, 111, 164; incest taboo 54, 75–76; lost object 62, 98; object choice 55, 61; omnipotence 84–85, 89, 93–95, 141, 159–161; phallus 14, 111–113, 115, 117, 128n9, 133–134, 136–137, 139, 160, 166; *see also* separation

Name-of-the-Father 100, 133–135, 137, 139, 144, 146–149, 151n7, 162–164, 170
narcissism 9, 13, 30, 45, 61–65, 68, 168
need 13, 15n21, 31, 38, 43, 46, 48–49, 51–52, 83–84, 87, 91, 95, 109, 125–126, 138–139, 161
negation 83, 93, 102n16, 140, 151n8
negativism 84, 94, 114
Newton, I. 4, 143
Nightingale, F. 4, 143
nihil negativum 86, 102n8
Nirvana principle 90, 141, 152n10
Nobus, D. 79n10
normative heterosexuality 12, 31, 71–72, 146
nothing, the 14, 82–86, 88–89, 91–95, 108, 110, 114, 116, 121, 126–127, 140–141, 148, 159–161, 164–165

object choice 6, 8, 10–11, 40–41, 47–52, 54–55, 60–61, 69–70; non-sexual 10, 14, 47, 53, 60, 63–64; sexual 7, 9, 10, 13, 37–38, 40–45, 49, 51, 53, 55, 60–63, 68–69, 75–76; *see also* idealization
objet petit a 10, 82–83, 85–87, 89–91, 98–101, 107–109, 111, 121, 123, 125, 140–141, 170; as the nothing 110, 116, 128n4, 128n13, 141, 148, 164–165, 170
obsessional neurosis 7, 72–73, 98, 121, 150

Oedipus complex 48, 51–54, 61, 63–64, 75, 77–78, 87, 93, 111–113, 157, 161, 169, 171
oral drive 84, 92, 140, 160
oral stage 41, 84, 94, 114, 126, 138–139, 160, 171
O'Reilly, Z. 3
Other, the 16n28, 41, 63, 82, 128n5, 128n8, 135; asexual relation to 14, 31, 49, 51, 61, 64, 69, 78, 87, 90, 92, 95, 123, 127, 166–167; desire of 11–12, 86, 110–111, 114–116, 121, 123, 136; first Other 14, 84–85, 89–90, 93, 95, 97–98, 125; Other-directed 6, 11, 13, 33, 52, 62, 82, 96, 117–118; sexual relation to 31, 76, 85, 96, 98, 100; *see also* reversal of dependence

Palomera, V. 121
paradox 14, 25, 37, 47, 62, 69, 72, 75, 86, 88–89, 92, 102n20, 109–110, 116, 118, 120, 140, 145, 159
Pardo, É. 30
paternal metaphor 113, 120, 137, 151n4, 151n7
pathology x–xi, 2, 13, 21, 23–24, 142
perversion 41, 48, 56n12, 123, 134–137, 151, 163
phallocentrism 136, 163
phallus 86, 114–115, 128n6, 128n9, 128n17, 137; annulled/foreclosed 91–92, 108, 110–111, 115–118, 137, 139, 141, 143, 146–149, 157, 162–164, 171; beyond the 167, 172n11; imaginary 11, 14, 111–113, 115, 117, 133–139, 146, 157, 160, 162–166, 168, 170–171; signifier of desire 11, 29, 90–91, 110–111, 114, 117, 139, 169–170; symbolic 29, 95, 112–115, 117, 135–137, 139–140, 146, 160, 162–164, 168, 170
phantasy 7, 10, 15n22, 30, 34n3, 71, 85–86, 88–89, 95, 107–108, 110–111, 116, 121–125, 128n3, 140–141, 164–165; *see also* fantasy; fundamental phantasy
Plato 100, 102n8
pleasure 5–7, 10–12, 15n21, 31, 33, 38–39, 41–42, 44–50, 55, 65–67, 69, 76, 85, 87, 90, 98, 117, 119, 128n6, 128n15, 148, 155, 168, 172n7
pleasure principle 15n21, 31, 44–45, 65–66, 69, 87

polymorphously perverse 39, 56n7
Pontalis, J-B. 90, 126, 129n22, 161
Prause, N. 21, 23
preconscious 49, 56n21
pre-Oedipal 14, 48, 54, 63, 67, 78, 90, 93, 98, 116, 127, 133, 137, 157–159, 163, 168, 171
primal father 120, 151n5
primordial 84, 94, 97, 99, 108–109, 134, 136–137, 141, 163
Przybylo, E. 5, 27–28, 57n25, 128n12, 128n14, 152n12, 166–167, 172n6
psychiatry 2
psychosis 13–14, 123, 133–137, 144, 147, 151, 162

queer theory 4, 40

Real, the 12, 29, 31, 83, 96–101, 102n9, 103n28, 117, 123–125, 134–135, 140–141, 143–144, 148–150, 151n7, 152n14, 161–163, 165, 167
reality principle 44, 66, 87
refusal 75–76, 83–84, 93, 95, 108, 114–115, 126–127, 128n8, 138, 140–141, 159, 161, 172n13
regression 49, 55, 60, 93, 115, 158–159, 161
rejecting intention 133, 139
religion, influence of 20–21, 38, 77, 100, 117, 119–120, 128n4, 129n21
repetition 50–51, 68, 89, 96–99, 141, 143
repression 8–9, 13, 32–33, 40, 48–49, 52–54, 57n22, 63–67, 69–74, 78, 93, 114, 118, 157–159, 161
resistance 9, 49, 69, 72, 77, 96, 99, 140, 159
reversal of dependence 13, 85, 89, 92–94, 98, 108, 112–113, 117, 126, 134, 140–141, 159–161, 163, 165
romantic relationships 1, 9, 12, 21, 24, 26, 124, 159
Rose, J. 102n18
Rothblum, E. D. 5
Roudinesco, É. 151n3

Salecl, R. 123
Scherrer, K. S. 16n26, 22–23, 26, 34n10, 142
Schopenhauer, A. 88, 102n13
sensuality 76–77
separation 113, 128n8, 133–134, 137, 140, 143, 146–147, 151n7, 161–164

sex-negative messages 77
sex-normative 33, 64, 87, 141, 149
sexual activity 1–2, 6, 8–9, 13, 20–21,
    23–25, 30, 34n7, 41, 45, 50, 53, 55, 66,
    75–77, 118; non-sexual 9, 29, 43, 75,
    118, 128n15
sexual arousal disorder 2–3
sexual attraction: absence of 1–3, 5–14,
    20–26, 28–29, 33, 34n10, 41, 46, 52,
    63, 66, 68–72, 76, 82–83, 86, 90, 96,
    107, 122, 126, 128n14, 138, 142, 149,
    156–157, 165–166, 171, 171n1
sexual drive 2, 7, 47–48, 55n2, 56n7,
    56n17, 60–61, 70, 75, 129; asexual
    9, 31–32, 40, 43–44, 53–54, 62–63,
    67, 71, 88, 108, 118, 157–158, 165,
    169, 171n1; object of 10, 37, 40–41;
    plasticity of 7, 39, 166; trauma of 8–9,
    11, 13, 52, 57n26, 64–67, 89–90,
    95–100, 107, 110, 112, 123, 125, 127,
    141, 156, 161, 164, 166; ubiquity of 2,
    7–8, 37, 40–41, 160; unpleasurable, as
    8–9, 41, 55, 64–67, 69–70, 75, 77, 155
sexual instinct 9, 41–43, 46–48, 51–54,
    61, 67, 72–73, 155, 159
sexual intercourse 1, 23–25
sexual relationship 32, 68, 100–101
sexual satisfaction 40–44, 46–47, 49–50,
    56n5, 62–63, 87–88, 118, 124, 158, 168
sexual normativity 4, 101
sinthome 12, 31, 135, 171; act of artifice,
    as 143, 145; asexuality and 14, 31,
    143, 147, 163–165, 167, 170; creation
    ex nihilo 150, 167; individuality of
    143–144, 150; Joycean 135–136, 144;
    nomination and 148; separation and
    146–147; sexuality and 146; signifier,
    as 144–150, 165; suppletion, as 149;
    universality 150
Soler, C. 12, 71, 94, 123–124
Spaltung 98, 110
Storms, M. 19–20, 27
subjectification 122–123, 165, 172n5
sublimation 9, 13, 31–32, 43–45, 53,
    60, 62, 67, 93, 107, 118, 125, 129n21,
    129n23, 147, 157–159, 165, 168–169;
    equivalence, as 118, 166–168; limit of
    45, 129n22, 158

sucking 48, 50, 93
super-ego 32, 63–64
symbolic annihilation 84
symbolic phallus see phallus
symptom 7, 12, 15n23, 22, 33, 49–50, 54,
    56n5, 56n22, 70–74, 77–78, 90, 94–95,
    112–113, 115–116, 121–124, 129n29,
    135–136, 139, 141, 144–151,
    158–159, 162

Thurston, L. 144
transference 64–65, 96–99, 103n25
trauma see sexual drive
tuché 97, 99

unconscious, the 7–8, 10, 13, 15n22, 34n3,
    39, 44, 46, 51, 54–55, 55n1, 63, 66, 69,
    74, 76–77, 79n10, 84–88, 92, 95–100,
    103, 108–109, 111, 113–114, 116, 127,
    128n3, 128n6, 133, 138–139, 142–143,
    146, 151, 157, 160–162, 164, 170;
    sexual reality of 96–98
unpleasure 7–8, 11, 14, 15n21, 40, 44, 47,
    55, 66–67, 69, 71, 74, 84, 87, 89, 95,
    99–100, 158

Vanheule, S. 122
Verhaeghe, P. 99, 120, 128n5, 139,
    148–150
Versagung 126–127, 138–139, 161–162
Verwerfung 133–135, 151n3
Vidal, G. 4, 144
Virgin Mary 4
void 89, 95, 107–108, 110, 121, 128n4,
    134, 141, 148, 160, 163, 165
Voruz, V. 124

Wajcman, G. 102n14, 129n29
Weeks, J. 55n1, 78n3
Wirklichkeit 141
Witty Butcher's Wife 124
Wrathall, N. 4

zero 83, 90–92, 102n15, 102n16, 102n17,
    102n19, 139, 141–142, 152n10,
    162, 165
Žižek, S. 89, 101n5, 129n21, 141, 152n10
Zupančič, A. 7, 118, 128n2

For Product Safety Concerns and Information please contact our EU
representative GPSR@taylorandfrancis.com
Taylor & Francis Verlag GmbH, Kaufingerstraße 24, 80331 München, Germany

9 7 8 1 0 3 2 1 0 3 5 8 7